NEW WORLD ORDER

THE ANCIENT PLAN OF SECRET SOCIETIES

William T. Still

Huntington House Publishers

Eleventh Printing

Huntington House Publishers
P.O. Box 53788
Lafayette, Louisiana 70505

Library of Congress Card Catalog Number 90-80397
ISBN 0-910311-64-1

Printed in USA

Contents

Acknowledgements

With any project of this magnitude, there are many to thank.

First of all to my parents, William and Mary Still, who helped in many ways, and second to my wife, Cynthia, who read and re-read, edited and re-edited, my sincere thanks.

In addition, thanks to Bob and Diane Still and Sam and Loya Wheatley for their support.

Valuable information and/or advice came from Dr. William Culbertson, Susan Doré, George Olmsted, Burt and Joan Collins, Len LeSourd, Bill McIlhany, Marshall Peters, Rev. Chris Parkins, Fran Overholt, Rev. Jim Shaw, Robert Garcia, and others who cannot be named.

Special thanks to Ron and Teresa Clark, Jesse and Cheryl James, Tom and Molly Todd, Dien and Maria Tran, Asa Moore and Arlene Janney, George Tiller, Marty Milrod, Woodrow W. Turner, Phil Spitzer (who now owes me a dinner), Roger Fones, F. Kirk Lininger, Jim Gibson, Dennis and Louise Gregg, John and Karen Russell, Gloria Lickey Schultz, Bill Michelmore, David Hazard, Pat and Drew Paulis, Ron Payne, Paul Meli, Jimmy and Sylvia Fleming, David and Tracey McCracken, Richard Edgerton, Jeff Book, Levant and Muriel DeWolf, Martha & Eloise Rogers, Kathy Taylor, Lanee Orrison, C.M. Piggott Jr., Joe Vilardi, Carl Shoemaker, Jerry and Pam Schonder, Don Schonder, John Janney, Don Pancoast, Mike Holden, Ruth Stenstrom, Rich Pollock, Eric Scudder, Mike Resnick, and my old history teachers, Colonel McClanahan and Kenny Rollins, all of whom played a role, whether they knew it or not.

Introduction

This book shows how an ancient plan has been hidden for centuries deep within secret societies. This scheme is designed to bring all of mankind under a single world government — a New World Order. This plan is of such antiquity that its result is even mentioned in the Bible — the rule of the Antichrist mentioned in the Revelation of Saint John the Divine.

Other works on the subject do not trace the plan beyond the founding of one of the most notorious of these secret societies, the German Illuminati, founded in 1776. Other works fail to see any continuity between the New World Order and secret societies at all. Still others don't connect the ancient secret societies to the modern versions.

This book shows what the secret societies are after and how they are going about it. It shows the symbols and emblems these groups have left down through the ages, subtly marking the path for their descendents.

This book shows why members of these secret societies can participate in something which will obviously lead to world despotism. It shows how their own members are tricked by them. It reveals enough of the secret rituals to establish credibility even with the most ardent members of these groups. Most importantly, the book demonstrates the profound influence secret societies have had on historical events through the centuries, their influences in the present day, and how they can best be thwarted in the future.

Among secret societies, I have focused primarily on Freemasonry, or Masonry, because it is the largest, oldest, and best documented of these groups. This does not mean Masonry is solely responsible in any way, or that all Masons are evil. Certainly the vast majority of Masons are not malevolent folk. Masonry is successful precisely because it has shielded an occult "inner doctrine" from all but a hand-picked elite. In this, Masonry follows the traditional pattern of other secret societies; attempting to attract the best in society with its benign "outer doctrine" while cleverly obscuring the dark secrets of its "inner doctrine."

It is not my intention to implicate all individuals involved in Masonic lodges. There are, no doubt, many well-meaning, community-minded people whose only purpose in joining a lodge is for fellowship and to contribute to the good of their communities. Some of their philanthropic endeavors include appreciable contributions to charitable organizations and financial support to their numerous burn centers, as well as to underprivileged children.

I in no way wish to vilify the many God-fearing members of Freemasonry. It is my intention to expose those at the top who are intentionally concealing their agenda.

This book is not primarily about Masonry, however, but about an ancient plan for world conquest. Most Masons who are aware of it sincerely believe that this "Great Plan" will someday usher in a new era of world peace and cooperation. However, the secret architects of this "Great Plan" are not benign humanitarians, as they would have us believe, but are men in the service of evil. Their "government of nations" is a deception, hiding, in reality, an iron-clad, world dictatorship.

This is where their New World Order is taking us, and unless we realize from whence the danger comes, our ability to oppose it will be unfocused and therefore ineffective.

ONE

OCTOBER 1973: THE NIXON COUP

My curiosity about secret societies began in the fall of 1973. As a young, aspiring reporter living near Washington, D.C., I stumbled across a startling story of political intrigue. Since then, I've slowly pursued this sometimes contradictory story, only gradually coming to understand its significance over the years. This book is the fruit of more than a decade of research that led inexorably into their shadowy realm.

On about October 15, 1973, I was given a memorandum by my father, Lt. Col. William L. Still, a retired Air Force officer, one of the architects of the military's defense communications network. On October 3, 1973 he was approached by an acquaintance, Joe Josephson, who claimed he had connections with the White House of President Richard M. Nixon. This acquaintance asked my father how he and his military friends would feel about a military takeover of the U.S. government.

The atmosphere in Washington at that time was thick with political intrigue. The CIA stood accused of domestic spying at home, and of *coup* d' état making in Chile. The Watergate hearings had gone on throughout the summer and now President Nixon was refusing to comply with court orders to surrender the White House tapes as evidence. The American Civil Liberties Union was taking out full-page ads in the *New York Times* urging impeachment of the president.

My father was dumbfounded by the suggestion that a coup was afoot. Fortunately, he was able to conceal his shock long enough to learn some of the details from his associate, Mr. Josephson. Shortly thereafter, he wrote a memorandum detailing the incident and circulated it in military intelligence and FBI channels. This startling memorandum reads as follows:

MEMORANDUM FOR THE RECORD

Subject: Rumor concerning planning for a Military Coup within the USA.

INTRODUCTION

My name is William L. Still, Lt. Col., USAF (Ret). I am not an alarmist, and consider myself to be intelligent, objective and an analyst of above average capability. I am writing this statement only after careful consideration of its potential impact on both the country and myself.

The following summary is a combination of fact, hearsay, and conjecture. I have limited the subjective data to those areas which I believe will aid in evaluating the source of the rumor, and make no comment on the rumor itself.

I have not included the names of pertinent personnel or organizations for their own protection. However, I will co-operate fully with any responsible investigators.

GIST OF RUMOR. (Hearsay)

A committee exists which is dedicated to the repeal of the 22nd Amendment to the Constitution. Its goal is to place Mr. Nixon in the White House for a third term. Connected in some manner with this organization is a second committee which has a super-patriotic name such as THE COMMITTEE FOR THE PRESERVATION OF CONSTITUTIONAL PROCESSES (I do not remember the exact name, however it was similar to this). It is to be used as a fall back cover in the event that the first committee cannot accomplish its goal by constitutional means. This second committee [despite its name] is dedicated to keeping Mr. Nixon in office by any means: ---- INCLUDING A MILITARY COUP BY HIGH RANKING OFFICERS!

I heard this rumor on 3 October 1973. The man from whom I heard this story stated that he had recently been "sounded out" on a writing job for the second committee, and that there was apparently unlimited money behind it as "price was no object" in salary discussions.

He gave the above rumor as the strategy of the organization. We then entered into a discussion on the tactics which could be used to execute such a coup. During the course of the discussion, I was questioned as to the feasibility of the plan and asked whether I thought senior military men could be enlisted for such an effort.

Upon reading this memorandum, I dropped everything and spent my time trying to convince other members of the press in Washington that this was a legitimate threat. What happened next was the stuff spy novels are made of - guns and car chases through Washington, as well as much more sophisticated spy games.

Due to my own intensifying paranoia, I eventually backed off the story, but not before the appropriate authorities, in both government and media, were aware of the situation. At that time, I had no additional facts. I was sure I was not just dealing with a run-of-the-mill Washington scandal. It was clear that those involved were capable of wielding great power, but more than that, there was a chilling feeling of antiquity that surrounded the situation. But with my limited resources, I had run into a dead end.

As the years have passed the story has continued to trickle out. Though much more research needs to be done in the area of the actual involvement of the Nixon administration in this unsuccessful coup, proving that involvement is not essential to my thesis. My thesis is that secret societies have had a major, yet little known impact on world events throughout history, and will undoubtedly attempt to influence world affairs in the future. I cannot prove that secret societies had anything to do with coup plotting in 1973-74, but the circumstantial evidence is certainly strong. I hope the publication of this book will stimulate the release of new data, which only the principals can supply.

Why would a U.S. president consider such drastic action, if, indeed he did? At first, it seemed that this was merely the act of a power-mad president, but the historical record has not borne out that hypothesis. The only logical alternative is very complex and requires an entire book to explain. In a nutshell, President Nixon was probably used and when proven no longer useful, discarded by the same group who brought us the American, French, and Russian revolutions in the eighteenth and twentieth centuries, and the World Wars, the United Nations, the Korean War, and Vietnam in the twentieth century.

The problem with identifying this group is that they hide behind numerous covers, but the motive is always the same—money and power. This group has no national affiliation; in fact, they are actively working to eliminate the concept of national boundaries altogether. Their goal is to inflict on the nations of the world an international government which they will control for their own gain. This book shows the history of this scheme throughout the centuries. Although it has been known by many names, like the "Great Plan," to Masonic occultists, it is now generally referred to as the New World Order.

What follows are the facts that have come out over the years relating to the Nixon-era coup. They are arranged roughly in chronological order.

WATERGATE — JUNE 1972

Former CIA employees under direction of the White House were caught breaking into Democratic National Headquarters at the Watergate office complex in Washington. An informed intelligence source has told me the burglars were working on a tip that there was evidence that Democratic presidential candidate Senator George McGovern had accepted substantial illegal contributions from Fidel Castro.

Nixon maneuvered successfully to keep an investigation of the incident relatively quiet until after the fall election. Then early in 1973, the famed Senate Watergate hearings started.

COMMITTEE TO REPEAL THE 22ND AMENDMENT
SUMMER OF 1973

Nixon loyalists floated what is known in Washington as a "trial balloon." They tipped off the local Washington media that a group of Americans who wanted Nixon to remain president for a third term, or even longer, had formed a group called "The Committee to Repeal the Twenty-second Amendment." A third term is forbidden by the Twenty-second Amendment to the Constitution. This group gained no immediate support in Washington, and so it quietly died after, at most, a week of local media mention.

However, local Washington Nixon watchers began to worry privately that the Committee to Repeal the Twenty-second Amendment signaled something more ominous brewing under the surface.

THE AGNEW AFFAIR — SEPTEMBER 1973

A mass-market paperback book entitled *The Glasshouse Tapes* was published by Louis Tackwood, who claimed that he was a member of a super-secret domestic intelligence unit of the Los Angeles Police Department which was working on a plan to create a chaotic domestic political situation in the U.S. that would give President Nixon the justification for declaring martial law.

Tackwood claimed that he helped set up a secret operation which would allow anti-war demonstrators to break onto the floor of the 1972 Republican convention, then scheduled to take place in San Diego, just as Vice-President Agnew began to speak. Tackwood and his accomplices would then cause a riot on the convention floor, with the demonstrators battling police. During the resulting uproar, the vice-president would be shot on nationwide TV to gain maximum impact.

This incident would be followed by a wave of nationwide bombings for which the revolutionary left would openly take credit. In response, President Nixon would then have the justification to declare a state of national emergency, and essentially suspend Constitutional rights.

As wild as this tale may sound, Tackwood's assertions are more believable today given what happened to Agnew. He was certainly considered expendable by the White House. Although Nixon did not replace him on the ticket in 1972, Agnew resigned on October 10, 1973, after allegations of corruption and bribery suddenly surfaced.

According to Senator Barry Goldwater's autobiography, Nixon never liked Agnew because his nomination had been forced upon him by the conservative wing of the Republican party:

> A lot of us in the GOP knew Nixon would have preferred Rockefeller or former Texas Governor John Connolly as his running mate in 1972, but *conservatives would not have tolerated that....I was positive of one thing: The White House itself was leaking some of the allegations against Agnew.*[1]

Nixon then selected Gerald Ford to replace Agnew as his vice-president. Ford later granted Nixon a presidential pardon from any future prosecution.

Former Nixon aide John Dean hinted that he may have been aware of this incident. In a December 1982 interview on ABC-TV's *After Hours*, Dean said that he knew about "these assassination plots" but said that he didn't know just what to make of them.

The idea in such an assassination strategy is, of course, to create a chaotic condition. This is usually considered a necessity in coup-making. At the peak of chaos, you move quickly and ruthlessly to seize power by force and kill your opposition during the turmoil. Although President Nixon's role remains uncertain, it is clear that some powerful group was trying to create a chaotic political situation in the United States in October of 1973.

CHILE — SEPTEMBER 11, 1973

The Marxist government of Salvadore Allende was overthrown in Chile. Many observers in Washington feared that the covert expertise gained in Chile by the CIA would soon come home to rest in the United States.

COUP CONTACT — OCTOBER 3, 1973

Colonel Still was asked how he and his military friends would feel about a military takeover of the U.S. government. Two weeks later, Colonel Still circulated his memo to the FBI, top intelligence officials, and the press.

HAIG AND THE SATURDAY NIGHT MASSACRE
OCTOBER 20, 1973

Watergate Special Prosecutor Archibald Cox was fired by President Nixon for continuing his Watergate investigations. Attorney General Elliot Richardson and Deputy Attorney General Ruckleshouse were fired by Nixon for refusing to fire Cox.

General Alexander Haig, Nixon's chief-of-staff at the time, testified before Congress at his confirmation hearings for Secretary of State on January 14, 1981 concerning these events. Although it went totally unnoticed by the assembled press corps, Haig dropped a bombshell that day concerning what has been called the "Saturday Night Massacre." He revealed that the firings were no surprise to the participants, although they were to the rest of the world. Haig claims that Attorney General Richardson knew his fate at least a day in advance, and that the firings were designed to prevent far more drastic scenarios.

Haig described Attorney General Richardson's bargain with the devil in agreeing to the plan. "Now I must say in fairness to him that his agreement the day before to implement the plan...in fact he helped to construct it...was an alternative to something that was far more drastic."[2]

Haig then explained what he meant by "far more drastic." He asserted that some people in Washington were "flirting with solutions which would have been extra-Constitutional."

Haig would later warn Archibald Cox's replacement, Leon Jaworski, "about the dangers to the nation that Watergate posed." Jaworski then warned the grand jury that if they indicted the president, that if they did, Nixon might use force to keep himself in office.[3] In June, 1982 Watergate grand juror Harold Evans appeared in a segment of the ABC news magazine 20/20 and said that Jaworski had warned the grand jury that if indicted, the president might have "surrounded the White House with armed forces."[4]

Reporter Seymour Hersh, in an August 1983 article in the *Atlantic Monthly* entitled "The Pardon," wrote that Haig "is known to have spread similar concerns inside the White House...."[5]

ROWAN BREAKS THE STORY — OCTOBER 26, 1973

Syndicated columnist Carl Rowan broke the story that President Nixon may well have been planning a military takeover of the government. On October 26, 1973, in a column in the *Washington Star* entitled "Has President Nixon Gone Crazy?," Rowan wrote:

> Those who wonder about the President's emotional balance have now begun to suspect that even in the face of a vote to impeach he might try, as "commander-in-chief," to use the military forces to keep himself in power.

NIXON APPEALS TO JOINT CHIEFS OF STAFF
DECEMBER 22, 1973

President Nixon met with the Joint Chiefs of Staff and tried to enlist their support in an extra-Constitutional action to keep him in power. According to Seymour Hersh, writing in the August 1983 edition of *Atlantic Monthly* in an article entitled, "The Pardon" (p. 69), one of the Chiefs of Staff recalled Nixon's speech with alarm:

> He kept on referring to the fact that he may be the last hope, [that] the eastern elite was out to get him. He kept saying, "This is our last and best hope. The last chance to resist the fascists" [of the left]. His words brought me straight up out of my chair. I felt the President, without the

words having been said, was trying to sound us out to see if we would support him in some extra-constitutional action. He was trying to find out whether in a crunch there was support to keep him in power.

Fears of a Nixon coup, however, did not end in 1973. We now know that throughout 1974, high-level government officials were worried that President Nixon might resort to "extra-Constitutional" measures, rather than be forced from office by impeachment due to the cover-up of the Watergate scandal.

SCHLESINGER SECURES MILITARY CHAIN OF COMMAND
AUGUST 27, 1974

On this date, the *Washington Post*, in a story entitled "Military Coup Fears Denied," reported that Secretary of Defense James Schlesinger had taken special measures to protect the military chain of command should any illegal orders come from President Nixon:

> Defense Secretary James Schlesinger requested a tight watch in the military chain of command to ensure that no extraordinary orders went out from the White House during the period of uncertainty.

> Pentagon officials have said that Schlesinger never feared that a coup would be successful even if attempted.

> Nevertheless, Defense Department officials said the word went out that no commanders of any forces should carry out orders which came from the White House, or elsewhere, outside the normal military channels.

> Department officials have confirmed that Schlesinger and Gen. George S. Brown, chairman of the Joint Chiefs of Staff, discussed among themselves how they should be aware of any illegal orders being issued to military units outside the formal chain of command structure.[6]

82ND AIRBORNE WOULD PROTECT WASHINGTON
JULY 1974

Secretary of Defense Schlesinger investigated how quickly the Army's 82nd Airborne Division could be brought to Washington, D.C. from Fort Bragg, North Carolina to counterbalance Marine contingents loyal to Nixon. Seymour Hersh, writing in the August 1983 edition of the *Atlantic Monthly* stated:

> Schlesinger began to investigate what forces could be assembled at his order as a counterweight to the Marines, if Nixon—in a crisis—chose to subvert the Constitution. The notion that Nixon could at any time resort to extraordinary steps to preserve his presidency was far more widespread in the government than the public perceived in the early days of Watergate or perceives today.[7]

Hersh even suggested the probable military leader responsible for helping plan the coup attempt. When Richard Nixon was vice-president under Eisenhower, he struck up a friendship with his military aide,

Robert Cushman. In 1971, it was General Cushman who, as deputy-director of the CIA, provided "unauthorized" CIA support to the illegal escapades of Watergate plumbers E. Howard Hunt and G. Gordon Liddy. By June 1974, Cushman had been appointed as the Marine representative on the Joint Chiefs of Staff, one of the five most powerful military men in the nation. Schlesinger watched Cushman closely for several months. The article in *Atlantic Monthly* continues:

> Schlesinger...continued to believe that Cushman, with his personal loyalty to Nixon, was a weak link in the new chain of command. He quietly investigated just which forces would be available to Nixon....The Marines...Cushman's troops—were by far the strongest presence in the Washington area.[8]

KISSINGER CONCERNED — AUGUST 2, 1974

Even Secretary of State Henry Kissinger claims that he was informed by chief-of-staff General Haig that the president was considering ringing the White House with troops. Kissinger asserts:

> This I said was nonsense; a Presidency could not be conducted from a White House ringed with bayonets. Haig said he agreed completely; as a military man it made him heartsick to think of the Army in that role; he simply wanted me to have a feel for the kinds of ideas being canvassed. [9]

OPERATION SURVIVAL — LIBERTY LOBBY
APRIL 1981

There has been a certain amount of crossfire between the extremes of the American political spectrum over this coup issue. The leftist *Mother Jones* magazine printed a story by Robert Eringer in April 1981 which reported that Robert Bartell, chairman of the anti-semitic "Liberty Lobby," presided over a secretive 1970 Liberty Lobby fundraiser for a project known as "Operation Survival." The stated goal of this project was to "finance a right-wing military dictatorship for the U.S."

According to the article, Bartell denied that this was the motivation, saying that "the fundraiser was to help prevent the U.S. climate from deteriorating into further 'chaos.' "

SENATOR BARRY GOLDWATER — July 9, 1981

On this date, Senator Barry Goldwater gave a television interview in which he mentioned he was aware of coup-planning in 1973 and 1974. Unfortunately, Goldwater has consistently refused to grant further interviews on the subject. Surprisingly, in his 1988 autobiography, *Goldwater*, he specifically denies coup-planning existed. "I do wish to stress that the hysterical rumors about a military coup were completely unfounded. Al Haig and I know that."[10]

First of all, General Haig is not exactly a totally objective witness. He was the White House Chief of Staff at the time of the Saturday Night

Massacre. In fact, many in Washington who were aware of the situation at the time felt that General Haig was one of the prime suspects.

Why would Senator Goldwater, the one-time "Mister Straight-shooter," mislead history in this regard? Senator Goldwater once had a solid reputation of doing things for the good of the nation and/or the Republican party. Perhaps he thinks if the coup story got out it would be blamed on Republicans. Perhaps he thinks it is in the national interest not to rehash what is undoubtedly one of America's most embarrassing political moments. In any case, it is interesting that he felt compelled to mention the coup at all in his autobiography.

It is also interesting to note that Goldwater is a Shriner, an upper-level branch of Freemasonry, [11] the significance of which will be shown later in detail.

SEVEN DAYS IN OCTOBER — SEPTEMBER 29, 1987

During the Senate confirmation hearings on Judge Bork in 1987, Senator Ted Kennedy (D-Mass.) reminded former Attorney General Elliot Richardson of the events surrounding October 20, 1973:

> But you and I lived through those days together, Mr. Richardson—seven days in October of 1973—and it was by no means clear to either of us that everything would turn out alright. The fire storm of public criticism had a great deal to do with the fact that everything did turn out alright....[12]

Unfortunately, Senator Kennedy has not answered requests from this author for an interview on the subject.

CONCLUSIONS

It is likely that this was no isolated incident involving a desperate president, or a power-hungry staff, but something associated with a larger plan. Certainly General Haig's Senate testimony indicates that there was significantly more planning going into the managing of events than anyone has previously indicated.

The most plausible theory is that some sort of timetable was in place, and then someone got a little anxious to eliminate Constitutional government as we know it in the United States. They not only significantly overestimated their own strength, but the forcefullness of the reaction to their plans.

Standing by itself, the allegation of a military coup being planned in the U.S. is difficult to believe. Therefore, this book attempts to meticulously build a case for it based on an explanation of concepts originating thousands of years ago with examples of world events which have taken place during the last 200 years.

What group was powerful enough to even consider an internal coup in the United States in the 1970s? Unfortunately, for years we have had to endure a wide variety of unsatisfying theories, primarily that the planned Nixon coup was a right-wing plot similar to the September 1973 overthrow of the Chilean government which took place only a month earlier.

In fact, Washington was rife with rumors at the time that the same clandestine group which had overseen the management of the Chilean coup in September 1973 turned its attentions to President Nixon's problems in the United States in October. However, these were only rumors. Where the truth lies cannot be ascertained at this juncture. We must leave it to the consciences of those individuals involved to shed further light on this important chapter in American history.

RIGHT? OR LEFT?

So, until now, those few who were aware of coup-plotting saw it as merely an obscure footnote in the overall struggle between the leftists in Congress and the "rightist" President Nixon over the Watergate scandal, and nothing more. But that just doesn't add up. There are too many unexplained contradictions. For example, President Nixon was not living up to the hard-line "right-wing" image he had been given by the press, but never earned. At the policy level, he was stunning even liberals with his swings toward the left.

Harvard historian and professed socialist John Kenneth Galbraith gleefully noted President Nixon's tilt to the left in an article in the September 1970 issue of *New York* magazine entitled "Richard Nixon and the Great Socialist Revival." Galbraith wrote that after gaining the presidency, Richard Nixon surrounded himself, not with leading conservatives, but with some of the leading socialist scholars of the day, who wasted no time in pushing the nation toward the left. Galbraith observed:

> Certainly the least predicted development under the Nixon Administration was this great new thrust to socialism. One encounters people who still aren't aware of it. Others must be rubbing their eyes, for certainly the portents seemed all to the contrary. As an opponent of socialism, Mr. Nixon seemed steadfast.[13]

In February 1968, Richard Nixon announced that he would run for president. What few people realized was that Nixon had spent the previous six years working for the law firm of John Mitchell, Nelson Rockefeller's personal attorney.[14] Later in this book, I document the Rockefeller family's involvement in both secret societies and pro-Soviet activities over a period of many years.

In 1960 Nixon suffered a narrow defeat in the presidential race against John F. Kennedy. He then ran for governor of California in 1962, only at the request of Nelson Rockefeller,[15] and soon disappeared into what most political observers thought would be political oblivion when he was defeated by Pat Brown. Supposedly Nixon was broke, both economically and politically, but soon, a remarkable rehabilitation began to take place. Researcher Gary Allen noted, however:

> When Nixon left Washington, he, by his own claim, had little more than an Oldsmobile automobile, Pat's respectable Republican cloth coat, and a government pension. While in law practice Nixon had an income of $200,000 per year....By 1968, he reported his net worth as $515, 830.[16]

During those years Nixon lived in a posh $100,000-a-year Manhattan apartment owned by Nelson Rockefeller.[17] And what did Nixon do from 1962 to 1968 to earn his $200,000-a-year salary? He "spent most of his time touring the country and the world, first rebuilding his political reputation and then campaigning to get the 1968 Republican nomination."[18]

In 1968, Nixon campaigned as the arch-enemy of Communism, yet after the elections, his actions quickly boggled the minds of most conservatives. Gary Allen wrote in 1971: "The Nixon Game Plan is infinitely more clever and dangerous than those of his predecessors because it masquerades as being the opposite of what it is."[19]

Even during his campaign, Nixon began proclaiming that if elected, he would pursue a program which he termed "new internationalism." "New internationalism" turned out to be a euphemism for the disastrous trade policy with the Soviet Union, also known as "détente," the likes of which had not been seen since President Franklin Roosevelt's Lend Lease policy of the early 1940s rebuilt the Soviet war machine into the dominant force that it is today.

This "new internationalism" was merely a prelude to the real goal of the secret societies, which they call the "New World Order," or even their "New Atlantis."

After Nixon was elected, his former boss, John Mitchell, took over as Attorney General. Nixon also appointed Dr. Henry Kissinger, another Rockefeller confidant, as his national security advisor. Kissinger was Rockefeller's personal advisor on foreign affairs and a paid staff member of the Council on Foreign Relations. The significance of this relationship is explained in later chapters as are the persistent allegations that Kissinger was a Soviet agent.

After the 1968 election, the Nixon team quickly moved to establish the most pro-Soviet program the United States had seen in twenty-five years. Outgoing President Lyndon Johnson was astonished by Nixon's sweeping turn to the left. In a December 1, 1971 article in the now-defunct *Washington Star* he said:

> Can't you see the uproar...if I had been responsible for Taiwan getting kicked out of the United Nations? Or if I had imposed sweeping national controls on prices and wages?...Nixon has gotten by with it.

Columnist Stewart Alsop certainly agreed:

> There is a sort of unconscious conspiracy between the President

and his natural enemies, the liberal Democrats, to conceal the extent to which his basic program...is really the liberal Democratic program.[20]

Syndicated columnist James Reston, writing on February 3, 1971, was surprised at Nixon's leftist economic approach. "The Nixon budget is so complex, so unlike the Nixon of the past, so un-Republican that it defies rational analysis....The Nixon budget is more planned, has more welfare in it, and has a bigger predicted deficit than any other budget of this century."[21]

What did this hard left turn mean? That is the topic of this book. Into what line of thought did Nixon suddenly become initiated? Twenty years after the fact, this once-inexplicable shift of political direction begins to make some sense if we look at Nixon as merely a pawn in the age-old game of secret societies.

It is probable that most of the public figures and military men involved in the scheme were unaware of the real goals, or who was really behind it. Even President Nixon was probably being manipulated. Perhaps Nixon will someday see fit to shed additional light on this subject.

What is certain is that elements of the left were being pitted against elements of the right to serve some other purpose. The so-called "left" was being provoked into stirring up revolt; the so-called "right" was being pushed into eliminating Constitutional guarantees to quell the disturbances. It is likely that another group was prepared to fill the power vacuum this domestic political chaos caused.

For example, there is some evidence that large business interests were promoting violent demonstrations in the streets. James Kunen, writing about the 1968 Students for a Democratic Society (SDS) national convention in his book, *The Strawberry Statement—Notes of a College Revolutionary*, notes that:

> At the convention, men from Business International Roundtables...tried to buy up a few radicals. These men are the world's leading industrialists and they convene to decide how our lives are going to go....They're the left wing of the ruling class....They offered to finance our demonstrations in Chicago. We were also offered Esso (Rockefeller) money. They want us to make a lot of radical commotion so they can look more in the center as they move to the left.[22]

Therefore, all this banter about political "rights" and "lefts" really doesn't make much sense. After all, rightists can be dictators. Leftists can be dictators. That is not the point. Once a condition of chaos is created in a government, then freedom inevitably suffers.

Once President Nixon resigned in August 1974, the coup option was dead. But the same planners who brought America to the verge of civil war quickly shifted gears and changed their direction of attack. Since they hadn't been able to eliminate Constitutional government by military means, they mounted a new onslaught to eliminate it by legislative means by convincing thirty-four state legislatures to call for a constitutional convention, as allowed for in Article Five.

It is not mere coincidence that in 1975, less than one year after the resignation of President Nixon, the first six states passed resolutions calling for a Constitutional Convention. Four years later, thirty states had passed resolutions. But in the decade of the 1980s, only two more states joined in, while two others, Florida and Alabama, withdrew their calls after citizens became aroused.

In 1984, in an attempt to get the final two states needed for the convention to proceed, James MacGregor Burns, a board member of the lead organization trying to bring about a Constitutional Convention, known as Committee on Constitutional Systems (CCS), made this shocking admission in urging his forces onward:

> Let us face reality. The framers [of the Constitution] have simply been too shrewd for us. They have outwitted us. They designed separate institutions that cannot be linked by mechanical linkages, frail bridges, [or] tinkering. If we are to turn the founders upside down...we must directly confront the Constitutional structure they erected.[23]

What changes can we expect if CCS succeeds? In 1974, Rexford Guy Tugwell, one of the original members of President Franklin D. Roosevelt's "Brain Trust," published the "Constitution for the Newstates of America." This new constitution proposed that:

> The government would be empowered to abridge freedom of expression, communication, movement and assembly in a "declared emergency." The practice of religion would be considered a "privilege."[24]

As this book will show, one of the major goals of secret societies is to bring all nations under a world government, a "New World Order." So what's bad about that? An effective world government would mean an end to war. Why would anyone want to stop a plan to eliminate wars? Because there is a deadly flaw in the logic of it all. Is there one shred of evidence to suggest that the old adage "power tends to corrupt and absolute power corrupts absolutely,"[25] first written by Britain's Lord Acton in 1887, would not apply to this newly-created world government?

Is there any evidence suggesting that such a government would not become as corrupt and dictatorial as that predicted in the last book of the Bible? There is not.

Certainly nationalism is a bad system for running world affairs. It is wasteful. It is the direct cause of countless wars, death, and poverty. But until someone with perfectly incorruptible wisdom emerges to head this world government, relinquishing national sovereignty to the "New World Order" promoted by secret societies could only lead to the most corrupt and ironclad dictatorship mankind has ever known.

We in America live in a golden bubble insulated from a very dangerous world. Life is so good in the United States that it seems impossible that it could ever change. Threats to our national security seem distant. The American system seems to be the most stable ever devised by man. It is difficult to believe that in the decade of the 1970s, this remarkable, hybrid form of government could have hung by such a surprisingly slender thread.

The life Americans lead is not the world norm. It is an aberration in world history. Never before has mankind enjoyed this degree of freedom or had so many options and liberties. But this golden bubble may be about to burst. Whether its destruction can be prevented, or at least minimized, may depend on how much we know about the secret societies determined to destroy it. So it is to the preservation of the United States that this book is dedicated. May God continue to bless America.

TWO

ANCIENT SECRET SOCIETIES

Secret societies have existed among all peoples, savage and civilized,
since the beginning of recorded history.
Manly P. Hall, *The Secret Destiny of America*, 1944

Masonry, or Freemasonry, is the largest and oldest of the secret societies, and still today is one of the most powerful groups on earth. Certainly in the past it was difficult to hold a position of power in most nations without having undergone the initiatory rites of Masonry, or one of the related secret societies.

One modern source lists seventeen American presidents as having been Masons: Washington, Madison, Monroe, Jackson, Polk, Buchanan, Andrew Johnson, Garfield, McKinley, Teddy Roosevelt, Taft, Harding, Franklin D. Roosevelt, Truman, Lyndon Johnson, Ford, and Reagan.[1] According to a 1951 edition of the *Holy Bible, Masonic Edition*, there is abundant evidence that Thomas Jefferson was a Mason, and Pierce and Taylor are also strongly suspected of having been members.[2]

Although Masonry claims members in every corner of the globe, the vast majority of the six million members worldwide reside in the United States and Great Britain. Masons themselves are proud of their influence. One high-ranking Mason, Manly Hall, wrote, "It is beyond question that the secret societies of all ages have exercised a considerable degree of political influence.... [3] Hall then urges his readers to, "...join those who are really the living powers behind the thrones of modern national and international affairs."[4]

The same implication comes from other Masonic sources. The *Masonic Bible* states that "for well over one hundred and fifty years, the destiny of this country has been determined largely by men who were members of the Masonic Fraternity."[5]

President Harry S. Truman in Masonic Apron
(Courtesy of Harry S. Truman Library, Independence, MO.)

Researcher and former Army counterintelligence officer Paul A. Fisher, in his meticulously documented work, *Behind The Lodge Door: Church State and Freemasonry in America*, says one Masonic journal claimed in 1948 that between ten and twenty percent of the U.S. "adult thinking population come directly within the circle of Masonic influence..."[6]

ANCIENT EGYPTIAN MASONRY

Masonry can be traced back more than 5,000 years to the secret societies of the ancient Egyptian priests. Masons who visit the tombs of ancient Egypt are astounded by the religious symbols painted upon the walls. There displayed before them are the same grips, signs, postures, symbols, and even the apron, used for their own initiation.[7]

But some Masonic authors claim even greater antiquity. One Masonic writer claims it is older than any religion today and states that it originated in "remote antiquity....The Order existed...as a compact, well organized body long before the building of the oldest pyramid."[8] According to General Albert Pike, head of American Masonry in the late 1800s, and still today regarded as the guiding light of modern Masonry:

> With her traditions reaching back to the earliest times, and her symbols dating farther back than even the monumental history of Egypt extends...it is [still the same as] it was in the cradle of the human race, when no human foot had trodden the soil of Assyria and Egypt.[9]

Manly Hall, a thirty-third degree Mason, even claims that Masonry originated in the mythical kingdom of Atlantis:

> The age of the Masonic school is not to be calculated by hundreds or even thousands of years, for it never had any origin in the worlds of form. It is a shadow of the great Atlantean Mystery School, which stood with all its splendor in the ancient City of the Golden Gates, where now the turbulent Atlantic rolls in unbroken sweep.[10]

THE MYSTERIES

The vast majority of Masons believe that the Craft is only a fraternal organization with ceremonial traditions. But according to Hall, the guiding lights of Masonry believe Masons are the guardians of the ancient secrets of life, collected and practiced by history's greatest philosophers and adepts, known as the "Mysteries." What are these "Mysteries?" They are the occult secrets based on ritual magic that aid its practitioners in learning how to gain power and wealth, how to control the fate of men and nations, and interestingly, how to achieve some measure of immortality. According to General Albert Pike:

> Masonry, successor of the Mysteries, still follows the ancient manner of teaching....Though Masonry is identical with the ancient Mysteries, it is so only in this qualified sense: that it presents but an imperfect image of their brilliancy, the ruins only of their grandeur, and a system that has experienced progressive alterations, the fruits of social events, political circumstances, and the ambitious imbecility of its improvers.[11]

OSIRIS AND ISIS

Essential to the history of ancient Masonry are the Egyptian gods Osiris and Isis. Masonic literature still abounds with references to both these figures.

Isis has always been seen as the guiding light of the profession of prostitution; Osiris the chief evil god. Author Robert K.G. Temple quotes an Egyptian "magical" papyrus as saying that "Osiris is a dark God," and that Isis is married to "He who is Lord in perfect black." Osiris was the god of the Egyptian underworld, the prince of the dead.[12]

THE EYE

One of the oldest, and most important symbols of Masonry is the Egyptian hieroglyph of the eye — or the "evil eye." It represents their god Osiris.[13] This "Eye of Osiris" is also the symbol of modern day Masonry. It dominates the top of most Masonic documents, and now dominates the back of the Great Seal of the United States, which is reproduced on every American one-dollar bill. I will demonstrate that its presence on the Great Seal suggests that secret societies were instrumental in creating the new nation of America, and still have an important influence in the present day.

The Star of "Eastern Star." F.A.T.A.L., reportedly stands for
"Fairest Among Thousands; Altogether Lovely."
(courtesy of the Library of Congress)

THE MAGICAL STAR

The controversial five-pointed star emblem of Masonry has a fascinating yet little-known background which is also rooted in ancient Egypt. Masonry's leader of a century ago, Albert Pike, admits that the

Masonic five-pointed star represents "Intelligence," as well as having a darker meaning connected with Sirius, the brightest star in our night sky. In 1871 Pike wrote, in what is still regarded as the manual of the Masonic order, *Morals and Dogma of the Ancient and Accepted Scottish Rite of Freemasonry*, this explanation of the Masonic five-pointed star:

> ...the BLAZING STAR of five points....Originally it represented SIRIUS, or the Dog-star, the forerunner of the inundation of the Nile;...the Blazing Star has been regarded as an emblem of Omniscience, or the All-seeing Eye, which to the Egyptian Initiates was the emblem of Osiris, the Creator.[14]

In ancient Egypt, gigantic temples were constructed to mark the first morning of the Egyptian new year, which depended on Sirius. At this time, Sirius, also known as Sothis to the Greeks, would appear rising as a bright red star just ahead of the sun. When seen high in the sky, Sirius is blue-white in color, but when low on the horizon, it is the only star in the heavens bright enough to be seen as red in color. This phenomenon still occurs today, and is due to the deflection of the light of Sirius through the earth's atmosphere.

Sirius was referred to as Rubeola, which means "red or rusty" in sixth century Latin texts.[15] This recently discovered Latin reference, that Sirius was known as a red star, has caused considerable confusion among modern day astronomers as they ponder how Sirius could possibly have changed from a red giant to a white dwarf in a mere 1,400 years (short by astronomical standards). Masons well-versed in Egyptology must derive considerable amusement from this astronomical confusion.

This predawn appearance of Sirius is known as the heliacal rising. This event was the basis for the Egyptian Sothic calendar, and, therefore one of the most basic symbols of the Egyptian religion, which in general terms we shall call "Illuminism" (not to be confused with the eighteenth-century group, the Illuminati). The days that followed the helical rising of Sirius became known as the "dog days," or the hottest days of summer in the Northern Hemisphere.[16]

THE SUN

The symbol which represents the Mason, personally, is the sun symbol, a circle with a dot in the center. According to Manly Hall, the sun symbol represents the "wisdom" which "radiates" from every Mason. It is symbolic of the belief of Masons that God lives within, and speaks through the mouths of "illuminated" Masons:

> The Master Mason is in truth a sun, a great reflector of light, who radiates through his organism, purified by ages of preparation, the glorious power which is the light of the Lodge. He, in truth, has become the spokesman of the Most High. He stands between the

glowing fire light and the world. Through him passes Hydra, the great snake, and from its mouth there pours to man the light of God. His symbol is the rising sun....[17] Masonry is eternal truth...patience is its warden, illumination its master.[18]

When a Mason has built all these powers into himself, there radiates from him a wonderful body of living fire, like that which surrounded the Master Jesus, at the moment of his transfiguration.[19]

NUMERICAL SYMBOLISM

Masonry places great emphasis on numerical symbolism. The numbers three, five, and seven are deemed of special importance. In fact, odd numbers in general are thought to have primarily male qualities. "Why do Odds make a Lodge? Because all Odds are Men's advantage."[20]

Therefore odd numbers are used whenever possible in Masonry to symbolize its male exclusivity, while even numbers are thought to possess feminine characteristics.[21] Here's an interesting example from a Masonic text:

> Seven is a particularly sacred number....It is engraved in your very being, for at the age of seven you first showed understanding, at the age of fourteen puberty is generally reached, at the age of twenty-one manhood is recognized, at the age of twenty-eight full growth attained and at the age of thirty-five, physical vigor is highest, at forty-two, this begins to decline; at forty-nine man should have reached the height of intellectual strength; and at seventy he has reached the ordinary limit of human life.[22]

Many Masons will find this sort of numerical hocus-pocus a bit silly, but those who have studied their literature cannot fail to run across this sort of symbolic material in abundance. It not only pervades Masonic literature, but Masonic art as well.

ILLUMINISM

Masonry, like other secret societies, advocates a "religion," which is sometimes termed Illuminism. This is merely a polite name for Luciferianism. Again, this is not to be confused with the Illuminati of the eighteenth century. Those who follow Illuminism are known as Illuminists or Luciferians. Illuminism differs substantially from Satanism. General Albert Pike said in his "Instructions" to the twenty-three Supreme Councils of World Masonry in 1889, "The Masonic religion should be, by all of us initiates of the high degrees, maintained in the purity of the Luciferian doctrine."[23]

In 1889 Pike simultaneously occupied the positions of Grand Master of the Central Directory of Washington, D.C. (the head of D.C. Masonry), Grand Commander of the Supreme Council of Charleston (head of American Masonry), and Sovereign Pontiff of Universal Freemasonry (head of world Masonry).[24]

MAN BECOMES GOD

Illuminism—the Luciferian religion—teaches that man can become God, that he can evolve, through initiatory steps, into a god state himself. Even though written in 1871, Pike's words are still regarded as the highest Masonic authority by virtue of the fact that *Morals and Dogma* is still required reading for Scottish Rite Masons. Pike said, "Whosoever aids the march of a Truth...writes in the same line with Moses, and Him who died upon the cross; and has an intellectual sympathy with the Diety Himself."[25]

Of course, once you have evolved into a god, you can make up your own rules, make up your own morality. This tired philosophy has been used through the centuries to justify countless crimes and debaucheries.

Illuminists feel that man can attain more wisdom and spiritual advancement by studying their secret knowledge than he can from any conventional religion. Masonic authority Manly Hall wrote:

> Freed of limitations of creed and sect, he [the Mason] stands master of all faiths. Freemasonry...is not a creed or doctrine but a universal expression of Divine Wisdom... a very secret and sacred philosophy that has existed for all time, and has been the inspiration of the great saints and sages of all ages, i.e., the perfect wisdom of God, revealing itself through a secret hierarchy of illumined minds.[26]

Determining the philosophy of Masonry is very difficult. Every aspect of Masonry seems to have both a good and a bad side to it—an evil interpretation and a benign interpretation. Those who wish to find a Christian interpretation in its symbols can find ample published Masonic justifications. Those who wish to show that Masonry is really a form of Deism—built for all religions and faiths—can easily do so. Even Muslims are well-aware of this Masonic, quasi-religious trickery:

> Therefore, if you find any truth in the Bible, the Mason says "that's Masonry." If a Muslim expounds upon the science of Al-Islam that science is called "Masonry." Some Masonic writers have [gone] as far as to say Adam was a Mason because the Bible says he covered his private area with leaves which represents the "Masonic Apron." Such claims are made by those who want to make the uninitiated think that the "wisdom of the ages" can only be found in Masonry.[27]

However, those who wish to show Masonry to be of Luciferian, or even of Satanic basis encounter difficulty finding references hidden in the more secretive source material, but they can be found. Masonry itself admits to the confusion. British Mason Colin F.W. Dyer wrote in his 1976 book, *Speculative Craft Masonry*:

> It is possible to give a Christian interpretation to the whole of Craft Masonry...but a non-Christian interpretation should also exist and be just as correct.

There is one fact which must always be borne in mind...as time passes, men...weave new legends round old customs, or import them from another school of belief. This tendency can be traced in Masonry in many ways. More than one meaning lies hidden in our silent emblems, and the ostensible explanation given in the ceremony is usually neither the original nor the most profound meaning attached to it.[28]

So, to the "Christian Mason," Masonry is an integral part of the Christian faith. According to Dyer; "The First Degree of Masonry teaches [the candidate] that his actions must be squared by the precepts contained in the Holy Bible, the constant study of which is strongly recommended." [29]

As we will see, however, the "Christian" candidate is slowly weaned off the Christian path, and without ever realizing it, gently set on the path of Deism — the forerunner of modern day Unitarianism.[30] Deists believe in a God who existed merely to create the universe, but then withdrew to meddle no more in the affairs of man. Therefore, Jesus is considered to have been at best a prophet or a wise man, and certainly not the Son of God. For in Deism, man needs no God and, in fact, through reason and secret initiated knowledge, or illumination, Deists believe that man can become as God.

INNER & OUTER DOCTRINE

How can some Masons believe Masonry is a Christian organization, while others understand its darker goals? The key to this confusion lies in the concept of the "inner" and the "outer" doctrine. Masonry, like other secret societies, is set up with an "outer" doctrine for consumption by the general public, and an "inner" secretive doctrine known only to an elect few.

To Masons, ananalogy is found in the concept of the onion. As you progress in Masonry, you peel away layer after layer until you finally reach the truth at the core. In the words of Adam Weishaupt, founder of an eighteenth-century German secret society, the Illuminati: "One must speak sometimes in one way, sometimes in another, so that our real purpose should remain impenetrable to our inferiors."[31]

In a book so scarce outside of Masonic circles that it could not be found in the prestigious collection of the Library of Congress, General Pike is very clear in revealing part of Masonry's inner doctrine claiming that it is an improvement on Christianity:

Christianity taught the doctrine of FRATERNITY; but repudiated that of political EQUALITY, by continually inculcating obedience to Caesar, and to those lawfully in authority. Masonry was the first apostle of EQUALITY.[32]

Pike also explained that Masonry must deceive its members in the first three degrees, called the "Blue Degrees."

> The Blue Degrees are but the outer court or portico of the Temple. Part of the symbols are displayed there to the Initiate, but he is intentionally misled by false interpretations. It is not intended that he shall understand them; but it is intended that he shall imagine he understands them. Their true explanation is reserved for the Adepts, the Princes of Masonry.[33]

This basic deception of Masonry is perfectly depicted by the Sphinx.

> It is well enough for the mass of those called Masons, to imagine that all is contained in the Blue Degrees; and whose attempts to undeceive them will labor in vain....Masonry is the veritable Sphinx, buried to the head in the sands heaped round it by the ages.[34]

Masons must swear oaths, known as "blood oaths," that they will never reveal the secrets of their order on pain of a barbaric death. After extensive memorization of Masonic lore and philosophy, the candidate is initiated into what is known as the lodge. At first, members are told little about the goals of their order. It is only gradually, as the member advances through the various degrees, or steps of initiation, that the true scope of Masonry is revealed. One Masonic source has said: "Masonry should be felt everywhere, but nowhere should it be un-veiled. The whole strength of Masonry lies in its discretion. Our enemies fear us all the more because we never reveal our methods of action."[35]

As the new Mason becomes more trusted and more involved, he gradually becomes able to accept the "truths" of his new-found relig-ion. The moment a Mason does not accept one of the new tenets of his "new morality," his advancement mysteriously freezes.

WHY SECRECY?

If Masonry were really purveying pure truth, as it claims, then why would it need to keep its ancient secrets hidden? For, as Jesus said in John 18:20, "I have always taught in synagogues and in the temple, where all Jews come together; I have said nothing secretly."[36]

In reality, there are two reasons for Masonic secrecy. First of all, if every Mason's wife knew the exact content of the "blood oaths" to which her husband had sworn, then Masonry would collapse in a single night. In the wider scope, anti-Masonic investigations, inquisitions, and purges have been launched whenever the order's secrets have been revealed.

Secondly, secrecy makes members feel that they are part of an elite group. This tends to better weld them into a unit. Adam Weishaupt, father of the eighteenth-century group which eventually consumed European Masonry, the Illuminati, wrote:

For our Order wishes to be secret, and to work in silence; for thus it is better secured from the oppression of the ruling powers, and because this secrecy gives a greater zest to the whole....The slightest observation shows that nothing will so much contribute to increase the zeal of the members as secret union.[37]

Ironically, most Masons never know the darkest secrets of their order because Masonry is constructed as a secret society within a secret society. The outer doctrine is constructed to have a mass appeal and to seem relatively harmless to the vast majority of members. After all, the goal of any successful organization must be to attract good men if it is to survive. The inner doctrine is only for the highest initiates.

One of the greatest secrets of Masonry, and of all the secret societies, is something called the "Great Plan," the details of which are known only to those with access to the inner doctrine. As one Masonic scholar explained:

Though the whole extent and origin of the plan was known only to an initiate few, members of the outer order were subjected to a selective system by which they could attain to numerous degrees and proportionately receive deeper insight into the work. This in turn spurred them to greater effort and endeavor in their various occupations and stations in life, and made them useful instruments.[38]

This outer doctrine allows the average member to see his organization as little more than a social fraternity involved in a few charitable works. However, for those who are judged ready, or "worthy" to accept it, the inner doctrine drops all pretense of this idealism. As we will see, this inner doctrine is nothing less than a cancer growing on civilization, unknowingly supported by the huge body of mostly innocent, dues-paying members.

The Masonry-Lucifer connection is further strengthened by occultist Mason Manly Hall, who says that when the Mason learns how to use this occult power "he has learned the mystery of his Craft. The seething energies of Lucifer are in his hands and before he may step onward and upward, he must prove his ability to properly apply energy."[39]

So, as we see, acquiring "the seething energies of Lucifer" is but the first step. To show that he is worthy to move up, the Mason must prove he can apply this knowledge. Hall recounts a typical example of Masonry's attitude toward religion:

Freemasonry is a philosophy which is essentially creedless. Its brothers bow to truth regardless of the bearer; they serve light, instead of wrangling over the one who brings it....No truer religion exists than that of world comradeship and brotherhood.[40] Freemasonry is not a material thing; it is a science of the soul...a divine symbolic language perpetuating [by] certain concrete symbols the sacred mysteries of the ancients.[41]

LUCIFER OR SATAN?

So are Masons Satanists? Not at all. Though few Masons know it, the god of Masonry is Lucifer. What's the difference between Lucifer and Satan? Luciferians think they are doing good. Satanists know they are evil. In the Bible, Lucifer was God's most important angel, "perfect in thy ways...full of wisdom and perfect beauty."[42]

Although he was the highest angel, Lucifer wanted more. He wanted to replace God, and so he led the first revolution and rebelled against God. God quickly cast Lucifer out of heaven, banishing one-third of all the angels with him.[43] Lucifer, the good angel of light, forevermore became Satan, the evil angel of darkness:

> How you are fallen from heaven, O Day Star, son of Dawn! How you are cut down to the ground, you who laid the nations low! You said in your heart, "I will ascend to heaven; above the stars of God."
> Isaiah 14:12-15

However, the essence of Masonry and of all Luciferian religions denies this biblical account. The real secret of all the secret societies is that they believe Lucifer never fell to earth; that Lucifer is really God, and has been since the dawn of creation. They derisively call the Christian God by the name Adonay, and believe that he is really the god of evil because he forces men to be subservient to his repressive dictates.

So to Luciferians, God has a dual nature; he is the good god, Lucifer, and the bad god, Adonay, both supposedly equal in power, yet opposite in intent. This idea is symbolized by the circular yin-yang symbol of the Buddhists, or the black-and-white checkerboard pattern seen on the floor of Masonic lodges, or buildings.

Lucifer is further subdivided into Isis, the female principal, and Osiris, the male principal. The myth that a benevolent Lucifer still exists, is at the core of all the secret societies. It paints Lucifer as being different from Satan—as some form of benevolent god who favors his followers on the basis of their level of "illumination." By comparison, Christianity teaches that faith in Jesus Christ is the determining factor in the attainment of everlasting spiritual life.

Masons have their own Luciferian-based calendar. Our Western calendar counts its years based on the number of years before and after Christ; B.C. for before Christ, and A.D., Anno Domini, meaning "in the year of the Lord," for the years after the birth of Christ. The Masonic calendar counts its years with the suffix A.L., meaning Anno Lucis or "Year of Light," the Masonic year of the Creation.[44] This can also be interpreted to mean "Year of Lucifer."

Masons don't count their years from the year of Christ's death because for a rather curious reason, they consider it a tragedy. In their initiation ceremony for the eighteenth degree, the Knight of the Rose

A Masonic diploma, recording the dates of the first three degrees. In five
places, the dates are specified in both A.D. and A.L., or "Anno Lucis."
(Courtesy: Library of Congress)

Crucis, also known as the Rose Croix, the Red Cross, or "the Rosicrucians,"[45] Masons symbolically drape the lodge room in black and sit on
the floor in silence resting their heads in their arms in mock grief around

an altar above which are three crosses. They grieve not for the death of the Son of God, but, according to the French Masonic historian Abbé Augusten de Barruel, they symbolically mourn because the day Jesus was crucified was the day Christianity was born, ever to be the antagonist of Masonry:

> It is the...time when the veil of the temple was rent asunder, when darkness and consternation was spread over the earth, when the light was darkened, when the implements of Masonry were broke, when the flaming star disappeared, when the cubic stone was broken, when the word was lost.[46]

It is a strange paradox that both Christians and Satanists believe the Bible is the word of God. Neither believe in Lucifer. Both Christians and Satanists believe that Lucifer existed only before his fall. Both believe that a benevolent Lucifer no longer exists; that he is now the demonic being known as Satan.

Satanists, however, worship evil and so they do the opposite of what the Bible teaches. Satanists know Satan is evil, and is merely trying to drag as many souls to hell with him as he can. They have no delusions that Satan is benefic in any way. They know that Lucifer is merely one of Satan's myths, trying to trick mankind away from following the real God and his tenets, using whatever deceptions prove to be effective.

So Luciferianism and Satanism have a basic difference: Luciferianism pretends to be good; Satanism admits it is bad, and says there is no "good." The results are the same. Lucifer and Satan are frequently confused, even by experts. For example, in 1908 French occultism expert Copin Albancelli confused Lucifer and Satan in describing the beliefs of the upper echelons of Masonry:

> Certain Masonic societies exist which are Satanic, not in the sense that the devil comes to preside at their meetings...but in that their initiates profess the cult of Lucifer. They adore him as the true God, and they are animated by an implacable hatred against the Christian God, whom they declare to be an imposter.[47]

According to Webster, Albancelli goes on to show that the Masonic motto changes from "To the glory of the Great Architect of the Universe," at the lower levels of Masonry, to "Glory and Love for Lucifer! Hatred! hatred! hatred! to God, accursed, accursed, accursed!"[48]

Albancelli also explained the view of the Ten Commandments held by one French version of Masonry:

> It is professed in these societies that all that the Christian God commands is disagreeable to Lucifer; that all that He forbids is, on the contrary, agreeable to Lucifer; that in consequence one must do all that the Christian God forbids and that one must shun like fire all that He commands.[49]

It should be noted here that some Masons, especially British and American Masons, vehemently deny that they embrace any Satanic or Luciferian doctrines. In fact, many claim that French Masonry is "bad" while British Masonry and its American derivative is benign. The truth is that all Masons, no matter which country they are in, have to swear to increasingly horrific "blood oaths" as they ascend through the degrees of initiation.

Masons complain bitterly that these oaths are merely ceremonial, and meaningless, at least in today's world. If this is so, then why perpetuate them? The similarities between Continental and Anglo/American Masonry are so substantial and so well-documented, while the demonstrable differences are so few, that at this point it is incumbent on the Masonic fraternity to prove there is a significant difference.

Both Lucifer and Satan incite revolution—revolution against all forms of authority, husband against wife, child against parent, citizen against government. Rebellion against supposedly unjust authority is the hallmark of all Masonry. The Bible, however, teaches obedience:

> Wives must submit to your husbands' leadership....Children, obey your parents and...obey every law of your government: those of the king as head of state and those of the king's officers, for he has sent them to punish all who do wrong, and to honor those who do right. [50]

Illuminism teaches the opposite of obedience—revolution. Illuminists are living the sad and ultimate deception of all mankind, believing that man does not need God, does not need obedience:

> For even Satan disguises himself as an angel of light. Therefore it is not surprising that his servants also disguise themselves as servants of righteousness; whose end shall be according to their deeds. [51]

This ancient struggle between Satan and God for the souls of men has affected every individual, in every nation, through every period of human history since the Garden of Eden, where Eve was successfully tempted and deceived by the serpent to "eat of the tree of the knowledge of good and evil—" because then she would attain deity. "Ye shall surely not die...for then your eyes shall be opened, and ye shall be as gods, knowing good and evil."[52]

All the secret societies play on this yearning of all men to seek immortality for themselves or their souls. The Luciferian doctrine promises enlightenment, via Lucifer. It promises that man can become a god through secret knowledge passed down through these societies.

THE ANCIENT GREEKS

The basic philosophies of Illuminism turn up in every culture, ancient or modern; only the names of their gods change. Isis and Osiris, and some of the other Egyptian gods, mutated into new identities as they passed into different nations and different eras.

In ancient Greece and Rome, Isis mutated into a variety of slightly different forms, such as Diana, Athena, Aphrodite, and Venus. Osiris became Zeus, Poseidon, and Mercury. Why is this mythology important? Because the worship of these pagan gods and goddesses still exists.

How are the societies' secrets kept secure? One of the methods of preserving secrecy in secret societies is the concept of common criminality. A prime example of this can be seen in one of the best documented scandals of the pre-Christian era. The cult of Isis flourished in ancient Greece, and her mysteries were, as always, kept by the secret societies. But the proverbial cat got out of the bag when the famous "Mystery Scandal" broke in ancient Athens.

It seems that a large group of aristocrats conspired to overthrow the Athenian democracy. In order to insure the secrecy of the operation among the extraordinarily large number of conspirators, a common crime was committed in which each member had to participate. Communal criminality has always been a necessary security measure for the highest "mysteries" of the secret societies.

One night the conspiring Athenians went out into the city streets armed with hammers and chisels and cut off the genitals of the many statues of the god Hermes gracing their city. In that day, nothing could have been a more public display of desecration, and would surely have been dealt with quite harshly. In this way, it was assured that if any member of the group was to betray the conspiracy, he would find himself charged with a crime with numerous influential witnesses testifying against him.

The case came to light only because of the public outrage. A thorough investigation was launched, and eventually the conspiratorial web was cracked. The perpetrators were discovered, publicly humiliated during a series of trials, and later exiled from Greece.

ATLANTIS

Secret societies have existed in most, if not all nations throughout history. Manly Hall claimed that a super-secret society superior to the Masonic order was the backbone of not only the ancient civilizations of Greece and later Rome, but also the civilizations of Islam and the Mongol empires. Hall calls this super-secret group the "Order of the Illumed Ones," the "Order of the Quest" or the "Order of the Ancient Philosophers."

Even in ancient times, scholars bound themselves with "mystic ties" into a worldwide fraternity, drawing candidates from all the Mystery Schools, the Masons, the Rosicrucians, the Kabbalists (Jewish Mystery School tradition), and others. These "priest-philosophers" from Egypt, Greece, India, China, and the rest of the ancient world were formed into a sovereign body to instruct and advise their leaders.[53]

Where did this ancient order originate? Hall claimed that it originated in the legendary Atlantis. He claimed that the Atlanteans devised a plan — a "Great Plan" — which would guide world events for millennia to come, and that it included a mysterious blueprint of what would later become America. Hall said that ancient Egyptian secret societies inherited this Great Plan and were well aware of the existence of the land mass in the Western Hemisphere which we now call America, long before it was "discovered" by Columbus.[54] Hall stated:

> The explorers who opened the New World operated from a master plan and were agents of re-discovery rather than discoverers.

> Time will reveal that the continent now known as America was actually discovered and, to a considerable degree, explored more than a thousand years before the beginning of the Christian era. The true story was in the keeping of the Mystery Schools, and passed from them to the Secret Societies of the medieval world. The Esoteric Orders of Europe, Asia, and the Near East were in at least irregular communication with the priesthoods of the more advanced Amerindian nations. Plans for the development of the Western Hemisphere were formulated in Alexandria, Mecca, Delhi, and Lhasa [in Tibet] long before most European statesmen were aware of the great Utopian program.[55]

Hall maintained that the unifying goal of these secret societies was to create a "New Atlantis" in America:

> The bold resolution was made that this western continent should become the site of the philosophic empire. Just when this was done it is impossible now to say, but certainly the decision was reached prior to the time of Plato, for a thinly veiled statement of this resolution is the substance of his treatise on the Atlantic Islands.[56]

America, according to this Great Plan, was to become the first nation to begin to establish a "universal democracy," or "world commonwealth of nations." This quest was said to be the most noble pursuit to which a man could devote himself. It is said to have been so perfectly inspired that it continues today:

> The mechanism for the accomplishment of this idea was set in motion in the ancient temples of Greece, Egypt, and India. So brilliant was the plan and so well was it administrated that it has survived to our time, and it will continue to function until the great work is accomplished.[57]

ILLUMINATION

So just what is illumination? I have mentioned it in vague terms such as "light" and "secret knowledge." However, illumination is not just the knowledge gained from reading books, or receiving oral instruction, or even the secretive knowledge gained from initiation. Illumination also involves a vivid flash of insight or understanding, regardless of what means are used to attain it:

> Wise men, the ancients believed, were a separate race, and to be born into this race it was necessary to develop the mind to a state of enlightened intelligence. The old philosophers taught that physical birth is an accident, for men are born into various races and nationalities according to the laws of generation; but there is a second birth, which is not an accident; it is the consequence of a proper intent. By this second birth, man is born by enlightened intelligence out of nation and out of race into an international nation and an international race. It is this larger and coming race that will some day inherit the earth. But unless a man be born again by enlightenment, he shall not be a part of the philosophic empire.[58]

Obviously, this is a hermetic version of the Christian "born-again" experience. This is a theme which runs throughout Masonry and all the other secret societies: that the acquisition of secret knowledge, or illumination, is man's salvation.

There are many ways to achieve illumination. The method most important to Illuminists is the mystical inspiration invoked by the performance of occult rituals. Illumination can be achieved by dancing to exhaustion to the rhythm of native drums. It can be brought on by sexual rituals, such as those practiced in Tantric Yoga. To the Satanist, it can be brought on by ritualistic sacrifice. Throughout history, mind-altering substances such as marijuana, hashish, peyote cactus, and LSD have been used to achieve this paranormal mystical experience. In fact, the Greek word for sorcery is *pharmakia* from whence came the word pharmaceuticals.

GNOSTICISM

Another branch of Illuminism which still survives is Gnosticism. It rose in the first and second centuries A.D., and taught that magical knowledge, known as gnosis, was the only path to salvation. One of the ways believers received access to these "divine mysteries" was through sexual orgies disguised as religious rites.

The general Gnostic emphasis on knowledge, received through magical inspiration, naturally led to a contempt for conventional morality, because according to Gnosticism, a man did not reach heaven by leading a good life, or through faith, but through possession of gnosis. A man who received gnosis had in effect evolved into a god, and could not be corrupted by anything he might do. Secure in godhead, Gnostics seduced their female disciples and indulged all the lusts of the flesh. Some Gnostics said that good and evil were meaningless labels and that the way to perfection was to experience everything.

Scholars of today call this "Experimentalism". It was widely seen in the "hippies" and "flower children" of the 1960s, though it is rarely understood in its historical perspective.

It is not a large leap from Gnosticism to Satanism. Researcher Richard Cavandish, author of *The Black Arts*, has written: "All these Gnostic ideas fit into the general pattern of Satanism, indeed, they largely established it."

Nesta Webster, noted British historian of the 1920s, reported that Gnostic rituals formed "the basis of black magic in the Middle Ages" including the "glorification of evil which plays so important a part in the modern revolutionary movement."[59] According to Webster, "the role of the Gnostics was to reduce perversion to a system by binding men together into sects working under the guise of enlightenment in order to obscure all recognized ideas of morality and religion."[60]

Gnostics were some of the first known advocates of the "ends-justify-the-means" philosophy. They believed that there was no such thing as an absolute morality; that evil deeds were justifiable if they served a higher purpose. Since the second century, the Christian concept of man reaching up to God has been under constant, yet subtle attack. Webster says:

> ... the secret society conception of man as God, needing no revelation from on high and no guidance but the law of his own nature. And since that nature is in itself divine, all that springs from it is praiseworthy, and those acts usually regarded as sins are not to be condemned. [61]

But Gnosticism has at its core the same belief in Lucifer that all the Illuminist philosophies do. Occult expert Edith Star Miller pointed out that Gnostics believe themselves to be gods. Writing in her 1933 book, *Occult Theocracy*, she said:

> Such was the excellency of their knowledge and Illumination who arrogantly styled themselves Gnostics, that they [feel they] are superior to Peter and Paul or any of Christ's other disciples. They only, have drunk up the supreme Knowledge, are above Principalities and Powers, secure of Salvation: and for that very Reason are free to debauch Women.[62]

The Gnostics set themselves up as gods, or demigods, enticing men to follow their system by sexual perversion, and/or the promise of secret knowledge. Are there links between Gnosticism and the Mystery School systems of the twentieth century? Indeed so. According to Miller:

> Gnosticism, as the Mother of Freemasonry, has imposed its mark in the very centre of the chief symbol of this association. The most conspicuous emblem which one notices on entering a Masonic temple, the one which figures on the seals, on the rituals, everywhere in fact, appears in the middle of the interlaced square and compass, it is the five pointed star framing the letter G.

Different explanations of this letter G are given to the initiates as they rise up from the lower levels. In the lower grades, one is taught that it signifies Geometry, then God, then Great Architect of the Universe:

> To the brothers frequenting the lodges admitting women as members, it is revealed that the mystic letter means Generation....Finally, to those found worthy to penetrate into the sanctuary of Knights Kadosch, the enigmatic letter becomes the initial of the doctrine of the perfect initiates which is Gnosticism.

> It is Gnosticism which is the real meaning of the G in the flamboyant star, for, after the grade of Kadosch the Freemasons dedicate themselves to the glorification of Gnosticism (or anti-christianity) which is defined by Albert Pike as "the soul and marrow of Freemasonry.[63]

THE ILLUMINATI

Popular history texts and encyclopedias generally paint the Illuminati as having its origins in 1776 in Bavaria. However, the origins go back much further. The Illuminati are tied directly through Masonry to the sun and Isis cults of ancient Egypt.

The term "Illuminati" was used by one early writer, Menendez Pelayo, as early as 1492 and is attributable to a group known as the "Alumbrados" of Spain. The Alumbrados were said to receive secret knowledge from an unknown higher source, resulting in superior human intelligence. This group was condemned by an edict of the Grand Inquisition in 1623, in what was another battle in the long-running war between the Catholic Church and the secret societies.[64]

Some writers claim that a group known as the "Illuminated Ones" was founded by Joachim of Floris in the eleventh century and taught a primitive, supposedly Christian doctrine of "poverty and equality." This tactic to disguise Illuminism behind a thin veil of Christianity is now a well-established theme. Later, this group is said to have become violent, plundering the rich and thereby discrediting Christianity as a whole.

Still other writers trace the Illuminati to the dreaded Ishmaelian sect of Islam, also known as the "Order of Assassins." Founded in 1090 by Hassan Sabah, this group combined the use of the drug hashish with murder as their main path to illumination.

Killing was a mystical experience to this branch of the Mystery Schools. They not only maintained their control by murder and threats of murder, they believed that the assassin could acquire the gnosis, or soul energy from the victim. This is the theory behind the human and animal sacrifices of Satanists throughout history.

Primitive religions get the same effect by dancing and drumbeating. Seeking this form of illumination was the main attraction of drugs like marijuana, hashish, and LSD to teenagers of the 1960s and 1970s. Buddhists can gain the same illumination through sexual rituals known as Tantric Yoga, or through the different forms of meditation. Witch-craft covens still meet in the nude and participate in group sexual rituals for the same effect. Mass participation in animal sacrifice is another way to scavenge gnosis.

The sad fact is that although sex, drugs, dancing, and drumbeating are believed to release a lot of gnosis, Satanists believe that sacrifices release more of it than anything else. Such are the dark and sordid machinations of the deluded souls who think their gnosis accumulations and illumination will give them some form of deity or immortality.

This is only a thumbnail sketch of the myriad forms Illumination has taken up to the eighteenth century A.D. It is important to realize however, that Illuminism is really the religion of a benevolent mythical Lucifer—not Satan. It is disguised as political idealism, bent on eradicating religion and monarchies in general, and Christianity in particular, and gaining global control for a "commonwealth of nations" featuring "universal democracy."

> "And no wonder, for even Satan disguises himself as an angel of light."[65]

THREE

THE GREAT ATLANTEAN PLAN

Destiny and the Mysteries must win,
for they are on the side of the Great Plan.
Manly P. Hall, 1951[1]

According to Masonic sources, the most important mystery of secret societies is an ancient plan, passed down for thousands of years by oral tradition, for the establishment of a world government—a "universal democracy"—a "New Atlantis." In the early 1600s, this plan for a new world order was in the keeping of Masons in the greatest commonwealth the world had ever known—the British Empire. English Masons believed that North America was the continent from which their New Atlantis would spring.

Most people believe that the legend of Atlantis is only a myth. Yet the similarities between the account of the destruction of Atlantis and the biblical account of the flood of Noah are really quite remarkable. They appear to be the same event. The difference may be just one of perspective. From the vantage point of secret societies the destruction of Atlantis was a tragedy. Manly Hall claimed that the Atlantean legend is central to the philosophy of all secret societies. He describes Masonry as, "... a university, teaching the liberal arts and sciences of the soul.... It is a shadow of the great Atlantean Mystery School, which stood with all its splendor in the ancient City of the Golden Gates." [2] From the biblical point of view its destruction was a necessity because the preflood world had become so corrupt:

> And God looked on the earth, and behold, it was corrupt; for all flesh had corrupted their way upon the earth....I am bringing the flood of water upon the earth....everything on the earth shall perish.[3]

Atlantean authority Ignatius Donnelly wrote in 1882 that the similarities were so significant as to mandate that they were one and the same event:

> The Deluge plainly refers to the destruction of Atlantis, and that it agrees in many important particulars with the account given by Plato. The people destroyed were, in both instances, the ancient race that had created civilization; they had formerly been in a happy and sinless condition; they had become great and wicked; they were destroyed for their sins—they were destroyed by water.[4]

Isn't it interesting that it is this corrupt preflood civilization that the secret societies are working so hard to reinstate? Interesting too, is the fact that the Bible tells us that Christ will return when the same kind of society exists again. Matthew 24:37-39 tells us:

> For the coming of the Son of Man will be just like the days of Noah. For as in those days which were before the flood they were eating and drinking, they were marrying and giving in marriage, until the day that Noah entered the ark.

Whether or not one believes in the Atlantean legend, it certainly exists in literature. There is only one source of the Atlantis legend outside of Masonic circles—the account written by Plato about 400 B.C. This account is said to be derived from an even earlier oral account originating with a Greek philosopher named Solon, known as the father of the Greek democracy.

Solon was told the story of Atlantis around 595 B.C. while studying with the priests of the Temple of Isis located in Sais, Egypt. The legend was passed in oral tradition for several generations before Plato heard it and wrote it down in the traditional form of the day, called a "dialogue." This dialogue is known as the *Critias*.

Although the account in the *Critias* is the oldest available reference to the legendary kingdom, it seems that additional information about Atlantis is still possessed by the highest initiates of the secret societies. Hall, a thirty-third degree Mason, the highest publicly-known Masonic ranking, gives us a detailed account of his own concerning just how Solon acquired his knowledge of Atlantis in his 1944 book, *The Secret Destiny of America*.

Although he does not provide the reader with the source of the story, Hall recounts that Solon, while visiting Egypt in search of wisdom, was accepted by the priests in the temple of Isis as a brother-initiate and was shown their secrets.

According to Hall's undocumented, yet interesting account, the priests took Solon down a long series of ancient steps, hewn from living rock, that eventually opened into a huge subterranean chamber through which flowed part of the Nile River. The party boarded a small boat that was rowed by blind men to a tiny island far underground. On this island were two pillars made of a rare metal, said to be orichalcum, the fabled indestructible Atlantean material, which neither rusted nor deteriorated with age. Upon these two huge, inviolable pillars were curious writings in a mysterious language unknown to Solon.[5]

Solon was told that the columns were placed there thousands of years earlier by a lost people who had vanished forever. He was told that the mysterious inscriptions on the columns were the laws of the Atlantean ancients, left there to steer mankind until the appointed time for the Atlantean civilization to flourish once again.

According to this account, at its peak, some 10,000 years before the Greek civilization, Atlantis was ruled in complete harmony by a cooperative commonwealth of ten kings, known as the Atlantic League. Seven of these kings ruled over the seven islands that actually made up what was called the "continent of Atlantis." The other three kings of the Atlantean kingdom ruled over the other three known continents: Europe, Asia, and Africa.[6]

One day the seven kings of Atlantis decided to conquer the other three continents. They invaded Greece and all of Europe about 10,000 B.C. This overt transgression of Atlantean law enraged the father of all the gods. In a single evening, Zeus caused the entire island of Atlantis, with some sixty million inhabitants, to sink beneath the waves.[7]

In fact, in the record of almost every civilization for which ancient legends exist, the one thing they all hold in common is a flood tradition in the distant past. In 1933, historian Immanuel Velikovsky attributed the flood to a common astronomical phenomenon—a close passage of either Venus or Mars to the Earth.

According to Hall, with the demise of Atlantis went the "ideal pattern of government," the secrets of which Masons have conserved through their oral traditions:

> So complete was this destruction, that men forgot there is a better way of life, and accepted the evils of war and crime and poverty as inevitable....The old Atlantis is gone, dissolved in a sea of human doubts. But the philosophical empire would come again, as a democracy of wise men.[8]

Solon was told that the mysterious columns were all that was left of the ancient Atlantean culture to guide the future "government of nations."[9] However, what Hall and Masons fail to point out is that this supposedly "ideal pattern of government" led to the destruction of old Atlantis. Can there be any doubt that if such a government *is* ever reinstalled, it will bring about the same tragic result?

Manly Hall explained why this Atlantean legend is so important to understanding the goals of those who are still striving to bring forth a new world order in America:

The league of the ten kings is the cooperative commonwealth of mankind, the natural and proper form of human government. The Atlantis [legend], therefore, is the archetype or the pattern of government, which existed in ancient days but was destroyed by the selfishness and ignorance of men.[10]

Today, the elite of secret societies are still taught that bringing forth a new cooperative commonwealth of mankind—a new Atlantic League—is the natural and proper form of human government, and the highest calling to which a person can dedicate himself.

Christians well-versed in the Bible believe that this so-called "commonwealth of mankind" is, in reality, the dictatorship of the Antichrist, predicted in the Bible's book of Revelation. In fact, there is a startling similarity between the Atlantean myth and biblical prophesy. Revelation 13:1 states:

> And I stood upon the sand of the sea, and saw a beast rise up out of the sea, having seven heads and ten horns, and upon his horns ten crowns, and upon his heads the name of blasphemy.

According to noted biblical scholar Charles Ryrie, the ten horns of the beast are the ten kings mentioned in Daniel 7:24, who will rule over ten nations. Ryrie interprets the Bible as saying that one of these kings will be different, more brutal than the others, and he shall destroy three of the other kings.[11] The Bible says that this most brutal king, referred to as the Antichrist, will "defy the Most High God, and wear down the saints with persecution, and try to change all laws, morals, and customs. God's people will be helpless in his hands for three and a half years.[12]

The Atlantean legend seems to set the ideological foundation upon which all the secret societies rest. Whether it is the "cooperative commonwealth of the ten kings," the "Philosophical Empire," the "New Atlantic League," the "New World Order," or the "New Atlantis," the meaning is always the same: to establish a so-called "enlightened" world government.

What is an "enlightened" world government? It takes a little digging, but the word "enlightened" is meant to describe a government free of religion, or, as its proponents usually explain, a government free of "religious persecution" or "superstition." Hall gave us the Masonic reasoning when he wrote the following in 1944 under the heading "The Democratic Tradition Preserved by Secret Societies":

> For more than three thousand years, secret societies have labored to create the background of knowledge necessary to the establishment of an enlightened democracy among the nations of the world...The rise of the Christian Church brought persecution...driving the guilds [the secret societies] into greater secrecy; but all have continued searching for human happiness under a variety of rituals and symbols; and they still exist.[13]

Today, this concept is remarkably widespread among leading politicians the world over, and is embodied in the spirit of the current United Nations. Now let's take a look at the role of the secret societies in the earliest origins of America.

SECRET SOCIETIES IN THE ANCIENT AMERICAS

Secret societies have been active in most civilizations since the beginning of recorded history. Primitive secret orders have existed among African tribes, among the Eskimos, and throughout the East Indies and northern Asia. American Indians, the Chinese, Hindus, and even Arabs have elaborate religious and fraternal organizations.

Wherever they sprang up, secrecy was maintained in these groups for two reasons. First was to prevent condemnation and persecution in the event the rites they practiced were made public. A second purpose for secret societies was to create a mechanism for the perpetuation, from generation to generation, of policies, principles, or systems of learning, confined to a limited group of selected and initiated persons.[14]

Ancient Masonic lodges have been discovered among the American Indians. Former newspaper editor and thirty-second degree Mason John Loughran recently found what he called an ancient Indian Masonic lodge at an Anasazi Indian archaeological site. Loughran writes:

> The furniture was placed the same [way], and the area where the main rituals took place seemed eighty percent identical to the Masonic lodges in America now. The only difference was that these temples were round. Then I did some research and found out that in northern Africa the Masonic temples started out round.[15]

In the ancient lodge, he was able to decipher symbols left by the Anasazi Masons that led him to a "locater device." That device, in turn, led to a hidden library. In this library, there were fifty rock and clay tablets, which he dates between 1000 and 1200 A.D., written in what appears to be Arabic. It is interesting to note that the name Anasazi means "ancient ones."

Even the name "America" may be the product of ancient American secret societies. In an 1895 edition of a magazine called *Lucifer*, published by the occult-promoting Theosophical Society, author James Pryse gave an interesting insight into the meaning of the word "America." He said that the supreme god of the Mayan culture of Central America, known as Quetzalcoatl elsewhere, was known in Peru as Amaru. Amaru's territory was known as Amaruca. According to Pryse:

> From the latter comes our word America. Amaruca is, literally translated, "Land of the Plumed Serpent." The Priests of this God of Peace once ruled the Americas. All the Red men who have remained true to the ancient religion are still under their sway.[16]

Most historians attribute the name America to explorer Amerigo Vespucci, but Manly Hall claims that since the serpent is frequently symbolic of Lucifer, it is no exaggeration to extrapolate from this that America may well mean "Land of Lucifer."

To the secret societies, Lucifer is always depicted as a benevolent, peace-loving god with nothing but the best intentions for the human race. In Greek mythology he was Prometheus, the titan who defied Zeus to bestow the gift of fire upon mankind, an act for which he was tortured mercilessly. Interestingly, the initiatory knowledge of secret societies is commonly referred to as "light" and associated with fire. Among Luciferans, God is seen as evil, trying to keep knowledge away from man. The same scenario was repeated in the Garden of Eden, when the snake explained to Adam and Eve that God didn't want them to have knowledge that would make them wise.

In Central and South America, a land of dark-skinned natives, Quetzalcoatl was said to be a white man with a strong body, broad forehead, large eyes, and a flowing beard. He wore a miter on his head similar to the headdress worn by the Egyptian goddess Isis in ancient Egyptian drawings.

Quetzalcoatl dressed in long white robes reaching to his feet, which were covered with a design of red crosses.[17] This brings to mind the garb of the British "crusaders" and, as we now know, the Rosy Cross symbol is the one employed by another modern day secret society, the Rosicrucians.

Quetzalcoatl left the Americas, and entrusted his teachings and the purpose of his mission to a secret "Order of Priests" until the day when he returned to rule again. This is why, when Spanish explorers first set foot in Central America, they were greeted as returning gods, because native legend had predicted the return of the white-faced Quetzalcoatl.

SIR FRANCIS BACON (1561-1626)

If one man can be singled out as the person most responsible for the colonization of America, the honor would certainly fall to the head of both Masonry and Rosecrucianism of his era, Sir Francis Bacon. In the early 1600s Bacon authored a novel entitled *New Atlantis*, which laid out the idea for a utopian society across the ocean from Europe where mankind could build a new civilization based upon the principles he believed to be those of the legendary lost continent of Atlantis, "cherishing as he did the dream of a great commonwealth in the New Atlantis."[18]

Marie Bauer Hall claims in *Collections of Emblemes, Ancient and Moderne* that:

Truly the Sixth great Empire of the Western world had its inception with the advent of Sir Francis Bacon...the true father of democracy, the

actual and true FOUNDER OF AMERICA...[and] wise guardian and
protector of its history during the last three hundred years.[19]

Born only sixty-nine years after Columbus "discovered" America,
Bacon's parentage is very controversial. He was born to Queen
Elizabeth's lady-in-waiting, Lady Ann Cooke-Bacon, wife of the Lord
High Chancellor of England. But some Bacon scholars now believe he
was, in reality, the first-born son of Queen Elizabeth and Lord Robert
Dudley, the Earl of Leicester, and was merely adopted at birth by the
Bacons, who had suffered the misfortune of a stillborn child at approxi-
mately the same time.[20] That would have made Bacon the grandson of
King Henry VII, and therefore the rightful heir to the British throne.

Why the switch? Bacon's father, Dudley, was secretly married to
Elizabeth before she became Queen in 1558 at age twenty-five.[21] It is
well known that Elizabeth wanted to marry Dudley openly, but it was
politically impossible because he was very unpopular. His first wife
died suddenly under suspicious circumstances in 1560, the year before
Bacon's birth. Throughout her reign, Elizabeth was haunted by this
persistent rumor that she had given birth to bastard children, Bacon
being the most prominent.[22]

In any case, at maturity, Bacon, an English lord, became well-versed
in the occult, and even claimed to be so mystically adept as to be in
possession of "all knowledge."[23] Marie Hall described Bacon in glowing terms:

> He is the Founder of Free Masonry...the guiding light of the
> Rosicrucion Order, the members of which kept the torch of true
> universal knowledge, the Secret Doctrine of the ages, alive during the
> dark night of the Middle-Ages.[24]

> Bacon had been initiated into the new liberalism represented
> throughout Europe by Secret Societies of intellectuals dedicated to
> civil and religious freedom....Later, when the moment was propitious,
> he threw the weight of his literary group with the English colonization
> plan for America...cherishing as he did the dream of a great
> commonwealth in the New Atlantis.[25]

Though born a half century after the death of Columbus, the ciphers
Columbus used were later to be called "Baconian ciphers." This secret
method of communication involved the seemingly random use of
italics, and the use of subtly different type styles to convey coded
messages. Sometimes even single letters within words were italicized
or had subtle font changes. Entire volumes have been devoted to the
deciphering of these coded messages, many of which are available only
in the rare books section of the Library of Congress.[26]

There is evidence suggesting that Columbus was a member of the
same secret society that Bacon led in his later days. The similarities
between the two are so remarkable that Lord Bacon has even been

referred to as the "little Columbus of literature."[27]

Bacon was very secretive. Although he strove mightily to propagate the "New Atlantis" idea, like many others involved in the plan since, he preferred to remain in the background as much as possible. The leaders

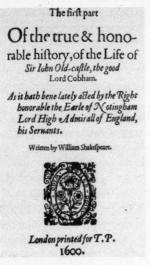

The first part

Of the true & hono-
rable history, of the Life of
Sir Iohn Old-castle, the good
Lord Cobham.

*As it hath bene lately acted by the Right
honorable the Earle of Notingham
Lord High Admirall of England,
his Seruants.*

Written by William Shakespeare.

London printed for T. P.
1600.

(courtesy of the
Library of Congress)

Original Shakespearian title page circa 1600.

of the Great Plan have always been strictly cautioned against trying to bring their plan to fulfillment too quickly:

> The Great Plan reached the Western Hemisphere through a series of incidents. Many early explorers and colonizers are known to have been associated with Secret Societies....Some of the colonizers were probably unaware of the parts they were playing, and the settlements which they founded remained for generations without the strength or security to advance ideological programs. The work, then as always, was in the hands and keeping of a few initiated leaders. They were responsible for the results, and they built slowly and wisely, thinking not of their own days or of their reputation, but of the future in which the Great Plan would be fulfilled.[28]

Bacon's novel, *New Atlantis*, was published the year after his death in 1627 by his trusted secretary, William Rawley. Hall described some of the hidden Masonic meanings contained in the *New Atlantis:*

> On the title page is a curious design. It shows the figure of an ancient creature representing Time drawing a female figure from a dark cavern. The meaning is obvious. Through time, the hidden truth shall be revealed. This figure is one of the most famous of the seals or symbols of the Order of the Quest. Contained within it is the whole promise of the resurrection of man, and the restitution of the divine theology.[29]

> TO THE
>
> # READER.
>
> His *Fable* my Lord devifed, to the end that he might exhibit therein a *Model*, or *Defcription* of a *Colledge*, inftituted for the Interpreting of *Nature*, and the producing of great and marvellous *Works* for the benefit of *Men*, under the Name of *Solomons* Houfe, or, *The Colledge of the Six daysWorks*. And even fo far his Lordfhip have proceeded as to finifh that Part. Certainly the Model is more vaft and high, than can poffibly be imitated in all things; notwithftanding moft things therein are within Mens power to effect. His Lordfhip thought alfo in this prefent Fable to have compofed a Frame of Laws, or of the beft State or Mould of a *Commonwealth* ; but fore-feeing it would be a long VVork, his defire of collecting the *Natural Hiftory* diverted him, which he preferred many degrees before it.
>
> This VVork of the *New Atlantis* (as much as concerneth the *Englifh Editions*) his Lordfhip defigned for this place, in regard it hath fo near affinity (in one part of it) with the preceding *Natural Hiftory.*
>
> *W. Rawley.*

William Rawley's Forward to Sir Francis Bacon's *New Atlantis, circa 1627*
(courtesy of the Library of Congress)

Baconian scholar and Masonic enthusiast Marie Bauer Hall believes this Great Plan has been perpetuated by an international group of only the highest initiates of the secret societies. She wrote:

> Perpetuation of the great plan was secured by secret tradition among an inner group of Initiates unknown to the outer Order at large, and patterned...in Bacon's "New Atlantis." This inner group counts a small number of members in all the countries of the Western Hemisphere. They have kept the lamp of the Muse burning during the last three hundred years.[30]

There is some controversy over why *New Atlantis* was never published in Bacon's lifetime. Although most authorities believe it was unfinished, Manly Hall offers another interesting view:

> The book was actually completed but was never published in full form because it told too much. The final sections of Bacon's fable are said to have revealed the entire pattern of the secret societies which had been working for thousands of years to achieve the ideal commonwealth in the political world.[31]

Bacon formulated a complex and far-reaching plan to reorder the world and everything in it. As revealed in another of his books, *Instauratio Magna*, the plan would reorganize the sciences and restore man to that mastery over nature that he was conceived to have lost by the fall of Adam. Bacon envisaged knowledge as a pyramid with natural history as its base, physics as the middle, and metaphysics as the vertical point.[32]

Some experts say that Bacon wrote a sequel, or at least a second part, to *New Atlantis* that included comprehensive details and timetables of how the Great Plan should be accomplished:

> It is well known among the secret societies of Europe that the second part of the New Atlantis exists. It includes a description of...the crests and the coats of arms of the governors of the philosophic empire. It may be for this reason that the writings were suppressed, for these crests and arms belonged to real persons who might have been subjected to persecution, as Sir Walter Raleigh was, if their association with the secret order had been openly announced.[33]

The initiated faithful believe that this secret document still exists and was brought to Jamestown in 1653 by his descendent, Nathaniel Bacon.[34] Nathaniel Bacon is said to have buried his ancestor's material in the new capitol of Virginia, then in Williamsburg, "in a great vault beneath the tower center of the first brick church in Bruton Parish."[35]

This is now known as the Bruton Vault and has been the subject of great speculation and treasure hunting ever since. Incidentally, it was Nathaniel Bacon who instigated the first "revolution" in America. Later that year, in 1676, exactly fifty years after Lord Bacon's death, and exactly a century before the American Declaration of Independence, Nathaniel Bacon burned Jamestown and seized the Virginia colony from England by force. This was known as Bacon's Rebellion. His short-lived revolution died shortly thereafter when he died unexpectedly.

Lord Bacon was revered by Thomas Jefferson as one of the three great men of history, along with Isaac Newton and John Locke.[36] Some Baconian scholars believe that Jefferson was the last to examine the contents of this vault, and that it has been lost since then.[37]

THE "NEW ATLANTIS"

British exploration in America began in 1585 when Sir Walter Raleigh, an adventuring British nobleman, mounted an expedition to colonize Roanoke Island, off the coast of what is now North Carolina. The twenty-four year-old Raleigh was already a member of a secret society which would later become known as the Baconian Circle. This circle, of course, believed that America was to be the glittering "New Atlantis" promised for centuries by secret societies.

So great was the clamor for the settlement of America which the

Baconian Circle had set up in England, that Raleigh had no trouble recruiting candidates for a new expedition as "every man in Europe had it 'on good authority' that the Indians used chamber pots of solid gold, encrusted with rubies and diamonds."[38]

Once they arrived, however, the new colonists found no gold like that which the Spanish had discovered in Central and South America. Under constant attack by hostile Indians, they were eventually wiped out.

After the failure of Sir Walter Raleigh's expedition in 1585, it took a generation before the British were ready to mount another attempt to colonize America. This time, the only way to stir interest in the new colonizing effort was to portray the expedition as a great work for God, through which the souls of countless Indian savages could be saved.

The "Virginia Company" was duly formed, with Francis Bacon as one of its early members. In the preamble to the Company's charter, King James I — who was also busy authorizing his own English translation of the Bible — justified the new expedition by stating that it had been organized for the "propagating of Christian religion to such people as yet live in darkness and miserable ignorance of the true knowledge and worship of God, and may in time bring the infidels and savages, living in these parts, to human civility and to a settled and quiet government.[39]

It is interesting to note, however, that of the first party of 144 men, only one minister, Rev. Robert Hunt, was included. The colonists landed in Jamestown on May 14, 1607. Fully half the party were English gentlemen in search of easy riches, who were totally unable to cope with the unbroken wilderness. Unfortunately, their code of conduct forbade them from doing any physical labor. Among the early arrivals were jewelers and a perfumer.

The Reverend Hunt tried in vain to rally the gentlemen to help with the necessary tasks of the colony, and put their faith in God instead of gold. But no crops were planted that summer. In fact, it would be twenty years before the colony would plant a crop large enough to sustain itself.

When food rations ran out, and the gentlemen grew hungry, they went to the Indians and traded for food. Were it not for the unusual tolerance of the mighty Indian chief, Powhatan, the little colony would surely have starved in the first few years. As it was, in less than two years, only thirty-eight of the initial 144 men remained alive in Jamestown.

Meanwhile, back home in England, the leaders of the secret societies were in an uproar. They tried to suppress letters and other accounts of what was really happening to the beleaguered Virginia colony, but the truth could not be quashed. As a result, fund-raising for a rescue mission to resupply Jamestown was very difficult. When finally launched in 1609, the nine-ship fleet managed to sail into a hurricane, and its flagship ran aground on the island of Bermuda.

Shakespeare's play, "The Tempest," which made its debut in 1611, was said to have been inspired by this incident. The theme of the famous drama was that there was a magical isle across the seas where nature brought forth such an abundance that no man would have to work, and the concept of personal property would be dissolved.[40] In the play, the "idealistic yet honest" old counselor, Gonzalo, muses that if he had a plantation on that luxuriant isle he would design it along communal lines and nature would supply the rest:

> All things in common Nature should produce
> Without sweat, or endeavor: treason, felony,
> Sword, pike, knife, gun, or need of any engine
> Would I not have: but Nature should bring forth
> Of its own kind, all foison, all abundance
> To feed my innocent people.[41]

SHAKESPEARE AND BACON

Over the centuries, hundreds of books have been written asserting that the plays attributed to William Shakespeare were in reality written by Lord Francis Bacon. The Library of Congress has an entire card catalog drawer full of hundreds of entries on the subject in its rare books section. If Bacon did write the Shakespeare material, and was able to keep it a secret for four centuries, then his importance to those who were privy to the secret in today's world would be greatly enhanced.

There is no doubt that someone named William Shakespeare did exist. There is no doubt, however, that he was a commoner, and little doubt that he was illiterate. Yet the plays attributed to him show a vast knowledge of English court etiquette, numerous foreign languages, and a masterful command of the English language. Critics of the Bacon-Shakespeare connection have trouble explaining away these discrepancies. Masonic researcher Marie Bauer Hall maintains:

> Sir Francis Bacon is the only man of his period who could have written the plays. William Shakespeare, the Stratford man, most definitely could not have written them, because it has been proved, time and again, beyond the shadow of a doubt that William Shakespeare could not read or write.[42]

In fact, the only evidence that William Shakespeare was literate at all consists of five alleged signatures appearing in his will.[43]

Mark Twain was certainly convinced that the historic William Shakespeare was not the real author of the Shakespeare material. In a 1909 booklet entitled *Is Shakespeare Dead*? he wrote:

"Nothing that even remotely indicates that he was ever anything more than a distinctly common-place person; an actor of inferior grade, a small trader in a small village that never regarded him as a person of any consequence, and had forgotten him before he was fairly cold in his grave."[44]

Why perpetrate such an elaborate hoax? Since many of the plays depicted real scandals in the British court involving Bacon's own estranged family, his authorship would have to be concealed.

For example, according to both Marie Bauer Hall and Baconian scholar Elizabeth Wells Gallup, Bacon had a younger brother, Robert Devereux, the second child of the union between Lord Dudley, the Earl of Leicester, and Queen Elizabeth. Devereux was also sent for adoption by the star-crossed couple. However, he himself later had an affair with Elizabeth, his mother, and the two may have conspired to kill Dudley.[45] When Bacon learned the facts of his birth, at about age sixteen, he confronted the Queen with them. In a fit of anger, she admitted her motherhood, but immediately sent Bacon to France, and took action which permanently barred him from the throne.

In an incredible irony, Devereux was later accused of treason for trying to raise the City of London in revolt against the Queen — his mother. For this he was tried and executed in 1601. During the trial, it fell upon Lord Bacon to serve as the Queen's attorney, prosecuting and condemning his own brother, Robert, to death.

Assuming all this is fact, Shakespeare's *Hamlet* takes on a stunning realism if considered as an attempt by Lord Bacon to recount the tragic story of his own family. What Bacon desperately needed was a cover. He needed a substitute author — a pen-name only, not a ghostwriter — to allow him to tell his incredible story in a manner that would not endanger either himself personally, or his mother's ability to maintain the throne of England. Hall claimed that such a stand-in would need to be:

> An ignorant outsider—who could take the consequence of authorship in case of possible detection....Such a man was found in William Shakespeare, a groom in the employ of Sir Francis Bacon's father, the Earl of Leicester.[46]

At some point, the historic William Shakespeare did come into a substantial sum of money. According to Marie Bauer Hall, "In 1602, he returned to Stratford a wealthy man and purchased one hundred seven acres of land....He [also] helped his father in the purchase of a coat of arms under false pretenses."[47]

Shakespeare died in 1616, at age fifty-two, supposedly after a drinking bout with Ben Jonson, the famed English playwright and poet.

Jonson was a close friend and contemporary of Lord Bacon, though eleven years his junior. Jonson was asked to terminate the deception by "retiring" the historical William Shakespeare prematurely. Hall stated that Jonson admitted he "put arsenic in the nitwit's beer."[48]

Jonson wrote of Bacon fondly, however: "Of greatness he could not want." But of the death of Shakespeare, supposedly the greatest playwright of all time, Jonson, and all his colleagues who should have known him well, would write nothing:

> [Shakespeare's] death was ignored by all contemporary authors, though his plays were glorified....At his death there was not a book or a desk in his possession. There is no mention of any manuscript in his will....The first folio was printed seven years after his death. At the time no relations or heirs made any claims. Seventeen plays were not published until after his death, yet no provisions are made in his will for these plays. Though miserly, he never sought remuneration for his plays.[49]

Elizabeth Wells Gallup, a cryptologist who spent years deciphering Bacon's coded messages in the seemingly random use of italicized words and letters in original editions of Bacon's and Shakespeare's works, came to the same conclusion. Writing in 1899, she said:

> The proofs are overwhelming and irresistible that Bacon was the author of the...immortal plays and poems put forth in Shakespeare's name....They came from the brain of the greatest student and writer of that age, and were not a "flash of genius" descended upon one of peasant birth, less noble history, and of no preparatory literary attainments.[50]

Why is Bacon's connection to Shakespeare so important? If true, then neither Lord Bacon's genius nor his influence on present day secret societies can be underestimated. Imagine, if you will, a man so clever that he could not only author the greatest body of literature produced, but keep his authorship a secret for centuries. It is no surprise then that secret societies of today are so respectful of his plan for a New Atlantis.

Manly Hall claims that a Baconian secret society was set up in America while Jamestown was still floundering. Membership soon spread into South America in the person of legendary revolutionary Simon Bolivar. Hall stated that the Bacon group was also very powerful in Germany, France, and the Netherlands. Although secret societies played a significant role in the British colonization of America, with colonization came a force that was to bedevil their well-laid plans for the New World Order — Christians. Unlike the greedy dandies of Jamestown, they came with a spirit of self-sacrifice, and consequently flourished. Today, as then, it is Christians who are the major stumbling block to the plans for the rise of their New World Order. Through the years, this concept has remained the same: to unite all nations under a single sovereign world government.

FOUR

EARLY AMERICA AND THE REVOLUTION

Although secret societies were very well organized and funded in early America, a formidable force arose to oppose them and quietly challenge their control of the developing nation. This force was the spiritual zeal of the Christian colonists.

Christianity came to America as a direct result of the first English translation of the Bible in 1381. In the early 1300s John Wycliffe, a professor of Divinity at Oxford University, realized that the major problem with the Church in England was that the Bible could only be read by the educated clergy and nobility because it was written in Latin. Although the common man was generally illiterate, Wycliffe decided that if an English translation of the Bible was available, then general literacy might be stimulated as well.

As Wycliffe translated the Latin text, he organized a group called the Order of Poor Preachers. They began distributing the new Bible throughout England to anyone who could read. For the first time, it was possible for the common man to know what the Bible actually said. Suddenly, peasants flocked to the village greens and country parsonages to hear preachers read aloud from the new English translation.

Opponents of Wycliffe's Order of Poor Preachers called them and their followers "Lollards," which means "idle babblers." The Lollards grew so quickly, not only among the country folk, but even the artisans and noblemen that one opponent wrote: "Every second man one meets is a Lollard."[1]

The Lollards made such an impact in Britain that eventually Wycliffe's works were banned and the Pope ordered him to Rome to undergo trial. Although Wycliffe died in 1384 of a stroke before he could undertake the journey, Lollardy continued to grow. By 1425, forty-one years after his death, the Roman Church was so infuriated with Wycliffe that they ordered his bones exhumed and burned together with 200 books he had written.

One hundred years later, scholar William Tyndale decided to translate the Bible from the original Greek versions into English, instead of using the Latin Bible as Wycliffe did. The English language had undergone dramatic changes in the 150 years since the first Wycliffe translation, so a new version was in order in any case.

Tyndale finished the New Testament but was prevented from publishing it in England, and so went to Germany instead, where it was printed in 1525. It wasn't until 1536 that he finished the Old Testament translation. But before he could have it printed and distributed, Tyndale was burned at the stake in Belgium as a religious heretic at the order of British monarch King Henry VIII.

A year later King Henry broke from the Catholic Church, formed the Church of England, and authorized the sale and reading of the Tyndale Bible throughout the kingdom.[2] So in 1537, for the first time in British history, owning and reading a Bible was legal for the common man.

By 1604, King James I of England decided that he needed his own translation of the Bible and authorized a committee of fifty scholars to do the job. They drew heavily, however, on the Tyndale version. The new King James version first appeared in 1611.

PILGRIMS AND PURITANS

Once the common man had his hands on a Bible written in English, two dissenting groups arose within the Christian Church. The first was dedicated to purifying the Church from within. These dissenters were known as the Puritans. Although the Church of England frowned on this rather large movement, their leaders were not persecuted or martyred.

The second group was considered much more dangerous. These were the "Separatists" who believed that the Church of England was corrupted beyond any possibility of reform. They believed that Jesus Christ should be the head of the Church, and therefore they could swear no religious allegiance to either Queen or Bishop. Many of these Separatists eventually went to America, where they were known as the Pilgrims.

As long as Elizabeth was Queen, few Separatists were persecuted, but when James I ascended to the throne, he chased the band out of England entirely. Led by William Bradford, the group sought sanctuary in Holland, where they toiled mercilessly at the most menial labor just to survive. After a dozen years in Leyden, in 1619 the Separatists decided that they would seek their religious freedom in the new land of America. They were able to gain backing for their venture from wealthy British merchants.

Even though stories of a fifty percent death rate at the Virginia settlement of Jamestown abounded in Europe, the Pilgrims became convinced that America was the direction in which God wanted them to move. Bradford wrote about the Separatists' decision to go to the New World:

> All great and honorable actions are accompanied with great difficulties, and must be enterprised and overcome with answerable courages. It was granted that the dangers were great, but not desperate, and the difficulties were many, but not invincible....And all of them, through the help of God, by fortitude and patience, might either be borne or overcome.[3]

The Pilgrims elected a pastor, John Robinson, who wrote that he felt the group was being called by God to journey to a new Jerusalem.[4] It is ironic that this group of Christians, as well as Bacon's Illuminists, both felt their migration to the new land of America was the fulfillment of prophesy—one to establish their New Atlantis, and the other their New Jerusalem.

PLYMOUTH

Although originally headed for Virginia, the ship carrying the Pilgrims, the *Mayflower*, was blown hundreds of miles off course and into the peninsula of Cape Cod. In December 1620, after tides and winds allowed them to go no farther, the group felt Providence had led them to that spot. Before disembarking, Pilgrim leaders Deacon Carver, Elder Brewster, and William Bradford decided to put a new plan for a civil government based on Christian principles on paper. This became known as the Mayflower Compact. It read in part:

> In the name of God, amen. We whose names are under-written...having undertaken, for the glory of God and advancement of the Christian Faith and honor of our King and country, a voyage to plant the first colony in the northern parts of Virginia.[5]

William Bradford later described the arrival of the Pilgrims in Massachusetts:

> Being thus arrived in a good harbor and brought safe to land, they fell upon their knees and blessed the God of heaven, who had brought them over the vast and furious ocean....The whole country, full of woods and thickets, represented a wild and savage hue....What could now sustain them but the Spirit of God and his grace?[6]

Unlike the colonists of Jamestown, the Pilgrims took their time choosing a well-watered campsite on a hill with a remarkably good twenty acres of ground already cleared and ready to plant, with abundant fresh water nearby. The area seemed too good to be true. Although there were no signs of recent agriculture, the area seemed abundantly fertile, yet abandoned.

The reason for this, as it turned out, was a truly remarkable coincidence. Only three or four years earlier, a plague had obliterated the indigenous Indian population, leaving a fertile, idyllic area, ripe for colonization. This was perhaps the only area within hundreds of miles where the colonists could have landed and not met fierce coastal Indian tribes. So, call it luck, or call it divine intervention, but the colonists had encountered a very narrow window of opportunity hundreds of miles from their intended destination.

During that first harsh winter, nearly half of the Pilgrims died. But when the *Mayflower* weighed anchor in the spring, none of the survivors opted to return to England. Due to the deaths of the other leaders, William Bradford, then only thirty years old, was elected the new governor of the colony.

Bradford soon realized that the system of communalism foisted on the colony by the London merchants who had financed the trip was not working. Everyone was fed from common stores. The lack of incentive was threatening to turn Plymouth into another Jamestown with each person doing only the work that was necessary to get by.

So Bradford instituted an incentive system. He assigned a plot of land to be worked by each family. From then on, the little community was never again in need of food. Bradford said, "This had very good success; for it made all hands very industrious."[7] From then on, there was never a famine at Plymouth.[8]

Bradford later lashed out in his writings at the communal, or communist system advocated by Plato, where all property was supposedly held in common by all residents:

> The vanity and conceit of Plato and other ancients...that the taking away of property, and bringing [it] in community...would make them happy and flourishing; as if they were wiser than God....[However, it] was found to breed much confusion and discontent, and retard much employment that would have been to their benefit and comfort.[9]

The first two colonies in America were excellent examples of two rival systems—one based on the concept of individually-held property driven by incentive, the other based on the communal theories of Plato and Francis Bacon.

Within ten years, buoyed by reports of plenty at Plymouth and prodded by renewed persecution from Britain's King Charles I and Archbishop Laud, the great Puritan exodus to America began. Unlike the outcast Pilgrims, the Puritans represented families of some standing in Britain. Some had considerable wealth, while others were influential ministers in the Church.

New England was now getting some of Britain's best and brightest intellects, and a considerable slice of its net worth. In fact, it has been estimated that if the persecution of the Puritans had continued for twelve years longer than it did, one-quarter of the riches of Britain would have made its way to the New England colonies.

During the balance of the seventeenth century, the tiny colonies struggled for survival. Jamestown was finally able to survive, but only after families were finally included, and a new policy was instituted that every person had to work, or go hungry. Crops were planted. Preachers came and began preaching. Not until hard work and family values were added into the mix did the colony become secure.

By the dawn of the 1700s, all along the Eastern seaboard, most of the important secret societies of Europe already had sturdy footholds in colonial America.[10] Manly Hall stated that "The brotherhoods met in their rooms over inns and similar public buildings, practicing their ancient rituals exactly according to the fashion in Europe and England."[11]

However by 1776, ninety-nine percent of the Europeans in the American population were still Christian.[12] Because of the dominant influence of Christianity, the Masons and the other secret schools were forced to modify their philosophies to include Christianity as they had done nowhere else in the world. For the first time, Christ was said to be the "Grand Master" of the lodges. The Bible became a part of the rituals of Masonry; however, it was always placed symbolically under, and therefore considered inferior to, the Masonic square and compass.

BENJAMIN FRANKLIN

Benjamin Franklin has the image of the benevolent grandfather of the American Revolutionary period, and interestingly, he was said to be the inventor of the concept of the "virtuous revolution." Franklin's wit and wisdom made him the most popular author of the day. As Minister to France, however, Franklin was well known for his love of the indulgences of the French Masonic halls. He may well have contracted the syphilis from which he eventually died as a result of these indiscretions.

Franklin was known as the "First American Gentleman," and held enormous sway over colonial politics. But, according to Manly Hall, "the source of his power lay in the secret societies to which he belonged and of which he was the appointed spokesman."[13]

Franklin became a Mason in 1731, at age twenty-five, and by age twenty-eight was Provisional Grand Master of all Masonry for Pennsylvania.[14] When he went to France as ambassador, he was honored at the top Masonic lodge, the Lodge of Perfection, and his signature, written in his own fine hand, is in their record ledger close to that of the Marquis de Lafayette.[15]

He was inducted into the French Lodge of Nine Muses, and even became its Master. According to researcher Paul A. Fisher, it was here that Franklin, by "the most carefully planned and most efficiently organized propaganda ever accomplished," made possible French support of the American Revolution.[16]

Even more importantly, Franklin became the father of the "virtuous revolution" theory and was responsible for spreading the idea throughout Europe.[17] According to French historian Bernard Fay, up to this time, the term "revolution" had always been regarded in a negative light—as a crime against society.[18] Nesta Webster described the atmosphere of the period:

> The people have never wished to do away with monarchy, they have always loved their kings. During the French Revolution the only popular and spontaneous movement was the rising of the peasants of La Vendée in defence of Louis XVI. In England they have always flocked to any display of royal splendour.[19]

Franklin's propagation of this theory, however, suddenly made revolutions acceptable as a natural part of the evolution of mankind.[20]

GEORGE WASHINGTON

George Washington (1732-1799) was a steadfast supporter of American Masonry. Although he took his first degrees in the lodge at Fredericksburg, Virginia on November 4, 1752 at age twenty, he was thereafter an infrequent attender of lodge meetings. Still, he publicly supported the Craft most of his life. Writing on August 22, 1790 to King David's Lodge #1 in Newport, Rhode Island he said:

> Being persuaded a just application of the principles on which Free Masonry is founded, must be promotive of virtue and public prosperity, I shall always be glad to advance the interests of this Society and be considered by them a deserving brother.[21]

Although Masons certainly make much of Washington's affiliation, he was offered the leadership of American Masonry at one point, and turned it down. In 1798, he severely criticized the Masonically-affiliated Jacobin Clubs and the notorious Illuminati as "diabolical" and "pernicious."[22] In a letter to the Reverend G.W. Snyder, written at Mount Vernon on September 25, 1798, only fifteen months before his death, Washington thanked Snyder for sending him a copy of Professor John Robinson's book, *Proofs of a Conspiracy*:

> I have heard much of the nefarious, and dangerous plan, and doctrines of the Illuminati, but never saw the Book until you were pleased to send it to me.... I must] correct an error you have run into, of my Presiding over the English lodges in this Country. The fact is, I preside over none, nor have I been in one more than once or twice, within the last thirty years.[23]

Washington also defended American Masonry, however, saying that in his opinion none of the American lodges were "contaminated with the principles ascribed to the society of the Illuminati." American Masons place great weight on the distinction between British Masonry, from which the American version sprang, and European, or Continental Masonry. Even Masonic critic and historian Nesta Webster acknowledged these differences:

> I have always clearly differentiated between British and Continental Masonry, showing the former to be an honorable association not only hostile to subversive doctrines but a strong supporter of law, order and religion.[24]

On October 24, 1798, Washington wrote Reverend Snyder again and felt compelled to offer a further explanation of his position:

> It was not my intention to doubt that, the Doctrines of the Illuminati, and principles of Jacobinism had not spread in the United States. On the contrary, no one is more truly satisfied of this fact than I am.[25]

Masonry was much more commonplace in those days than it is today. In fact, most of America's "founding fathers" were Masons. According to Manly Hall, "Of the fifty-five members of the Constitutional Convention, all but five were Masons."[26]

According to a 1951 Masonic edition of the *Holy Bible* twenty-four of George Washington's major generals were Masons, as were thirty of his thirty-three brigadier generals. Of fifty-six signers of the Declaration of Independence, fifty-three were Master Masons.[27] According to the Masonic publication, *New Age*, "It was Masons who brought on the war, and it was Masonic generals who carried it through to a successful conclusion. In fact, the famous Boston Tea Party, which precipitated the war, was actually a recessed meeting of a Masonic Lodge."[28]

According to Hall, the Boston Tea Party "was arranged around a chowder supper at the home of the Bradlee brothers, who were Masons. Mother Bradlee kept the water hot so that they could wash off the disguises." The participants were from the St. Andrews Lodge in Boston and were led by the Junior Warden, Paul Revere.[29] French historian Bernard Fay said a band of "Redskins" was seen leaving a tavern known as the "Green Dragon or the Arms of Freemasonry" on the afternoon of December 16, 1773, and then seen returning, yet none were seen to leave again.[30]

Does this mean that most of America's founding fathers were part of some gigantic, evil conspiracy? Not at all. The secrecy of the Masonic Lodge was the perfect cover for revolutionary activities. Few of these men, if any, knew of the "plan" of which only the leaders of Masonry were aware. Most believed that they were simply involved in the cause of gaining independence from a tyrant. Masonry was to most of them, as it is to most of the membership today, merely a fraternal organization promoting social skills and providing fellowship to its members. The majority were well-meaning Christians. Masonry in America had merely adjusted its tone appropriately to suit its audience. Adam Weishaupt, the leader of the eighteenth-century Illuminati, the most notorious of all the secret societies of that day, described this adaptive philosophy:

> I have contrived an explanation which has every advantage; is inviting to Christians of every communion; gradually frees them from religious prejudices [and] cultivates the social virtues....My means are effectual, and irresistible. Our secret Association works in a way that nothing can withstand.[31]

But what siren song could have been used to convince some of the most intelligent and idealistic men in predominantly Christian America? Again Weishaupt's exact words:

> Jesus of Nazareth, the Grand Master of our Order, appeared at a time when the world was in the utmost disorder, and among a people who for ages had groaned under the yoke of bondage. He taught them the lessons of reason. To be more effective, he took in the aid of Religion — of opinions which were current — and, in a very clever manner, he combined his secret doctrines with the popular religion.... He concealed the precious meaning and consequences of his doctrines; but fully disclosed them to a chosen few. A chosen few received the doctrines in secret, and they have been handed down to us by the Free Masons.[32]

These clever tactics were able to deceive most of the elite of the American Revolution, as well as Christian Masons today, making Masonry out to be the salvation of Christendom, and promising liberty and happiness for mankind. But Professor John Robison, Masonic expert of the late 1700s and contemporary of Weishaupt's, was not fooled. "The happiness of mankind was, like Weishaupt's Christianity, a mere tool, a tool which Regents [the ruling council of the Illuminati] made a joke of."[33]

Although secret societies were generally able to guide the course of political change in colonial America, the vast majority of the population was Christian in its religious orientation. In fact, according to Constitutional scholar John W. Whitehead, when the Constitution was adopted in 1787, the population of the United States numbered about 3.25 million, of whom at least two million were Christians.[34]

On April 25, 1799, Dr. Jedediah Morse, the leading geographer of revolutionary America and father of Samuel Morse, inventor of the telegraph, aptly explained the relationship between Christianity and freedom from despotism:

> To the kindly influence of Christianity we owe that degree of civil freedom and political and social happiness which mankind now

enjoys. In proportion as the genuine effects of Christianity are diminished in any nation, either through unbelief, or the corruption of its doctrines, or the neglect of its institutions; in the same proportion will the people of that nation recede from the blessings of genuine freedom, and approximate the miseries of complete despotism.[35]

This view was widely held in the colonies. The Bible, in fact, was the acknowledged great political textbook of the patriots. In 1777, the Continental Congress directed the Committee of Commerce to import twenty thousand copies of the Bible.[36] When reading was taught, the Bible was frequently the text used. When reading books began to be published, such as the *New England Primer*, biblical references predominated.

Famed orator and attorney Daniel Webster, speaking at Plymouth, Massachusetts in 1820, on the occasion of the bicentennial celebration of the first landing of the Pilgrims, ended his address with this admonition:

> Finally, let us not forget the religious character of our origin. Our fathers were brought hither by their high veneration for the Christian religion. They journeyed by its light, and labored in its hope. They sought to incorporate its principles with the elements of their society, and to diffuse its influence through all their institutions, civil, political or literary. Let us cherish these sentiments, and extend this influence still more widely; in the full conviction, that that is the happiest society which partakes in the highest degree of the mild and peaceful spirit of Christianity.[37]

Although most of the important leaders of the American Revolution were Masons, Christianity exerted an equal and opposite influence. A good example of this dichotomy was in the struggle over the wording of the Declaration of Independence.

Thomas Jefferson came to the Second Continental Congress with references to "nature's God" in his first draft of the Declaration of Independence—a traditional Deist concept taken from the atheistic work of French philosopher Jean Jacques Rousseau (1712-1778) who, at that time, was at the zenith of his power in the lodges of the secret societies of Europe.

But the delegates were overwhelmingly Christian and soon made changes in Jefferson's draft to include compromise wording such as "appealing to the Supreme Judge of the World," and "with a firm reliance on the protection of divine Providence." This is a far cry from any direct reference to the totally Christian nation which America was at that time, but the influence of the secret societies had discouraged the inclusion of direct references to Christianity on the grounds of imbuing the new nation with a spirit of "religious tolerance," or neutrality.

Another important battle over wording in the Declaration of Independence was waged over the Jeffersonian phrase, "Life, Liberty and the Pursuit of Happiness." Few today realize that this was a subtle manipulation of the true motto of colonial America of that day. Throughout the colonies, the motto was "Life, Liberty and Property."

The vast majority of the colonists had come from conditions of relative serfdom in Europe. Few had owned property in their respective "old countries." The colonial experience had shown clearly that colonies flourished when men owned property. The concept of individual ownership of property was considered vital to personal liberty. According to James Madison in an essay entitled "Property":

> In a word, as a man is said to have a right to his property, he may be equally said to have a property to his rights....Government is instituted to protect property of every sort....[38]

In 1765, the battle cry of those opposed to the Stamp Act was "Liberty, Property, and no Stamps!"[39] Throughout the colonies, "life, liberty, and property" were spoken of as a single concept. This was at least partially due to the influence of the English philosopher John Locke, whose writings were widely read throughout the colonies. In his famous treatise *Of Civil Government*, published in 1689, Locke spoke of men's "Lives, Liberties, and Estates, which I call by the general Name, Property." He asserted that the "great and chief end therefore, of men's uniting into commonwealths, and putting themselves under government, is the preservation of their property."[40]

Locke explained that the Tenth Commandment forbids the coveting of another person's property, and the Eighth Commandment, "Thou shalt not steal," establishes that people certainly have the biblical right to hold property. Locke explained:

> Though the Earth and all inferior Creatures be common to all Men, yet every Man has a Property in his own Person: This no Body has any right to but himself. The Labour of his Body, and the Work of his Hands, we may say, are properly his. Whatsoever then he removes out of the State that Nature hath provided, and left it in, he hath mixed his Labour with, and joined to it something that is his own, and thereby makes it his Property.[41]

In 1774, the first resolution of the *Declaration and Resolves of the First Continental Congress* was that the colonies "are entitled to life, liberty, and property...." Less than two years later, Jefferson's master work contrived to change this phrase for the first time to "life, liberty and the pursuit of happiness," and thus it has been in the United States ever since.

The ideal government which Locke and Madison envisioned was one which would protect an individual's private property. It was this influence of Illuminism — not only the Illuminati, but the principles underlying all secret societies — that brought America a government dominated by a usurious central banking system and its attendant punitive taxation.

SYMBOLISM OF THE GREAT SEAL OF THE UNITED STATES

Anyone familiar with Masonic illustrations can easily see that the Great Seal of the United States is cluttered with the symbolism of secret societies. Although many have claimed to be able to interpret the significance of the Great Seal of the United States, little that is credible has ever been written about it.

On the front, or obverse side of the Seal, is what appears to be an eagle. However, the small tuft at the back of the head indicates a hybrid combination of an eagle and the mythical phoenix. This is hardly a revolutionary discovery. The eagle was not the original bird pictured on many coins of early America. For example, a good coin book will show photos of the New York Excelsior copper coin of 1787. This coin does not show the rugged, familiar lines of the American bald eagle, but the thin, long-necked, crested profile of the phoenix.

What is the significance of the phoenix being used on the seal? It was one of the most familiar symbols of both the Egyptian and Atlantean cultures. Although it resembles the eagle in size and general shape, there are certain distinctive differences.

According to legend, the body of the phoenix is covered with glossy purple feathers, and the plumes in its tail are alternately blue and red. Circling its distinctively long neck is a ring of golden plumage, and the back of the head has the familiar crest of brilliantly-colored plumage which is not present in the eagle.

Only one of these birds is said to exist at any given time. Its nest, in the "distant parts of Arabia," is said to be made of frankincense and myrrh. After its 500-year lifespan comes to an end, at death its body opens and a newborn phoenix emerges. For this reason, it is held by the secret societies as a representation of immortality and resurrection. To them, the phoenix represents the initiate who has been "reborn" or "twice-born" as a result of his initiation. Of course, this is the counterfeit of the Christian's spiritual rebirth. But primarily, it serves as the symbol of Atlantis reborn in America. Belief in the phoenix also occurs in China, representing the same concepts, as it does in the form of the Thunderbird of the American Indians.[42]

Apparently, throughout the years, there has been an effort to try either to hide, or tone down the Masonic origins of some of the founding symbols of America, and so the eagle has been gradually substituted for the phoenix. But many representations of the phoenix still exist, especially in the older buildings in Washington, D.C. For example, in the Old Senate Chamber of the U.S. Capitol building, high over the dais, is a depiction of a huge eagle. Elsewhere throughout the room, however, are depictions of the longer-necked, crested phoenix, or hybrids of the two.

There can be no doubt that the original feathered symbol of the new republic was a phoenix, and not the American eagle. The beak is shaped differently, the neck is longer, and the small tuft of feathers at the back of the head leaves little doubt.

But if the phoenix is not evidence enough to show the influence of the secret societies on the founding symbols of America, then the design on the back or reverse side of the Great Seal can be interpreted in no other way. It depicts a pyramid, composed of thirteen rows of masonry. The pyramid is without a cap stone, and above its upper platform floats a typically Masonic triangle—the Delta in Greek— containing the All-Seeing Eye surrounded by rays of light.

The All-Seeing Eye symbol has also been used in U.S. coinage. Known as the Nova Constellatio coppers, these coins were struck in fairly large quantities and dated 1783 and 1785 by Gouverneur Morris, the Assistant Financier of the Confederation.

The initial design of the Great Seal met with great resistance. It was so blatantly Masonic that scholars of the day fumed in open displeasure. Professor Charles Eliot Norton of Harvard said: "The device adopted by Congress is practically incapable of effective treatment; it can hardly (however artistically treated by the designer) look otherwise than as a dull emblem of a Masonic Fraternity."[43]

The pyramid of Gizah was believed by the ancient Egyptians to be the shrine tomb of the god Hermes, also known as Thot, the personification of universal wisdom. No trace has ever been found of the capstone. A flat platform about thirty feet square gives no indication that this part of the structure was ever finished.

According to Manly Hall it was built this way because it is complete only when a Master Mason stands on the apex. In fact, in one drawing in Hall's *The Lost Keys of Freemasonry* a Master Mason is seen performing Masonic rituals atop a capless pyramid. Hall commented upon that symbolism:

> The Master Mason becomes the capstone of the Universal Temple. He stands alone on the pinnacle of the temple. One stone must yet be placed, but this he cannot find. Somewhere it lies concealed. In prayer he kneels, asking the powers that be to aid him in his search. The light of the sun shines upon him and bathes him in a splendor celestial. Suddenly a voice speaks from the Heavens, saying, "The temple is finished and in my faithful Master is found the missing stone."[44]

Here, atop this capless pyramid, the essence of Masonry is revealed once and for all. Masonry believes that each Master Mason is the link between heaven and earth—the intercessor—a counterfeit Jesus Christ:

> The Master Mason embodies the power of the human mind, that connecting link which binds heaven and earth together in an endless chain.

> He...has become the spokesman of the Most High. He stands between the glowing fire light of the world [the sun]. Through him passes Hydra, the great snake, and from its mouth there pours to man the light of God. His symbol is the rising sun...illuminating the immortal East.[45]

Even at the level of the thirty-third degree Hall shows just how deeply his personal deception with Masonry goes:

> Truth always comes to man through man.... Obviously, the Great Schools, functioning through their trained and appointed messengers, constitute the highest leadership available to man or required by man.[46]

The pyramid symbol has its roots firmly fixed in the legend of Atlantis. Secret societies believe that in Atlantis stood a great university where most of the arts and sciences originated. The structure that housed this university was an immense pyramid with many galleries and corridors, with an observatory for the study of the stars sitting on its immense apex:

> This temple to the sciences in the old Atlantis is [symbolized] in the seal of the new Atlantis. Was it the society of the unknown philosophers who sealed the new nation with the eternal emblems, that all nations might know the purpose for which the new country had been founded!

> There is only one possible origin for these symbols, and that is the secret societies which came to this country 150 years before the Revolutionary War.

> The monogram of the new Atlantis reveals this continent as set apart for the accomplishment of the great work—here is to arise the pyramid of human aspiration, the school of the secret societies.[47]

On the front of the Great Seal in the beak of what is now the eagle, flows a scroll inscribed with "E pluribus unum," or "one out of many." This has a double meaning; both the unification of the American states into the American nation, and the ultimate goal, a unification of nations into one world state.

But it is the Latin phrase on the reverse side of the Seal, under the pyramid, that is the most controversial: "Novus Ordo Seclorum," or "New Order of the Ages." From this, Illuminists of the present day derive their favorite phrase to describe their work: New World Order.

Although the design was approved by Congress on June 20, 1782, the reverse side of the Great Seal of the United States was very rarely used and did not appear publicly until it suddenly showed up on the back of the one dollar bill, starting with series 1935A.

Many observe that the American one dollar bill also contains the phrase "In God We Trust." This phrase did not appear on paper currency, however, until 1957, and only then as the result of a one-man campaign waged by Mathew Rothert, a businessman from Camden, Arkansas. Congress finally passed the bill introduced by Arkansas Senator William Fulbright in June of 1955. Later the bill survived a court challenge by atheist Madalyn Murray O'Hair when the Supreme Court refused to hear the case.

This Great Plan of the secret societies has falsely fired the imaginations of many visionaries. For example, some forty years after the American Revolution, the famed "liberator" of South America, General Simon Bolivar (1783-1830), was convinced that he too was involved in this Great Plan to fulfill the secret destiny of South America.

He brought revolution to Venezuela, Equador, and Peru, and was the founder of Bolivia. He had direct contact with the European secret societies, and, in fact, while traveling in Europe, joined the Masonic Order.[48] In 1823, he wrote:

> America...is the highest and most irrefutable assignment of destiny....The nations I have founded will, after prolonged and bitter agony, go into an eclipse, but will later emerge as states of the one great republic, AMERICA.[49]

As will be shown later, after guiding the American Revolution, secret societies engineered a bloody revolution in France from 1789 to 1794. They then returned to America to attempt a second revolution, known as the Whiskey Rebellion. President Washington quickly brought in the Army to crush them, then publicly denounced the secret societies responsible.

Though Masonry was very popular in revolutionary America, its nature was tempered by the predominantly Christian character of the population. But it is safe to say that this moderation is only a facade to encourage membership. Good men won't join bad organizations. However, this neither makes Masonry harmless, nor desirable. It is still Deist in nature at best, Atheistic or Satanic at worst.

It is this Christian character of America which has forced secret societies to constantly attenuate their plans to dominate the nation and bring it into their new world order. Only an informed citizenry, vigilant of where the real battle lines lie, can postpone for a while longer the inevitable reign of the Antichrist, and provide yet another generation of Americans with the chance not only to live in this, the most kindly and benevolent society the earth has ever seen, but to have a chance to attain *true* salvation.

FIVE

WEISHAUPT'S ILLUMINATI

Founded by German law professor Adam Weishaupt in 1776, the Illuminati was the most infamous of all secret societies. The lack of information on the Illuminati in most current history texts is surprising given the fame and influence of the group. Weishaupt was as much the father of revolutionary Communism as was Karl Marx, who wrote the *Communist Manifesto* seventy-five years later. Frequently, the available information is quite superficial, describing the Illuminati as:

> A short-lived movement...founded as a secret society in 1776 in Bavaria by Adam Weishaupt, professor of canon law at the University of Ingolstadt and a former Jesuit. Its aim was to replace Christianity by a religion of reason. It was banned by the Bavarian government in 1785.[1]

With a little digging, however, more complete information can be found. Adam Weishaupt was born on February 6, 1748 in what is now Germany. Though a professor at a Jesuit university, he never joined the Jesuit order. He came to hate not only the Jesuits, but vowed to destroy the Catholic Church, and the Christianity it represented.[2]

Weishaupt adopted the teachings of radical French philosophers such as Jean Jacques Rousseau (1712-1778) and the anti-Christian doctrines of the Manicheans. He was indoctrinated in Egyptian occultism in 1771 by a merchant of unknown origin named Kolmer, who was said to have traveled Europe in search of converts. For the next five years Weishaupt formulated a plan by which all occult systems could be reduced to a single, powerful organization. On May Day, 1776, Weishaupt launched his Order of the Illuminati.[3]

Among other things, Weishaupt, like Rousseau before him, claimed that civilization was a mistake—that the salvation of mankind lay in a return to nature. He taught that mankind had been free and happy in his natural state, and that it was the paralyzing influence of civilization that had forced him from his natural Garden of Eden. Weishaupt also claimed that the chief impediment to this natural state of harmony was the invention of the concept of property, of owning things. Rousseau theorized:

> The first man who bethought himself of saying, "This is mine," and found people simple enough to believe him, was the real founder of civil society. What crimes, what wars, what murders, what miseries and horrors would he have spared the human race [if someone would have warned;]..."Beware of listening to this imposter; you are lost if you forget that the fruits of the earth belong to all and the earth to no one."[4]

British historian Nesta Webster, author of *World Revolution*, observed that Rousseau's writings embodied all of the principles which would later be known as Communism. In what is perhaps the most brilliant refutation ever devised of the Communist error in logic, Webster wrote:

> Ownership of property...is not peculiar to the human race. The bird has its nest, the dog has its bone that it will savagely defend....If everything were divided up today all would be unequal again tomorrow. One man would fritter away his share, another would double it by turning it to good account, the practical and energetic would soon be more prosperous than the idler or the wastral. The parable of the ten talents perfectly illustrates the differing capacity of men to deal with money.[6]

According to Weishaupt, this concept of property was the result of men giving up their nomadic life to live in a fixed residence. Therefore, the first step toward man regaining his natural "liberty and equality" was to renounce the notion of ownership of property and surrender his possessions. There is no evidence, however, that Weishaupt ever put this philosophy into practice.

Weishaupt's theory also held that patriotism, the love of country, and even the love of one's family, had to be abolished. He taught that these allegiances should be replaced by a universal love among men and nations which would "make the human race one good and happy family."[7] In 1921 Webster explained:

> This is the precise language of internationalists today, and it is of course easy to point out the evils of exaggerated patriotism. But it will not be found that the man who loves his country is less able to respect foreign patriots any more than that the man who loves his family is a worse neighbor than one who cares little for his wife and children.[8]

As Webster pointed out, it is much more likely that our primitive ancestors fought barbarically among themselves with crude flint weapons, than that they lived in a state of "equality" and "universal love." After all, since Cain killed Abel, murder has been tragically commonplace among men.

Even the "sacred" Masonic trinity, "Liberty, Equality, Fraternity," which Weishaupt adopted for Illuminism, contains a basic, important contradiction that fosters revolution and chaos, rather than peace and harmony:

> It is impossible to have complete liberty and equality, the two are mutually exclusive. It is possible to have a system of complete liberty in which every man is free to behave as he pleases, to rob or to murder, to live, according to the law of the jungle, rule by the strongest...there is no equality there. Or one may have a system of absolute equality, of cutting every one down to the same dead level, of crushing all incentive in man to rise above his fellows, but there is no liberty there.[9]

The tenets of the Illuminati are then summarized in the following five points:

1. Abolition of monarchies and all ordered government.
2. Abolition of private property and inheritances.
3. Abolition of patriotism and nationalism
4. Abolition of family life and the institution of marriage, and the establishment of communal education of children.
5. Abolition of all religion.[10]

This shocking agenda formed:

> A programme hitherto unprecedented in the history of civilization. Communistic theories had been held by isolated thinkers or groups of thinkers since the days of Plato, but no one, as far as we know, had ever yet seriously proposed to destroy everything for which civilization stands. Moreover...the plan of Illuminism as codified by the above five points has continued up to the present day to form the exact programme of the World Revolution.[11]

With regard to government, Weishaupt felt that a republic, where the citizens elect representatives to make the laws for them, should not be endured because it would eventually become despotic. He only tolerated the concept of a democracy because, by definition, the people could overthrow it on a whim.

Weishaupt believed that people should be taught to do without any controlling authority at all, to follow no laws or any civil codes. Of course, this is what we today would call anarchy. Yet his Illuminati, and the consequent governmental systems it would bring about were known for their absolute and dictatorial control.

True to his revolution-making agenda, Weishaupt began his secretive conquest of Europe by attacking monarchies. "Princes and nations shall vanish from the Earth," he said.[12] Although much is made of the differences between the Illuminati and the Anglo/American version of Masonry today, some Masons will verify that it is not incorrect to say that their goals, in this case, are identical. The difference is that in the case of the Illuminati, once a monarch was dethroned, then all civil government was targeted for destruction, because, in the end, anarchy and chaos—Weishaupt's idea of a "return to nature"— were their ultimate goals. The leaders of Masonry today would suggest that a world democracy is the form of government best suited to mankind. Granted, the difference is a technical point only, because in reality, either system results in a dictatorship, but enthusiasts of the New World Order still cling desperately to this point.

Weishaupt was well aware what the real consequences of his hollow political theories would be. He envisioned a dictatorship with himself and his Illuminati brethren at its head. But he also realized that he could accomplish nothing unless he could eliminate the bedrock of civilization—religion. Thus, he taught that religion should be eliminated and replaced with the worship of reason:

> [In] the secret schools of wisdom...through which Man will be rescued from his fall. Mankind will become one family...and reason will be the only law of Man. When at last Reason becomes the religion of Man, then will the problem be solved.[13]

Weishaupt's primary contemporary expositor was Professor John Robison. Robison was a highly respected British historian, professor of "Natural Philosophy" at Edinburgh University, and Mason for many years. Robison's book on the Illuminati, *Proofs of a Conspiracy*, published in 1798 in New York, caused a sensation in the United States. This was the book sent to George Washington by the Reverend G.W. Snyder in the same year. Robison reported on his growing concern with the connection between Illuminism and Masonry:

> I have found that the covert [secrecy] of a Mason Lodge had been employed in every country for venting and propagating sentiments in religion and politics, that could not have circulated in public without exposing the author to great danger.

> I found, that this impunity had gradually encouraged men of licentious principles to become more bold, and to teach doctrines subversive of all our notions of morality...of all our confidence in the moral government of the universe...

> I have been able to trace these attempts, made...under the specious pretext of enlightening the world by the torch of philosophy, and of dispelling the clouds of civil and religious superstition which keep the nations of Europe in darkness and slavery.

> I have observed these doctrines gradually diffusing and mixing with all the different systems of Free Masonry till, at last, AN ASSOCIATION HAS BEEN FORMED FOR THE EXPRESS PURPOSE OF ROOTING OUT ALL THE RELIGIOUS ESTABLISHMENTS, AND OVERTURNING ALL THE EXISTING GOVERNMENTS OF EUROPE.[14]

The publishers of Robison's book defined the Illuminati in the forward to the modern edition:

> The Illuminati were conceived, organized, and activated by professionals and intellectuals, many of them brilliant but cunning and clever, who decided to put their minds in the service of total evil; a conspiracy conceived not by Masons as Masons, but by evil men using Freemasonry as a vehicle for their own purposes.[15]

Because the true purposes of Illuminism were so shocking, Weishaupt constantly encouraged the secretive nature of the order. No member was ever to allow himself to be identified as an Illuminati. The words Illuminism or Illuminati were never to be used in correspondence, but were to be replaced by the astrological symbol for the sun, a circle with a dot in the middle. Weishaupt explained his organization in letters to the brethren:

> Secrecy gives greater zest to the whole....the slightest observation shows that nothing will so much contribute to increase the zeal of the members as secret union.

> The great strength of our Order lies in its concealment: let it never appear in any place in its own name, but always covered by another name, and another occupation. None is fitter than the three lower degrees of Free Masonry; the public is accustomed to it, expect little from it, and therefore takes little notice of it. Next to this, the form of a learned or literary society is best suited to our purpose, and had Free Masonry not existed, this cover would have been employed; and it may be much more than a cover, it may be a powerful engine in our hands. By establishing reading societies, and subscription libraries ...we may turn the public mind which way we will.

> In like manner we must try to obtain an influence in...all offices which have any effect, either in forming, or in managing, or even in directing the mind of man.[16]

It is obvious that the very existence of the Order was meant to be concealed with the greatest care, and that its true objectives were to be hidden, even from the vast majority of those who naively supported it in Masonic lodges everywhere. If total secrecy proved to be impossible, then, according to Webster, the Illuminati would portray itself in the press as "an unimportant philanthropic movement." This attempt to paint secret societies as merely philanthropic organizations continues unabated into the present day.

Interestingly, this is exactly the way Thomas Jefferson described Weishaupt and the Illuminati in the face of the widespread public alarm caused by Robison's book. Perhaps he innocently believed the propaganda of Illuminism. But in Charleston, South Carolina, the Reverend Jedediah Morse didn't see it that way. He declared Jefferson to be "an Illuminatus." Even in the face of these charges, Jefferson strenuously defended the Illuminati, and described Weinhaupt as "an enthusiastic philanthropist."[17]

Jefferson also strenuously attacked those who wrote exposures of the Illuminati. Nesta Webster wrote, "The very violence of these disclaimers shows how truly the shafts had gone home. The line of defense had been laid down some ten years earlier by Weishaupt." That line of defense was that the Order no longer existed, and that the former members had all renounced all their conspiracies, "and that in reality Illuminism was an unimportant and transitory movement, which finally ended with its suppression in Bavaria in 1786."[18]

To paint the Illuminati as a philanthropic movement is, of course, ludicrous. As we shall see from private correspondence captured during the Bavarian government's crackdown on Illuminism, there was not a single hint of concern for the world's poor and suffering, no hint of true social reform, only the use of these covers to hide the true work of the Order: world revolution, world domination, and according to Webster, "sheer love of destruction."

Secrecy in the Illuminati was enforced in the same way it was in the Greek mystery schools, and no doubt as it is today in the super-Masonic organizations. The candidates were required to confess compromising information about themselves, like sexual indiscretions, or previously hidden criminal behavior, as if he were confessing his sins to a Catholic priest. If confessions of a sufficiently embarrassing nature were not available, then common criminality, as we saw with the Greeks, was an option. If one of Weishaupt's initiates were to break the code of silence, his credibility would be questioned by damning evidence that would, at the very least, destroy his reputation in the community, if not send him to prison.

To enhance the secrecy of written communications, and perhaps to give members a sense of historical perspective, all members took "antique" names. Weishaupt himself assumed the name of Spartacus, the greatest of all the Roman gladiators. Spartacus led the insurrection of slaves which kept Rome in terror and uproar for three years around 73 B.C. This name, Spartacus, has been frequently invoked by revolutionaries since then.[19]

A key Illuminist, Herr von Zwack, privy counselor to Prince von Salm, took the name Cato; Baron von Knigge was Philo; the Marquis di Contanza became Diomedes; Herr Massenhausen, Ajax; Herr Hertel became Marius; the Baron von Schroeckenstein became Mahomed; and so on.

Weishaupt's great genius was at structuring his system of Illuminism to attract candidates, and then misleading them until he felt that they were ready to accept the true nature of his plans. Candidates for the order, who were almost always drawn from Masonic lodges of the day, were always assured that the Order was working for the benefit of mankind. The candidates were initiated step-by-step into the higher "mysteries," whereby the true purposes of the Order were revealed. Nesta Webster explained that:

> ... the greatest caution was to be exercised not to reveal to the novice, doctrines that might be likely to revolt him. For this purpose the initiators must acquire the habit of 'talking backwards and forwards' so as not to commit themselves...so that our real purpose should remain impenetrable to our inferiors. [20]

"PERFECTING" CHRISTIANITY

A key goal behind these initiatory rites is to provide a system to gradually and gently realign a man's religious beliefs. Thus, a Christian is slowly encouraged to become a Deist; a Deist becomes an Atheist; an Atheist to a Satanist. In this religious aspect, the best Anglo/American Masonry can hope to achieve is the first step, from Christian to Deist. A Deist is one who believes that a God exists who created the world, but that He thereafter lost interest in man, and so consequently, man has no responsibility to God. Professor Robison explained that:

> The Deist, thus led on, has not far to go before he becomes a Naturalist or Atheist; and then the eternal sleep of death crowns all his humble hopes.[21]

The candidate would then be told that the religion of the Order "is the perfection of Christianity." He was told that Jesus of Nazareth was the originator of Illuminism, and that his walk on earth was really a secret mission to restore to men the original liberty and equality they had lost in the fall in the Garden of Eden. The candidate was convinced that Christianity was really the foundation of the Order. Weishaupt stated that "Jesus of Nazareth, the Grand Master of our Order, appeared at a time when the world was in the utmost disorder, and among a people who for ages had groaned under the yoke of bondage. He taught them the lessons of reason."[22]

Here we see Weishaupt's desperate attempt to connect Christ with Illuminism's creed of secret knowledge. Weishaupt even tried to justify secrecy of the Order in terms of Christianity:

> To be more effective, he [Jesus] took in the aid of Religion... and, in a very clever manner, he combined his secret doctrines with the popular religion...Never did any prophet lead men so easily and so securely along the road of liberty. He concealed the precious meaning and consequences of his doctrines; but fully disclosed them to a chosen few. Let us only take Liberty and Equality as the great aim of his doctrines, and Morality as the way to attain it, and every thing in the New Testament will be comprehensible; and Jesus will appear as the Redeemer of slaves. Man is fallen from the condition of Liberty and Equality, the STATE OF PURE NATURE. He is under

subordination and civil bondage, arising from the vices of man. This is the FALL, and ORIGINAL SIN. The KINGDOM OF GRACE is that restoration which may be brought about by Illumination and a just Morality. This is the NEW BIRTH.[23]

This doctrine is the basis of York Rite Masonry in general, and the modern day Knights Templar in particular. This is not to say that Weishaupt invented either, but he was no doubt exposed to the code of the Templars of his day.

Of course, Jesus made no mention of Illuminism or secret knowledge as being a conduit for grace or forgiveness of sins, nor did he come to physically free slaves and end slavery or establish liberty and equality on earth.

Weishaupt insisted that he got these doctrines from Masons.[24] Whether York or Scottish Rite, the two main branches of modern day Masonry, members believe their craft is an improvement on Christianity. In the York Rite, only Christians can be members. In the Scottish Rite, nominal Christians are initially told that Jesus Christ is actually the "Grand Master" of their lodge. Albert Pike, Grand Commander of Supreme Council and head of Scottish Rite Masonry in the U.S. explained in 1871:

> Christianity taught the doctrine of FRATERNITY; but repudiated that of political EQUALITY; by continually inculcating obedience to Caesar, and to those lawfully in authority.

> Masonry was the first apostle of EQUALITY. In the Monastery there is fraternity and equality, but no liberty. Masonry added that also, and claimed for man the three-fold heritage, LIBERTY, EQUALITY, and FRATERNITY.[25]

Documents captured in later years would show how members of the Illuminati tried to develop a believable rationale that could be used to convince honest, upstanding Christians that the need for secrecy was legitimate and Christ-like. lluminatus Philo wrote this to Weishaupt's closest associate, Cato, who in reality was the lawyer Herr von Zwack:

> Jesus Christ established no new Religion; he would only set Religion and Reason in their ancient rights....Many therefore were called, but few were chosen. To these elect were entrusted the most important secrets; and even among them there were degrees of information. There was a seventy, and a twelve. All this was in the natural order of things, and according to the habits of the Jews, and indeed of all antiquity....the doctrines of Christianity were...kept up, only in hidden societies, who handed them down to posterity; and they are now possessed by the genuine Free Masons.[26]

But in writing to Cato, Weishaupt revealed the deception. Speaking of the new Priests degree of the Illuminati that he had just invented, Weishaupt bragged that it was such a clever imitation of Christianity that even the most dedicated clergy would be fooled:

> I say that Free Masonry is concealed Christianity...and as I explain things, no man need be ashamed of being a Christian. Indeed I afterwards throw away this name, and substitute Reason.[27]

In the same letter, Weishaupt divulged how he was secretly laughing at those he had taken in. He poked fun at one poor Protestant priest who had attained the Illuminati's Priests degree:

> You can't imagine what respect and curiosity my priest-degree has raised; ... a famous Protestant divine, who is now of the Order, is persuaded that the religion contained in it is the true sense of Christianity. O MAN, MAN! TO WHAT MAY'ST THOU NOT BE PERSUADED. Who would imagine that I was to be the founder of a new religion.[28]

However, others in Weishaupt's Order wrote of their difficulties in seducing candidates away from Christianity. Philo (Baron von Knigge) had problems convincing some members of the Order that their goal was not to abolish Christianity:

> I have been at unwearied pains to remove the fears of some who imagine that our Superiors want to abolish Christianity....Were I to let them know that our General holds all Religion to be a lie, and uses even Deism ... only to lead men by the nose.[29]

Philo then candidly explained why initiates must have the true nature of the Order kept from them: "Should I mention our fundamental principles, so unquestionably dangerous to the world, who would remain?"[30]

After one to three years of intense scrutiny, the candidate would be admitted into the Order. At this time, the consequences of betraying the Order were made crystal clear. Taking a naked sword from the table, the person performing the initiation held the point of the sword against the heart of the novice and told him that if he was a traitor to the Order:

> All our brothers are called upon to arm themselves against you. Do not hope to escape or to find a place of safety. Wherever you are, shame, remorse, and the vengeance of the brothers unknown to you will pursue you and torment you to the inner-most recesses of your entrails.[31]

Only gradually would the Initiates have the "higher mysteries" revealed to them. One of the first lessons was to get the novice to believe the idea that the ends justify the means, that evil methods were justifiable if the ultimate outcome was for good. This allowed a member of the Illuminati to be excused for using any means to achieve his goals because the goals of the Order were held to be superior to every other consideration.

The groundwork was now laid to announce to the Initiate, moving up into the higher mysteries of the Order, that he had been lied to previously. Of course, he was told that these deceptions were all necessary and for the good of the Order. According to John Robison the Order was devised so that "the squeamish and gullible never rose higher than the lowest degrees...while the bold, ruthless and cynical, those ready and willing to dispense with religion, morality, patriotism and any other hindrances, rose to the top." Weishaupt explained:

> We must first gradually explain away all our preparatory pious frauds. And when persons of discernment find fault, we must desire them to consider the end of all our labor. This sanctifies our means...because they procured us a patient hearing, when otherwise men would have turned away from us like petted children.[33]

The Initiate is next told that religion is unnecessary and that "Reason will be the code of laws to all mankind. This is our GREAT SECRET."[34] Once the impediment of religion is dispensed with, the way is open for a world dictatorship, ruled by Illuminism. One of the great attractions of membership in a secret society in those days was as it is today — greed. Today, many still join Masonry because it has a reputation in assisting its membership attain worldly success. The Illuminati was very successful at placing its members in key positions because:

> Through its connections and intrigues, the conspiracy was able to place its selected members in positions of influence and power where they could enjoy all the glories of worldly success, provided they used that success to work unceasingly for the advancement of the Order.

Once the candidate achieved a certain level of advancement, his superiors helped him bring his talents into action and placed him in situations "most favorable for their exertion, so that he may be assured of success."[35] Weishaupt continues:

> The pupils are convinced that the Order will rule the world. Every member therefore becomes a ruler. We all think of ourselves as qualified to rule. It is therefore an alluring thought both to good and bad men. By this lure the Order will spread.[36]

The famous magician and occultist, Cagliostro, was initiated into the Illuminati in 1783. Many years later, he told Catholic priests about his initiation. The initiation took place in an underground room near Frankfort, Germany:

> An iron box filled with papers was opened. The introducers took from it a manuscript book [which] on the first page...read: "We, Grand Masters of the Templars..."then followed a form of oath, traced in blood. The book stated that Illuminism was a conspiracy directed against thrones and altars, and that the first blows were to attain France, that after the fall of the French Monarchy, Rome must be attacked.[37]

Cagliostro was told that the Order possessed vast wealth dispersed in the banks of Amsterdam, Rotterdam, London, Genoa, and Venice. He was given a substantial sum of cash for the expenses of his first mission, to help start the elimination of the French monarchy. He helped set in motion the scandalous "Affair of the Necklace" in 1785 and 1786 where Marie-Antoinette, Queen of France and wife of Louis XVI, was falsely charged with having an immoral relationship with a Roman Catholic cardinal. The scandal discredited the monarchy, which added fuel to the fires of the impending French Revolution and caused the nobles to oppose all the financial reforms that might otherwise have prevented it.

With so many powerful and corrupt men engaging in a highly secretive organization, it is logical to assume that there were bound to be internal power struggles. There were. In fact, it was an internal struggle that eventually led to the public exposure and temporary downfall of the Order.

As thoroughly documented by Robison in *Proofs of a Conspiracy*, Weishaupt and an Illuminatus named Minos, as well as others, wanted to immediately introduce Atheism to the members of the lower degrees. The third-ranking member of the Illuminati, Philo, disagreed, saying that the teaching of Satanism or Atheism openly to the members of the lower degrees would scare many of them off. Weishaupt persisted, saying that it would be easier to come right out and teach atheism from the start, because it would be:

> ... easier to show at once that Atheism was friendly to society, [rather] than to [have to] explain all their Masonic Christianity, which they were afterwards to show to be a bundle of lies.

> It required the constant efforts of Philo to prevent bare or flat Atheism from being uniformly taught in their degrees. He [Philo] complains of Mino's cramming irreligion down their throats in every meeting, and says, that he frightened many from entering the Order. Spartacus complains much of the squeamishness of Philo; yet Philo is not a great deal behind him in irreligion.[38]

Philo (Knigge) believed only that it was better to "defer the development of the bold principles till we had firmly secured the man."[39] He revealed his suspicions that Weishaupt was inventing the highest degrees of Illuminism to be nothing more than a medium for pure Satan worship and explained that it was this realization that led to their eventual split:

> Spartacus...painted his three favorite mystery degrees, which were to be conferred by him alone, in colours which had fascinated his own fancy. But they were the colors of hell, and would have scared the most intrepid; and because I represented the danger of this, and by force obtained the omission of this picture, he became my implacable enemy. I abhor treachery and profligacy, and leave him to blow himself and his Order in the air.[40]

Here we see the perfect example of why the outward teaching of Satanism was, and is, avoided. Even the number-three man of the Illuminati was revolted when he found out for certain that Weishaupt was worshipping the powers of Hell.

Philo left the Order, probably in 1783. In 1784, the Bavarian government, having been informed that the Order constituted a danger to the State and that its followers were said to have declared that "the Illuminati must in time rule the world," published an edict forbidding all secret societies.[41]

In April 1785, four other Illuminati who were also professors left the society, disgusted by Weishaupt and his tyrannical Order. They were summoned before a court of inquiry to give an account of the doctrines and methods of the Order. The evidence presented by these men left no further room for doubt concerning the diabolical nature of Illuminism. Their testimony revealed a sweeping scope:

> All religion, all love of country and loyalty to sovereigns, were to be annihilated...every effort was to be made to create discord not only between princes and their subjects but...even between parents and children, whilst suicide was to be encouraged by inculcating in men's minds the idea that the act of killing oneself afforded a certain voluptuous pleasure.[42]

Finally, on October 11, 1786, the Bavarian authorities descended on the house of the lawyer, Zwack, known as Cato to Illuminists, and seized documents which:

> ... laid bare the methods of the conspirators. Here were found descriptions of a strong box for safeguarding papers which if forced open should blow up...a composition which should blind or kill if squirted in the face; a method of counterfeiting seals; recipes for...poisonous perfumes that would fill a bedroom with pestilential vapours, and a tea to procure abortion. A defense of atheism and materialism entitled "Better than Horus" was also discovered, and a paper in the handwriting of Zwack describing the plan for enlisting women...[43]

Weishaupt had already decreed that bringing women into the Order should be a goal, so that the philosophy of the new liberated woman could be developed. This concept was devised to aid in his plan for the breakup of the family by generally developing rationales which would sow discord between men and women. He initially achieved this by painting the plight of women as a downtrodden class. This rhetoric can still be seen in the "women's liberation" movement of today. But now we see that Illuminism had other, even more "practical" uses for this downtrodden, female class:

> It will be of great service and procure much information and money, and will suit charmingly the taste of many of our truest members who are lovers of the sex. It should consist of two classes, the

virtuous and the dissolute...They must not know each other, and must be under the direction of men, but without knowing it.[44]

These seized documents from the houses of Illuminists in 1786 are the primary source of the material quoted in this chapter. Even though the revelation and subsequent government-sponsored publication of these documents must have caused considerable damage to the cause of the Order, the Illuminati still proclaimed their innocence. Though they never denied the authenticity of these seized documents, they claimed they had been misinterpreted and reaffirmed that the real purpose of the Order was to make the human race "one good and happy family."

Despite the protestations of innocence by the Illuminati, the Bavarian government was now armed with numerous incriminating documents. They launched a thorough investigation of the Order and became convinced that the Illuminati were planning to take over the world by what we now call revolutionary Communism. The Bavarian government decided that the best way to proceed was to warn other governments by publishing the papers of the Illuminati, and circulating them as widely as possible. The document, entitled "Original Writings of the Order of the Illuminati," was sent to every government in Europe. Unfortunately, the rulers of Europe, possibly out of pride, and possibly out of the unbelievability of such an extravagant scheme, refused to take the Bavarian government's warning, or the Illuminati, seriously.

The Bavarian government continued its prosecution of the Order and several members were arrested. Zwack left the country for England, while Weishaupt, with a price on his head, fled to Switzerland. He eventually returned to Germany when one of his royal followers, the Duke of Saxe-Gotha, offered him sanctuary in his household.

Although the suppression of Illuminism made Weishaupt and other members of the Order flee Bavaria, the Illuminati had taken firm root among the rich and powerful of Europe, including, possibly, the wealthiest of all, the first international bankers and railway kings, the German brothers Rothschild. Weishaupt had made plans for the eventuality of discovery and repression, and even arrogantly outlined his plans on paper. He wrote in a letter to Cato:

> I have considered everything and so prepared it that if the Order should this day go to ruin, I shall in a year re-establish it more brilliant than ever. By this plan we shall direct all mankind. In this manner and by the simplest means, we shall set all in motion and in flames.[45]

Even though the Illuminati faded from public view, the monolithic apparatus set in motion by Weishaupt may still exist today. Certainly, the goals and methods of operation still exist. Whether the name Illuminati still exists is really irrelevant.

MASONRY AND ILLUMINATI JOINED

In light of these revelations, Masons should be shocked to discover that at least Continental Masonry and the Illuminati were formally wedded in July 1782. After lengthy negotiations between Weishaupt and members of Masonry, an agreement was reached on December 20, 1781 to combine the two Orders. The outside world will never know what really occurred at the Congress of Wilhelmsbad because even the honorable men who had been unwittingly drawn into the movement were under oath to reveal nothing. One such honest Freemason, the Comte de Virieu, said in his biography that he had brought back:

> tragic secrets. I will not confide them to you. I can only tell you that all this is very much more serious than you think. The conspiracy which is being woven is so well thought out that it will be...impossible for the Monarchy and the Church to escape it.[46]

From this point on, according to his biographer, M. Costa de Beauregard, "the Comte de Virieu could only speak of Freemasonry with horror."[47] In 1782, the headquarters of illuminized Freemasonry was moved to Frankfurt, the stronghold of German finance, and controlled by the Rothschilds. For the first time, Jews were admitted into the Order. Previously, Jews had only been admitted to a division of the Order called "The small and constant Sanhedrin of Europe."[48]

These new members brought new money and energy to Weishaupt's system. Once provided for financially, Weishaupt's mighty engine was ready to run. From the Frankfurt lodge, the gigantic plan of world revolution was carried forward. During a large Masonic congress in 1786 it was later said by two French Freemasons that the deaths of Louis XVI [the French monarch] and Gustavus III of Sweden were decreed.[49]

The facts show that the Illuminati, and its lower house, Masonry, was a secret society within a secret society. The outer doctrine, for the consumption of the masses, said Illuminism was merely a "perfected" form of Christianity, while the inner doctrine called for world conquest by any means, with Atheism or outright Satanism as its real creed. John Robison summed up the goals of Illuminism quite prophetically almost 200 years ago when he wrote:

> Their first and immediate aim is to get the possession of riches, power and influence, without industry [i.e., without working for it]; and, to accomplish this, they want to abolish Christianity; and then...universal profligacy will procure them the adherence of all the wicked, and enable them to overturn all the civil governments of Europe; after which they will think of farther conquests, and extend their operations to the other quarters of the globe.[50]

Nesta Webster did not exaggerate when she said of the Illuminati:

> It is by this terrible and formidable sect that the gigantic plan of World Revolution was worked out under the leadership of the man whom Louis Blanc [the radical Socialist who helped lead the 1848 French Revolution] has truly described as "the profoundest conspirator that has ever existed."[51]

SIX

THE FRENCH REVOLUTION

Illuminists, buoyed by their perceived success in Revolutionary America, soon turned their attentions to France. Although the French monarchy was considered to be second only to the British monarchy in its benevolence toward its subjects,[1] secret societies opposed it, and contrived its downfall.

Professor Douglas Johnson, in his 1970 book, *The French Revolution*, remarked that the eighteenth century had not been bad for France. The population was expanding, there had been no great plagues, and no wars had been fought on French soil. The French people loved their monarch; "no signs of disloyalty to it could be detected...."[2] We see in the French Revolution the first time where grievances were systematically created in order to exploit them.[3]

Most history texts tell us that the French Revolution of the late 1700s was a popular uprising sparked by a starving population, rioting in protest of a bankrupt government. We are also told that fewer than 50,000 lives were lost. The truth is, however, that the revolution was deliberately contrived by the machinations of the secret societies, rampant in France at that time, and the death toll was at least 300,000.[4]

The French Revolution was the first example of what we would later come to know as Soviet-style revolutionary Communism. As Russia's revolutionary leader Prince Peter Kropotkine, wrote in 1908, the "Great Revolution" as he called it "was the source and origin of all the present communist, anarchist, and socialist conceptions,"[5]

Some of America's founding fathers were equally enthralled with the "Great Revolution," becoming caught up in the popular Masonic fervor for liberty at any cost. John Marshall, Chief Justice of the U.S. Supreme Court from 1801 to 1835, stated that, "In no other part of the globe was this revolution hailed with more joy than in America."[6]

Who spearheaded this Great Revolution, and why? The answer is clear. In 1783, three years before the suppression of the Illuminati in Bavaria, its adherents had already begun their work in France. In 1790, only five years after the Bavarian suppression, the magician Cagliostro revealed at his own interrogatory before the Holy See in Rome, that the Illuminati was not dead, but actively working to ignite a revolution in France.

Cagliostro recounted that at the time of his entry into the Illuminati, in 1783, his initiators followed rituals read from an ancient manuscript which stated that Illuminism was a conspiracy directed against thrones and altars, and that the first blows were to be struck against the French monarchy, followed by a direct attack on the heart of Christianity of that day, the Catholic Church.[7] Cagliostro explained how the Germans had secretly been infiltrating the French Masonic lodges for years, in hopes of eventually bringing them under the control of the Illuminati:

> By March 1789, the 266 lodges controlled by the [French] Grand Orient were all "illuminized" without knowing it, for the Freemasons in general, were not told the name of the sect that brought them these mysteries, and only a very small number were really initiated into the secret....In the following month the Revolution broke out.[8]

The French monarchy of Louis XVI was not totally blameless. It certainly needed some reforms, but even Arthur Young, the nineteenth-century British historian, always quoted in historical circles as the strongest critic of the "Old Regime," asserted that "the old government of France, with all its faults, was certainly the best enjoyed by any considerable country in Europe, England alone excepted."[9]

Even Thomas Jefferson, who would later become one of the greatest admirers of the bloodshed that was soon to destroy the French nation, wrote in a letter to Lafayette in 1787 during a visit to France: "I have been pleased to find among the people a less degree of physical misery than I had expected. They are generally well clothed, and have plenty of food."[10]

Jefferson was obviously surprised to find that the French people enjoyed such a high standard of living, having been told in the circles of American Illuminized Masonry that the monarchy was brutal and repressive. Unfortunately for the unsuspecting French people, the relatively good times of the 1700s were not to continue. The revolutionaries, led and financed by the Illuminized Masonic lodges of France, began to initiate their plan to bring about a contrived state of chaos — a condition needed for any "revolution."

JACOBIN CLUBS

After their recent exposures in Bavaria, the Illuminati had been driven even further underground, taking on a variety of names, such as

The French Revolutionary Club. As radicals flocked into these new varieties of Illuminism, a larger meeting hall was needed. The Hall of the Jacobins Convent was leased, and it was from this hall that they eventually derived their new name, the Jacobin Club.

The Jacobin Club met in secret and eventually boasted of having some of the best-educated and most influential men in France among its 1,300 members. The Jacobins vowed to destroy the monarchy, as well as other existing institutions, and sought to establish what they called a "New World Order," or "Universal Republic."[11]

In order to achieve proper revolutionary zeal, the Jacobins began searching for an issue to justify revolution. Soon they came upon the formula that has been used in most revolutions since then. First, they encouraged lawlessness through a group of radical thugs. Then their more influential members raised a strident call for "law and order," and thousands of Frenchmen were sent to the guillotine. This set the stage with an atmosphere of repression.[12]

Webster presented compelling evidence that what was to follow was contrived by powerfully placed Jacobins:

> The Jacobin Clubs...were organized by the revolutionary committee...under the direct inspiration of the Bavarian Illuminati, who taught them their "method of doing business, of managing their correspondence, and of procuring and training pupils." It was thus that at a given signal, insurrections could be engineered simultaneously in all parts of the country.[13]

So complete was the organization of the Jacobin Clubs in France that between 1791 and 1792 all the Masonic lodges of France were closed down. The reason for this was that once the Jacobins felt that they were in control of the nation, they were fearful that Masonry might be used — as they had used it earlier — as a cover for a counter-revolutionary scheme.[14] This aspect of history repeated itself in Nazi Germany 150 years later when Hitler suppressed the very Masonry that helped him rise to power.

In the spring and summer of 1789, an artificial shortage of grain was created by Illuminist manipulations of the grain market. This produced a famine so intense that it brought the nation to the edge of revolt. One of the leading figures in this scheme was the Duc d'Orleans, the Grand Master of the Grand Orient lodges. The Illuminists claimed that their revolution would be "for the benefit of the bourgeoisie with the people as instruments...." But in reality the conspirators held up the food supplies and blocked all reforms in the National Assembly to exacerbate the situation, and the populace starved.[15]

By July 14, the Bastille was stormed, from which a grand total of only seven prisoners were "liberated."[16] Even French historians now acknowledge that the purpose of the revolutionaries was not to destroy the Bastille or liberate the prisoners, but to steal arms and gunpowder.[17] Thus armed, on July 22, 1789, the Jacobins set into motion one of the most elaborately timed revolutionary exercises ever attempted. It would later be known as "The Great Fear."

A panic was created simultaneously around the nation. Horsemen rode from town to town telling the citizens that "brigands" were approaching and that everyone should take up arms. Citizens were instructed that the conspirators were being harboured in the larger estates, the chateaux, and that by edict of the King all should be torched. The people, obedient to their monarch, complied. Soon, the flames of destruction were soon burning out of control. Anarchy continued to grow as citizens began raiding and pillaging — and not only for food.[18]

The scene in Paris was even worse. The city was running riot with criminals. The American minister in Paris, Gouverneur Morris, who had been one of the architects of the U.S. Constitution, wrote that Paris in July of 1789 was a country "as near to anarchy as society can approach without dissolution....The authority of the King and the nobility is completely subdued....I tremble for the constitution."[19]

For the next three years the chaos continued. Then, on August 10, 1792, a band of rioters broke into the royal palace and killed the king's famous Swiss Guards, who had been ordered not to fire on the people. The King was imprisoned and he and his family were eventually executed.[20] It was not, however, until after the overthrow of the monarchy on the tenth of August that the work of demolition began on the vast scale planned by Weishaupt.

"From the 10th of August onwards," stated Webster, "we find the [French] tricolour replaced by the red flag of the social revolution, whilst the cry of "Vive notre roi d'Orleans!" [Long live the King of Orleans] gives way to the masonic watchword "Liberty, Equality, Fraternity!"[21]

Remarkably, even today, "Liberty, Equality, Fraternity" remains the French motto. During the massacres in the prisons that followed in September, the assassins were observed to make Masonic signs to the victims and to spare those who knew how to reply.[22]

Terror was rampant in the streets of Paris. The full horror of government by Satanism was being played out, complete with human butcherings and cannibalism. The following brutal passages suggest the horror of the times. Although some may find them offensive, it is better to read to what extent these revolutions are carried, than to unwittingly help bring them to your town. Researcher William P. Hoar described the following scene on the streets of Paris:

A wretched undercook, who had not time to escape, was seized by these tigers, thrust into a copper, and in this state exposed to the heat of the furnace...monsters with human faces collected in hundreds under the porch of the Escalier du Midi and danced amidst torrents of blood and wine. A murderer played the violin besides the corpses, and thieves, with their pockets full of gold, hanged other thieves on the banisters.[23]

Illuminism, as pure Satanism, was now out in the open for all to view. Not surprisingly, in November 1793 a campaign against religion was inaugurated by a massacre of the priests all over France. In the cemeteries the cherished motto of the Illuminati, "Death is an eternal sleep," was posted by order of the Illuminatus "Anaxagoras" Chaumette. In the churches of Paris, Feasts of Reason were celebrated where women of easy morals were enthroned as goddesses. These were also known as "Eroterion," and were modelled on Weishaupt's plan to honor the god of Love.[24]

This was of course no revolution of liberation, but one of oppression, hiding behind a shallow, meaningless facade of "democracy." A century and a half later the Nazi idealogue Goebbels would pay homage to the French Revolution for "all the possibilities of life and development which it had brought to the people. In this sense, if you like, I am a democrat." In fact, Hitler called the Nazi revolt "the exact counterpart of the French Revolution."[25]

And what did America's patron saint of "democracy," Thomas Jefferson, have to say of the revolution? In 1791, after returning to the United States from a three-year stint as minister to France, he described the carnage as "so beautiful a revolution" and stated that he hoped it would sweep the world. He claimed to believe that "most Frenchmen were Jacobins. Their excesses, if one called them such, reflected that national will."[26]

This was certainly news to the French revolutionaries of that era. The revolution did not have popular support. The monarchy did. According to one revolutionary observer, writing in 1792:

> The Republicans are an infinitesimal minority...the rest of France is attached to the monarchy. Actually it was the liberality of King Louis in his regard for the French people that led to his downfall; each reform to which he acceded, each change, was followed by new demands—and when violence broke out the King hesitated to send troops against his own people.[27]

Treasury Secretary Alexander Hamilton openly criticized Jefferson when he was still minister to France. Hamilton charged that Jefferson had helped to foment the French Revolution, and, in fact, Jefferson did draft a Charter of Rights to be presented to the king. In a letter dated May 26, 1792, Hamilton wrote to a friend that Jefferson "drank freely of the French philosophy, in religion, in science, in politics.[28] He came from France in the moment of fermentation, which he had a share in exciting."[29]

Even though Jefferson did make significant and positive contributions to the nation, it is beyond question that he supported the methods and goals of the Jacobin Clubs. He wrote to Brissot de Warville from Philadelphia in a letter dated May 8, 1793 that he was "eternally attached to the principles" of the French Revolution.[30]

In light of this evidence, Jefferson's place in American history may eventually be reconsidered and memorials to him may well be inappropriate.

When the Revolution broke out, Illuminists from all over Europe came in droves to witness the spectacle. Among these was Weishaupt's hand picked representative, Prussian baron Anacharsis Clootz.

Clootz entered Paris when revolution broke out in 1789. He quickly became a member of the Club of the Jacobins. Not a man given to modesty, Clootz took charge of the band of thirty-six Illuminist foreigners who had come to Paris to participate in the orgy of blood and proclaimed that they were the "embassy of the human race." He addressed the revolutionary National Assembly on June 17, 1791 declaring that the whole world adhered to the democratic ideals of the Revolution. He titled himself "The Orator of Mankind" and adopted the pseudonym "Anarcharsis."[31]

By 1792, Clootz called on the National Convention to "liberate" the rest of Europe and soon France was at war with most of the European powers. As Nesta Webster explained:

> Historians, unaware of the sources whence Clootz drew his theories, or anxious to conceal the role of Illuminism in the revolutionary movement, describe him as an amiable eccentric of no importance. In reality Clootz was one of the most important figures of the whole Revolution...for it was he alone of all his day who embodied the spirit of anti-patriotism and internationalism which, defeated France in 1793, [and] finally secured its triumph on the ruins of the Russian Empire of 1917.[32]

It was Clootz who played the most active part in the Revolution's campaign against religion. Clootz ordered the slaughter of hundreds of imprisoned priests during one September of the Revolution. Later he remarked that he was sorry he had not "septemberized" more priests and openly declared himself "the personal enemy of Jesus Christ."[33]

Clootz and his Revolution abolished all Christian holidays such as Easter, Christmas, and All Saints Day. In fact, they even abolished Sunday, and attempted to create a new calendar which gave the people only one half day of rest every ten days. This new week was called a "decadi." In tongue-in-cheek fashion, an article in the French *Moniteur* for September 9, 1794 said: "All is new in France—weather, mankind, the earth, and the sea....The Republican year gives to work four months more than the papal and monarchic year."[34]

By 1793, much of France lay in ruin. Industries were decimated, libraries burned, the bourgeoisie all but wiped out. Even the great chemist Lavoisier had been guillotined on the excuse that "the Republic has no need of chemists."

DEPOPULATION

The French economy was in shambles. Unemployment was rampant. Toward the end of 1793, the new revolutionary Republic found itself faced with hundreds of thousands of working men for whom it could not find employment. The revolutionary leaders embarked upon a fearful new project that was to be copied by tyrants ever after, called "depopulation."

The idea was to reduce France's population of twenty-five million down to either eight or sixteen million, depending on which source you believe. Maximilien Robespierre believed depopulation to be "indispensable." "The system of the Terror was thus the answer to the problem of unemployment—unemployment brought about on a vast scale by the destruction of the luxury trades."[35]

In France members of the revolutionary committees in charge of the extermination toiled day and night over maps, calculating just how many heads must be sacrificed in each town. Fearful Revolutionary Tribunals tried to determine who would be killed, and a never-ending stream of victims marched to a variety of deaths. In Nantes, 500 children were killed in one butchery, and 144 poor women who sewed shirts for the army were thrown into the river.[36] Stone quarries were a favorite site for mass extermination because of their precipitous drops and rocky floors, and it was said that many quarry operators had to shut down due to the piles of bodies.

And what did Thomas Jefferson have to say of this extermination policy? Nothing would please me more than to report that over the years, Jefferson's enthusiasm for the bloody revolution mellowed. However, in 1793, Secretary of State Jefferson wrote that rather than see the French Revolution fail:

> I would have seen half the earth desolated. Were there but an Adam & Eve left in every country, & left free, it would be better than it now is....The liberty of the whole earth was depending on the issue of the contest. [37]

If taken literally, the incredibility of this statement cannot be over-emphasized. Was Jefferson merely exaggerating for effect, or is this what he really meant? Would he really rather have seen the entire population of not only France, but of every nation on earth, reduced to but a single couple rather than see the revolution fail? He certainly knew the results of the revolution on France. In 1789, while still in Paris, he wrote to John Jay:

> The city [Paris] is as yet not entirely quieted. Every now and then summary execution is done on individuals by individuals, and nobody is in condition to ask for what, and by whom....The details from the country are as distressing as I had apprehended they would be....Abundance of chateaux are certainly burnt and burning, and not a few lives sacrificed.[38]

Interestingly enough, during the visit of Soviet leader Mikhail Gorbachev and his wife to the United States in 1987, Jefferson was the only one of the founding fathers singled out for praise. Mrs. Raisa Gorbachev took a limousine tour of the Washington, D.C. monuments on December 8, 1987, her first day in town. She stopped only at the Jefferson Memorial. It was the only place where she spoke to the press. In the shadow of the nineteen-foot-high statue of Jefferson she proclaimed, "It's good you built a monument to one of the world's greatest thinkers." As we will see in later chapters, the Soviets revered the French Revolution as the model for their own.[39]

Although the revolution never fulfilled its hoped-for goal of killing off eight million French citizens, estimates of the final death toll at the time ran around 300,000.[40] The Revolution finally burned itself out, not for lack of revolutionary zeal, but because it consumed or destroyed the resources needed to sustain it.

Edmund Burke, the conservative British statesman who was one of the greatest supporters of the Americans during their revolution, abhorred the results of the French Revolution. In his 1790 book, *Reflections on the Revolution in France*, he said:

> Oh! what a revolution!...little did I dream that I should have lived to see disasters fallen upon [the Queen of France] in a nation of gallant men, in a nation of men of honour....But the age of chivalry is gone. That of sophisters, economists, and calculators, has succeeded; and the glory of Europe is extinguished for ever.

Eight years after the end of the Terror, in 1802, an Englishman named Redhead Yorke travelled through France and noted that it was still in a state of sickening desolation:

> France still bleeds at every pore—she is a vast mourning family, clad in sackcloth. It is impossible at this time for a contemplative mind to be gay in France. At every footstep the merciless and sanguinary route of fanatical barbarians disgust the sight and sicken humanity— on all sides ruins obtrude themselves on the eye and compel the question, For what and for whom are all this havoc and desolation?[41]

Many believed that the first French Revolution was a "bourgeois movement." Webster pointed out:

> It is true that it was made by bourgeois, and at the beginning also by aristocrats—[but] the people throughout were the chief sufferers; but this has been the case in every outbreak of the World Revolution. All revolutionary leaders or writers have been bourgeois....No man of the people has ever taken a prominent part in the movement. But in the French "Terror," as in Russia today, the bourgeoisie were the victims.[42]

As has been the case in every incident of social revolution since, the kings are dethroned as per the Masonic motto, but new aristocrats just take their place—less exposed, and more hidden from public view. "The conception of France rising like a phoenix from that great welter of blood and horror is as mythical as the allegory from which it is taken and has existed only in the minds of posterity." As Webster wrote:

> Not a single contemporary who lived through the Revolution has ever pretended that it was anything but a ghastly failure. The conspiracy of history alone has created the myth. [43]

Alloys Hoffman, the editor of the *Journal de Vienna*, wrote in 1793: "I shall never cease to repeat that the Revolution has come from masonry and that it was made by writers and the Illuminati."[44]

Whose interests did the French Revolution serve? Certainly not those of the citizens in whose name it was waged. The idea for this revolution, remember, came from the German Illuminati, and although Illuminism's ultimate goals are international in scope, German nationalism could have played a role. After all, in a single decade, hundreds of years of French civilization was reduced to rubble and chaos — something German armies were never able to accomplish. This certainly did not serve the national interests of France, but it did serve the national interests of Germany.

So the first French Revolution was not the benign, spontaneous uprising historians would like us to believe. It was spawned in Masonry and its inner order, the Illuminati. There was nothing about it that was idealistic, utopian, or uplifting. It was an exercise in anarchy, driven by Satanism, destined for pure destruction. But the revolution went far beyond mere nationalistic rivalries. One contemporary observer said in 1793:

> Hitherto the basis of human polity was religion, the Supreme Being was everywhere adored, and the great maxims of morality respected; but when the order of civil society had attained a degree of perfection unknown in former ages, we see endeavours...put in practice to destroy it, Atheism rising against Religion, Anarchy against government.[45]

SEVEN

AMERICAN JACOBINS

After their successes in France, the Jacobins tried to bring their Illuminated revolution to the struggling nation of America in the early 1800s. They succeeded in winning a large measure of popular support by painting a false picture of the bloody reality of the French Revolution.

The United States was in a frenzy of ill-informed enthusiasm over what had happened in France. In Boston a celebration was held to honor the perpetrators of the French Revolution. A tax of three dollars per person was imposed to pay for a great civic feast in honor of the French "comrades." Most Bostonians paid the tax rather than be denounced as aristocrats and suffer the same fate as the French aristocrats. It is said that in America, more gunpowder was fired in celebrating French triumphs than the French ever spent in achieving them.[1]

In one Philadelphia waxworks, the most popular exhibit was a reproduction of the execution of Louis XVI. Families were horrified to see the guillotine fall and the King's lips turn from red to blue. Children were admitted at half price. John Adams was disgusted by the new revolutionary furor and called it all "sound and fury." By contrast, Thomas Jefferson applauded it saying, "It was music."[2]

On July 16, 1782, the year after the British surrendered to the Americans, representatives of the world's secret societies convened the Congress of Wilhelmsbad in Europe and formally joined Masonry and the Illuminati. In the next four years the Order was able to secretly establish several lodges in America. In 1785, for example, the Columbian Lodge of the Order of the Illuminati was established in New York City. Its members included Governor DeWitt Clinton, Clinton Roosevelt, and Horace Greeley.[3]

True to the teachings of Weishaupt, Clinton Roosevelt wrote a book entitled *Science of Government Founded on Natural Law*, wherein he explained his philosophy: "There is no God of justice to order things aright on earth; if there be a God, he is a malicious and revengeful being, who created us for misery."[4] This is the Luciferian doctrine in its purest form.

In his book, Clinton Roosevelt refers to himself and other members of his order as "the enlightened ones." He further explained that the U.S. Constitution was a "leaky vessel" which was "hastily put together when we left the British flag," and therefore in need of drastic revision.[5] This theme, that the U.S. Constitution is fatally flawed by too many checks and balances, has been often repeated ever since and wholesale constitutional revision remains one of the most important objectives of secret societies.

It is interesting to note that few have done more to further the plans of Illuminism and Communism than Clinton Roosevelt's descendent, Franklin D. Roosevelt. In fact, what is probably the most influential Masonic lodge in modern day France is known as the Franklin Roosevelt Lodge in Paris.[6]

GENÊT

In April of 1793, the French sent over their new ambassador, the youthful Edmond Genêt. Genêt had been expelled from Russia less than a year earlier for revolutionary activities. Officially, Genêt had orders to seek repayment of part of the American debt incurred during the American Revolution. The idea was that the monies collected would help finance a war with England to further spread revolution there.

Some wonder why France, a nation already on the verge of self-destruction, would at this point in its history want to go to war with the most powerful nation on earth. Could it really serve French interests? Of course not. It served the national interests of France's historic enemy, Germany, but more importantly, it served the interests of Illuminism's plan for world revolution. From this point on, the history of Europe can only be completely understood in light of this continuing World Revolution movement marching across its face.

Genêt began agitating for French ships to be able to use American crews to raid the colonies of Britain and Spain. He also began to "tamper with American domestic politics for whatever advantage might accrue to France."[7] Against the advice of Secretary of State Jefferson, President Washington prohibited the outfitting of French privateers with American crews. Washington, during his presidency (1789-1797), grew increasingly uneasy with the French role in his young, struggling nation, and would soon begin a series of ever stronger denunciations against the Jacobins, and eventually, the Illuminati.

In the meantime, Genêt was busy at work in the American countryside organizing what he called "Democratic Clubs." The problem grew so extreme that at one gathering in Philadelphia, guests toasted Genêt but refused to extend the same courtesy to President Washington.[8]

Noah Webster, the great American educator and journalist who won fame for compiling a dictionary in the late 1700s, warned that the so-called Democratic Clubs were a group "which must be crushed in its infancy or it would certainly crush the government."[9]

John Quincy Adams, the sixth president of the United States, had no love for Masonry in general, and was under no misguided impressions as to the links between the Democratic Clubs and the European Illuminati. He cautioned that "the Masonic oath, obligations and penalties cannot possibly be reconciled to the laws of morality, of Christianity, or of the land."[10] He said that the Democratic Clubs "are so perfectly affiliated with the Parisian Jacobins that their origin from a common parent cannot possibly be mistaken."[11]

Washington reached the same conclusion, saying that the Democratic Clubs were meant to:

> ... sow seeds of jealousy and distrust among the people. I gave it as my opinion to the confidential characters around me that if these societies were not counteracted (not by prosecutions, the ready way to make them grow stronger), or did not fall into disesteem...they would shake the government to its foundations.[12]

Washington also believed that the Democratic Clubs were responsible for the so-called Whiskey Rebellion. In the early 1790s, the new Secretary of the Treasury, Alexander Hamilton, also a Mason, successfully urged Congress to levy a tax on distilled liquors. The purpose of the tax was not only to collect some much-needed funds for the debt-ridden federal government, but also to consolidate the power of the new nation at its western limits. Of course, Hamilton, being one of the most religious of our founding fathers, may also have thought it appropriate to tax corn liquor due to its status as a biblically reproved sin.

The new tax hit the western frontiersmen the hardest because frontier roads were little more than rough forest trails on which corn, their primary crop, was transported with great difficulty to markets in the more settled areas. Distilling the corn into whiskey reduced the volume of material which had to be transported to market. Consequently, whiskey was the most important cash crop for many farmers who lived on the frontier.

Genêt and his Democratic Clubs used the issue to try to stir up trouble in the Western regions of youthful America, which at that time extended no farther than western Pennsylvania. Soon, a mini-revolution broke out in Harrisburg. This was the first military challenge the new government had faced. President Washington, dressed in his military uniform, reviewed a hastily-gathered federal army of 15,000 troops before he sent them off to crush the rebellion. Secretary of the Treasury Hamilton personally accompanied the troops. The rebels were obviously not prepared for such a show of force, and the insurrection quickly melted away. When the federal troops entered Harrisburg, they found the French flag flying over the courthouse.

President Washington chastised the rebellion, its Illuminist sponsors in Congress, and the French in no uncertain terms:

> I consider this insurrection as the first formidable fruit of the Democratic Societies...instituted by artful and designing members [of Congress]....I see, under a display of popular and fascinating guises, the most diabolical attempts to destroy...the government.

> That they have been the fomenters of the western disturbance admits of no doubt. [If] this daring and factious spirit [is not crushed,] adieu to all government in this country, except mob and club government.[13]

Several years afterwards, in his Farewell Address to the American people, Washington confirmed his distrust for revolution as a general remedy for a nation's problems, and he urged nations to abide by their constitutions:

> The basis of our political systems is the right of the people to make and to alter their Constitutions of Government. But...let it be corrected by an amendment in the way which the Constitution designates. But let there be no change by usurpation; for though this, in one instance, may be the instrument of good, it is the customary weapon by which free governments are destroyed.

He then attacked the concept of the separation of church and state, which had recently been foisted on the new nation by Thomas Jefferson et al., saying:

> Of all the dispositions and habits which lead to political prosperity, Religion and morality are indispensable supports. In vain would that man claim the tribute of Patriotism, who should labour to subvert these great Pillars of human happiness, these firmest props of the duties of Men and citizens.

Washington then retired from public life for two years, until his nation called upon him again in 1798, when war with France threatened. So great was their fear of the Illuminati in the guise of the French Jacobins, that Washington, along with President John Adams, a non-Mason, and the majority of the members of Congress passed protective laws. These laws, known as the Alien and Sedition Acts, were "designed to protect the United States from the extensive French Jacobin conspiracy, paid agents of which were even in high places in the government."[14]

The Alien and Sedition laws were similar to laws passed by many European countries who feared the domestic subversion the Illuminati had demonstrated it could create at will. They authorized the president to expel any alien considered dangerous. In addition, the acts raised the waiting period for naturalization from five to fourteen years, and permitted the detention of anyone from an "enemy" nation. The Frenchmen who had flocked to America to stir up revolution in support of Jefferson were hit hard and many had to flee the country. The Sedition Act also prohibited the publication of false or malicious writings against the government.

Years later, former president John Adams would still be scolding former president Jefferson about his support of the French revolution and Genet's malevolent activities in the United States. In a letter dated June 30, 1813, Adams wrote to Jefferson:

> You certainly never felt the terrorism excited by Genêt, in 1793...when ten thousand people in the streets of Philadelphia, day after day threatened to drag [President] Washington out of his house, and effect a revolution...nothing but [a miracle]...could have saved the United States from a fatal revolution of government.[15]

So concerned was Washington over the Jacobin threat that he came out of retirement and again accepted the appointment of Commander-in-Chief of the Army and publicly supported the Acts. In a letter written to Rev. G.W. Snyder at Mount Vernon on October 24, 1798 he apologized for giving the impression previously that American Masons were not involved in the rebellion:

> It was not my intention to doubt that, the Doctrines of the Illuminati, and principles of Jacobinism had not spread in the United States. On the contrary, no one is more truly satisfied of this fact than I am. The idea that I meant to convey, was, that I did not believe that the Lodges of Free Masons in this Country had, as Societies, endeavored to propagate the diabolical tenants of the first, or pernicious principles of the latter.[16]

Washington went on to say that there was no doubt that the Illuminati was trying to separate in America, "the People from their Government." Soon after the passage of the Alien and Sedition Acts, the threat of war subsided. Unfortunately, a year later, on December 14, 1799, Washington died.

But did this unprecedented chastisement from the "father" of the new American nation put an end to the Jacobian ideals, or the goals of Illuminism? Hardly. Washington's comments did not fall on deaf ears, however, and the term "Illuminism" was well known in that day. Harvard's Houghton Library contains numerous sermons, pamphlets, and books denouncing Illuminism, or the Illuminati during the late 1790s and early 1800s. For example, in an 1812 sermon, given in Lancaster, New Hampshire, Rev. Joseph Willard said:

There is sufficient evidence that a number of Societies, of the Illuminati, have been established, in this land of Gospel light and civil liberty, which were first organized from the grand Society in France. They are doubtless, secretly striving to undermine all our ancient institutions, civil and sacred. These societies are closely leagued with those of the same order, in Europe; they have all the same object in view.

What is the difference between the American Revolution and the European revolutions, including that which occurred in Russia in 1917? The difference is that in America, Christianity was too strong to be erased by the revolutionary fervor. Americans did revolt against taxation without representation; however, they didn't throw out English law, they incorporated most of it and moved quickly to establish a stable, constitutional republic. Whether that is adequate justification for any revolution is a matter for debate elsewhere.

EIGHT

AMERICAN MASONRY

The radical philosophies which found such fertile ground in France and Germany did not easily take root in America. While the French Masons sought to destroy the monarchy and every scrap of its government, in America the essence of the British constitution was preserved and improved upon. Many American Masons honestly believed their craft to be essentially Christian, and they strove to keep it that way.

The concern over the influence of secret societies in the United States grew steadily until an anti-Masonic explosion erupted in 1826, after the murder of one Captain William Morgan, of Batavia, New York. Morgan was killed by Masons shortly after obtaining a copyright for an exposé on Masonry. Morgan's crime was that he was the first to publish the complete rituals, including the oaths and secret passwords of the first three degrees of Masonry, known as the Blue Lodge.

THE AIMS OF MASONRY

Masonry appears harmless on its surface, at least to the vast majority of its members. Yet there can be no doubt that Masonry and Christianity have been locked in an irreconcilable ideological battle since the time of Jesus. In *Les Sectes et Sociétiés Secrètes*, Masonic author Le Couteulx de Canteleu wrote in 1863 about the aim of secret societies.

> As a whole [it] was, is and will always be the struggle against the Church and the Christian religion, and the struggle of those who have not against those who have....All secret societies have almost analogous initiations, from the Egyptian to the Illuminati, and most of them form a chain and give rise to others.[1]

Another authority, Vicomte Leon de Poncins, explained that the aim of Freemasonry was to pervert the Christian nature of Western civilization into a Masonic "religion" he called "atheist rationalism." According to de Poncins, the destruction of Christianity is "indispensable" to Masonry in order to establish this "new political and social city... in its place.[2] ...the deeper meaning of the struggle is religious. It is a conflict between God and man lead by reason alone."[3]

Then, in what may be the most beautifully composed denunciation of Masonry ever written, de Poncins wrote:

> The great task of freemasonry is to spread ideas sometimes noble and beautiful in appearance but in reality destructive, of which the prototype is the famous motto: Liberty, equality, fraternity.
>
> Masonry, a vast organism of propaganda, acts by slow suggestion, spreading the revolutionary ferment in an insidious manner. The heads sow it among the inner lodges, these transmit it to the lower lodges whence it penetrates into the affiliated institutions and into the press, which takes in hand the public.
>
> Tirelessly and during the necessary number of years, the suggestion...works upon public opinion and fashions it to wish for the reforms from which nations die. In 1789 and 1848 [the years of the French Revolutions], freemasonry, in its momentary command of power, failed in its supreme endeavour. Taught by these experiences, its progress has become slower and surer. When once the revolutionary preparation is obtained and judged sufficient, masonry leaves the field to the militant organizations, Carbonari, Bolshevists, or other open or secret societies, and retires into shadows in the background. There it is not compromised; in case of check, it seems to have remained apart, and is all the better able to continue or take up again its work, like a gnawing worm, obscure and destroying.
>
> Masonry never works in the full light of day. Every one knows of its existence, its meeting places and of many of its adepts, but one is ignorant of its real aims, its real means, its real leaders. The immense majority of masons themselves are in that position. They are only the blind machinery of the sect which they serve....Many honest masons are so blind that they would be stupefied if they knew for what they are being used.[4]

He went on to explain that very few Freemasons know what the ultimate goals of the Order are. The work of Masonry is subdivided and compartmentalized. Each group "does the work assigned to them [but] remain ignorant of the place [it] occupies in the general scheme."[5]

THE MASONIC RITUAL REVEALED

Every Mason swears to a set of oaths so ancient that a separate term has been set aside to describe them. These are called "blood oaths."

Masonry, as we know it today in America, is thought of as having thirty-three degrees, or levels. Many offshoot organizations have developed over the years that have attempted to add additional degrees above the publicly known thirty-three. Mormonism is one such offshoot. As shown in a later chapter, its founder, Joseph Smith, and most, if not all of his initial circle of supporters were Masons. He borrowed heavily from Masonic ritual for his newly-created Mormon ceremonies.

With each successive degree, the Mason must swear to ever more cruel and barbarous oaths. The following details of the initiation oaths of the first three degrees of Masonry are closely-guarded Masonic secrets. In fact, every Mason must swear to kill any fellow Mason who reveals them. Fortunately for humanity, however, several brave souls in the last 200 years have felt compelled to speak out, publishing this "secret work" for the world to see. It is thanks to these courageous men that we have the exact wording and rituals of at least the first three degrees.

FIRST DEGREE

Before a "lodge" opens for business, appointed members ensure that the meeting room is secure from the prying eyes and ears of non-members with a series of rituals. This is why most of the older lodge meeting halls are on at least the second floor of the building. The leader of the lodge, known as the "Worshipful Master," then opens the meeting by silently displaying what is known as the penal sign, as follows:

> The Master then draws his right hand across his throat, the hand open, with the thumb next to his throat, and drops it down by his side. This is called the penal sign of an Entered Apprentice Mason, and alludes to the penalty of the obligation.[6]

This is followed by a prayer that is intended to confuse any candidate with religious proclivities, and serves as the foundation from which the initiate is progressively moved up the Luciferian ladder toward Deism and beyond. Those who balk at any point are judged unworthy for the higher mysteries and move up no further. The prayer hints at Christianity, yet only mentions God as "the great architect of the Universe."

> Most holy and glorious God! The Great Architect of the Universe; the giver of all good gifts and graces: Thou hast promised that 'Where two or three are gathered together in thy name, thou wilt be in the midst of them and bless them.' In thy name, we assemble, most humbly beseeching thee to bless us in all our undertakings; that we may know and serve thee aright, and that all our actions may tend to thy glory and our advancement in knowledge and virtue. And we beseech thee, O Lord God, to bless our present assembling; and to illuminate our minds through the influence of the Son of Rightness, that we may walk in the light of thy countenance; and when the trials of our probationary state are over, be admitted into the temple, not made with hands, eternal in the heavens. Amen. So mote it be.[7]

The meeting then progresses to the point where candidates, if any, are initiated. In the first degree, when the candidate is ready for initiation, he is blindfolded and asked to put on a special pair of pants, or drawers, that contain no metal. This pair of drawers is rolled up to just above the left knee only. The candidate's shirt is partially removed to uncover his left arm and breast. He is given a slipper for his right foot only. Then a rope noose, called a "Cable-tow," is put around his neck, and in some cases around his left shoulder.

After a series of memorized questions and answers, the candidate enters the hall where the members are assembled. As the candidate enters:

> ...the Senior Deacon at the same time pressing his naked left breast with the point of the compass, and asks the candidate, "Did you feel anything?"
>
> Ans. " I did."
>
> Senior Deacon to candidate, "What was it?"
>
> Ans. "A torture."
>
> The Senior Deacon, "As this is a torture to your flesh, so may it ever be to your mind and conscience if ever you should attempt to reveal the secrets of Masonry unlawfully."[8]

After a prayer, the Master of the Lodge asks the candidate, "In whom do you put your trust?" The candidate then answers, "In God." The Master then takes the candidate by the right hand and says, "Since in God you put your trust, arise follow your leader and fear no danger."

After being led, still blindfolded, around the lodge three times the Master asks him from whence he came and whither he is traveling. The candidate answers, "From the west and traveling to the east." The Master inquires, "Why do you leave the west and travel to the east?" The candidate answers, "In search of light."

From whence does this "light" come? As we will later see in the section on the Shriners, the "East" refers to Mecca, Saudia Arabia, the holiest city in Islam, showing conclusively that Masonry's philosophical base is eastern mysticism.

The candidate then kneels, assuming a position with his legs that symbolizes the Masonic "square and compass." The Master says:

> Mr. ...., you are now placed in a proper position to take upon you the solemn oath or obligation of an Entered Apprentice Mason, which I assure you is neither to affect your religion or politics. If you are willing to take it, repeat your name and say after me:
>
> I, ..., of my own free will and accord, and in the presence of Almighty God and this worshipful lodge of Free and Accepted Masons, dedicated to God, and held forth to the holy order of St. John, do hereby and hereon most solemnly and sincerely promise and swear that I will always hail, ever conceal and never reveal any part or parts, or any art or arts, point or points of the secret arts and mysteries of ancient Freemasonry which I have received, am about to receive, or may hereafter be instructed in, to any person or persons of the known world.

The lengthy affirmation goes on as the initiate promises not to "write, print, stamp, stain, hew, cut, carve, indent, paint, or engrave" any of the Masonic secrets on anything "movable or unmovable under the whole canopy of heaven whereby or whereon the least letter, figure, character, mark, stain, shadow, or resemblance of the same may become legible or intelligible to myself or any other person in the known world, whereby the secrets of Masonry may be unlawfully obtained."[10]

In other words, the deepest secrets of Masonry are never to be printed, only handed down from one Mason to another by ancient oral rituals and recitations. Keep in mind that Jesus forbade us from swearing to oaths at all. In Matthew 5:34 Jesus says:

> But I say to you, make no oath at all, either by heaven, for it is the throne of God, or by earth....But let your statement be, 'Yes, yes' or 'No, no'; and anything beyond these is of evil.[11]

The oath for the First Degree, however, concludes with these words::

> To all of which I do most solemnly and sincerely promise and swear, without the least equivocation, mental reservation, or evasion of mind in me whatever; binding myself under no less penalty than to have my throat cut across, my tongue torn out by the roots, and my body buried in the rough sands of the sea at low water-mark, where the tide ebbs and flows twice in twenty-four hours; so help me God, and keep me steadfast in the due performance of the same.[12]

The candidate, who has been blindfolded the entire time, is then asked what he most desires and he answers, "Light." Then the group forms a circle around him and the Master says, "And God said let there be light, and there was light."

At this time all the brethren clap their hands and stomp on the floor with their right foot as hard as they can, and at the same time, the blindfold is suddenly pulled off the initiate and he is temporarily blinded by the very brightly lit room. The effect is said to be so alarming as to cause fainting in some cases.[13]

After the candidate is "brought to light," he is told that the three great "lights" of Masonry are the Holy Bible, the Square, and the Compass.

The initiate is then taught the aforementioned penal sign, also known as the "due guard," which accompanies his new status, that of an Entered Apprentice Mason. He is also shown the secret handshake or the "grip of an Entered Apprentice Mason." This grip is performed as follows:

> The right hands are joined together as in shaking hands and each sticks his thumb nail into the third joint or upper end of the forefinger; the name of this grip is Boaz....It is the name of the left hand pillar of the porch of King Solomon's temple.[14]

The initiate then swears to support God and country, but both of these allegiances are overlooked in later degrees.[15]

SECOND DEGREE

In the second degree, or "fellowcraft degree," the candidate enters the lodge by benefit of the secret password "Shibboleth" and takes additional oaths. In this degree, the penalty for violation of the oaths is as follows:

> Binding myself under no less penalty than to have my left breast torn open and my heart and vitals taken from thence and thrown over my left shoulder and carried into the valley of Jehosaphat, there to become a prey to the wild beasts of the field, and vulture of the air, if ever I should prove willfully guilty of violating any part of this my solemn oath or obligation of a Fellow Craft Mason; so help me God, and keep me steadfast in the due performance of the same.[16]

Certainly carrying human hearts and vitals to the Valley of Jehosaphat could become prohibitively expensive, not to mention difficult, even for the powerful world of Masonry. In at least one example, though, it appeared that Masonry failed to follow through on its promises of exotic retribution for betrayal. The source of the present information, Captain Morgan, was simply and unceremoniously drowned in Lake Erie.

The candidate is now shown a new greeting sign, or "due guard," and a new secret hand grip, or "pass-grip."

> The pass-grip, is given by taking each other by the right hand, as though going to shake hands, and each putting his thumb between the fore and second fingers where they join the hand, and pressing the thumb between the joints. This is the pass grip of a Fellow Craft Mason, the name of it is Shibboleth.

They are also shown another hand grip called the "real grip."

> The real grip of a Fellow Craft Mason is given by putting the thumb on the joint of the second finger where it joins the hand, and crooking your thumb so that each can stick the nail of his thumb into the joint of the other;...the name of it is Jachin.

If one Mason wishes to "examine" another when giving this grip, for example, to see if he is some sort of spy, the following questioning and the proper responses are given, while the grip is maintained:

Q. "What is this?"

A. "A grip."

Q. "A grip of what?"

A. "The grip of a Fellow Craft Mason."

Q. "Has it a name?"

A. "It has."

Q. "Will you give it to me?"

A. "I did not so receive it, neither can I so impart it."

Q. "What will you do with it?"

A. "I'll letter it or halve it."

Q. "Halve it and you begin."

A. "No, begin you."

Q. "You begin."

A. "J. A."

Q. "CHIN."

A. "JACHIN."

Q. "Right, brother, Jachin, I greet you."[17]

As ridiculous as all this seems to laymen, it all serves to provide the lodge with a good measure of protection against intrusion. Remember, this is all memorized. None of this, the secret work, is ever written down. Supposedly, it has been handed down for hundreds, if not thousands of years. Captain Morgan, the first American to commit these secrets to writing, paid with his life. However, the repercussions from Captain Morgan's murder were such that Masonry was all but exterminated during the 1830s.

Of course, Masons of today try to tell us that their craft began in the 1700s. However, in the Masonic lecture delivered to the candidate only minutes after he is taught the new grips, the lecturer explains the following:

> Brother, we have worked in speculative Masonry, but our forefathers wrought both in speculative and operative Masonry; they worked at the building of King Solomon's temple, and many other Masonic edifices...Brother, the first thing that attracts our attention are two large columns, or pillars, one on the left hand and the other on the right; the name of the one on the left hand is Boaz, and denotes strength; the name of the one on the right hand is Jachin, and denotes establishment; they collectively allude to a passage in Scripture wherein God has declared in his word, "In strength shall this House be established."[18]

So, in this lecture alone, Masonry dates its work back to the temple of Solomon (approximately 1000 B.C.). The lecture goes on to explain the various symbolic meanings of Masonry, which would be of interest to those who wish to pursue further reading on the subject.

THIRD DEGREE

In the third degree, or Master Mason's Degree, the candidate enters the lodge by the password "Tubal Cain." Before administering the oath, and after much symbolic liturgy, the Master refers to death in one passage as "the silver cord be loosed, or the golden bowl be broken...."

Now we get down to the oaths of this degree. The third degree oath is where we start to see some subtle, yet noticeable deviations from what

Christianity teaches. The oath is very lengthy. One part of it reads:

> Furthermore do I promise and swear that I will not wrong this lodge, nor a brother of this degree to the value of one cent, knowingly, myself, or suffer it to be done by others, if in my power to prevent it.

Notice that they swear not to cheat a brother Mason, yet no mention is made of the rest of the world.

> Furthermore do I promise and swear that I will not speak evil of a brother Master Mason, neither behind his back nor before his face, but will apprise him of all approaching danger, if in my power.

This oath lays the foundation for one of Masonry's major evils. Although Masons say they never try to recruit members, it is made clear that acquiring members who work in the judiciary and enforcement branches of the government of any town, state, or nation would be highly desirable. Therefore, fellow Master Masons caught in any illegality can almost certainly be assured of immunity from prosecution by brother Masons strategically placed in the legal system. This is reaffirmed in a higher degree to which members of the legal branches at all levels of government are encouraged to aspire, the seventh, or Royal Arch Degree. Strict obedience is demanded from the initiate of the Third Degree.

> Furthermore do I promise and swear that I will obey all regular signs, summonses, or tokens given, handed, sent, or thrown to me from the hand of a brother Master Mason, or from the body of a just and lawfully constituted lodge of such.

> Furthermore do I promise and swear that a Master Mason's secrets, given to me in charge as such, and I knowing them to be such, shall remain as secure and inviolable in my breast as in his own, when communicated to me, murder and treason excepted; and they left to my own election. [emphasis mine]

In other words, if a Master Mason tells another that he has murdered someone, or is committing an act of treason against his country, and asks him to keep it secret, then they are not encouraged to inform the authorities, they are told that it is up to them. By the time the initiate attains the Royal Arch degree, this option is unavailable as the Order demands increasingly strict obedience to those who rise. Rev. C.G. Finney wrote in 1869, "Freemasonry waxes worse and worse as you ascend from the lower to the higher degrees."

Finally, the penalty oath for the third degree:

> Binding myself under no less penalty than to have my body severed in two in the midst, and divided to the north and south, my bowels burnt to ashes in the center, and the ashes scattered before the four winds of heaven, that there might not the least track or trace of remembrance remain among men or Masons, of so vile and perjured a wretch as I should be, were I ever to prove willfully guilty of violating any part of this my solemn oath or obligation of a Master

Mason. So help me God, and keep me steadfast in the performance of the same.[19]

Then the candidate is shown the "Grand Hailing Sign of Distress." The sign is given by raising both hands so the arms extend perpendicularly from the body then bend ninety-degrees at the elbows so the hands point straight upward. The words accompanying this sign, in case of distress, are "O Lord, my God! is there no help for the widow's son?" As the last words drop from the lips of the candidate, his hands fall, "in that manner best calculated to indicate solemnity."[20]

This is supposedly the sign given and the words spoken by Hiram Abiff, the master builder of the Temple of Solomon, considered to be the greatest Master Mason of all times, shortly before he was killed by three apprentice Masons, known as the Juwes, who attempted to force him to reveal the location of the sacred treasure of Enoch which he had accidentally uncovered during excavations for the Temple. The treasure consisted of:

> Gold and brass plates engraved with Egyptian hieroglyphics giving the history of the world and ancient mysteries of God, which [Enoch] preserved by putting them in a vault in the hill....Enoch buried the sacred record to preserve it just before a great disaster [the Flood], foreseeing that after the deluge an Israelitish descendent would discover anew the sacred buried treasure.[21]

Masonic lore is filled with references to this "widow's son." The origin is obscure, dating back to Egyptian occultism. The widow is the Egyptian goddess, Isis, after the death of her husband, Osiris. The penal sign for the third degree is made by putting the right hand to the left side of the bowels, the hand open, with the thumb next to the belly, and drawing it across the belly, and letting it fall. This is done very quickly. This alludes to the penalty of the obligation: Having one's body severed in twain.[22]

Then the pass-grip is given by pressing the thumb between the joints of the second and third fingers where they join the hand, "the word, or name is Tubal Cain. It is the pass word to the Master's degree."[23]

The membership then acts out the death of Hiram Abiff, and the candidate is shown yet another hand grip, the "Lion's Paw," or "Master's Grip," said to have been used to raise Hiram from the dead. The Master's grip is given by taking hold of each other's hand as though you were going to shake hands, and sticking the nails of each of your fingers into the joint of the other's wrist where it unites with the hand.[24]

The symbolism is that after being in the grave for several days, Hiram Abiff's flesh on his hands had began to rot, and so a grip had to be devised to pull him up and out of the grave—the Masonic version of resurrection.

It is interesting to note that this grip is so important to the basic concepts of secret societies that it is used in the witchcraft rituals of Wicca, where it is known as "The Strong Grip of the Lion of the Tribe of Juhad." It is also used in another initiation not usually associated with either secret societies or Masonry. In the Temple initiations of Mormonism (Church of Jesus Christ of Latter-day Saints) the same grip is taught as the "Second Token of the Melchizedek Priesthood" and is similarly named the "Strong Grip of the Lion's Paw."

After extensive additional oral instruction, the ceremony ends and the first three degrees of Masonry have been obtained by the initiate. It is said that seventy-five percent of Masons never go beyond this point.

Revealing these secret rites is what Captain Morgan died for. But what of his kidnapers? The precise details of the murder were not known until 1848 when one of the three Masons involved in the crime confessed to his doctor from his deathbed in hopes of religious absolution. The story broke in early 1849 in the press under the headline "Confession. The murder of William Morgan, confessed by the man who, with his own hands, pushed him out of the boat into Niagara River." The confessor, Henry L. Valance, said that since that dark night, he had been very unhappy and depressed.

> Go where I would, or do what I would, it was impossible for me to throw off the consciousness of crime. If the mark of Cain was not upon me, the curse of the first murderer was—the blood-stain was upon my hands and could not be washed out.[25]

The conspirators kidnapped Captain Morgan and his publisher in Batavia, New York, but the publisher was later rescued after outraged citizens of Batavia pursued the kidnapers. Morgan was not so lucky, however, and Masons went to extraordinary lengths to insure that as much confusion as possible would surround the matter.

> The courts of justice found themselves entirely unable to make any headway against the wide-spread conspiracy that was formed among Masons....It was found that they could do nothing with the courts, with the sheriffs, with the witnesses, or with the jurors.
>
> Masons themselves...published two spurious editions of Morgan's book, and circulated them as the true edition which Morgan had published. These editions were designed to deceive Masons who had never seen Morgan's edition, and thus to enable them to say that it was not a true revelation of Masonry.[26]

Captain Morgan paid for his exposures with his life, but the affect of his revelations on American Masonry was profound. In 1826, when Morgan published his book, there were estimated to be 50,000 Freemasons in the United States. It is said that as a result of the book, 45,000 of these left the order,[27] and as many as 2,000 lodges closed.[28] Author

William J. Whalen, writing in 1958, explained:

> As a result of this scandal, the anti-Masonic party was formed. It polled 128,000 votes in the 1830 election and carried Vermont in the 1832 presidential election. Rhode Island and Vermont passed laws against blood oaths. Thousands of Masons burned their aprons. In a few years time, membership in the New York lodges dropped from 30,000 to 300 as a direct result of the Morgan incident.[29]

One of those who left the Order was Millard Fillmore, a young attorney from Buffalo, New York who would later become the thirteenth president of the United States. Fillmore joined the Anti-Masonic Party in 1828.[30] According to one author, ex-Mason Fillmore once warned: "The Masonic fraternity tramples upon our rights, defeats the administration of justice, and bids defiance to every government which it cannot control."[31]

The New York State Senate launched an investigation of Masonry, reporting in 1829 that it was composed of powerful and wealthy men whose members held office in almost "every place where power is of any importance." They also criticized the role of the press, or the lack thereof, saying the press had been "...silent as the grave. This self-proclaimed sentinel of freedom, has felt the force of masonic influence, or has been smitten with the rod of its power."[32]

Five years later, in 1834, a Joint Committee of the Massachusetts legislature investigated the Craft. It found that Freemasonry was "a distinct independent government within our own government, and beyond the control of the laws of the land by means of its secrecy."[33]

In England, the Morgan revelations had no such negative impact, however. At the end of the 1700s, there were about 320 English lodges. By 1864, they numbered 1,000, and this number had doubled only nineteen years later. By 1903, lodge number 3,000 opened, the same year Winston Churchill was initiated into British Masonry. Lodge #4,000 opened in 1919; #5,000 in 1926; #6,000 in 1944; #7,000 in 1950; and by 1981, 9,003 British lodges were warranted, for an estimated membership of about 500,000 British Masons, about one-tenth of the current estimated U.S. Masonic population.[34]

It is said that even today, many town halls in Great Britain have private function rooms used for Masonic meetings, including New Scotland Yard, the headquarters of the Metropolitan Police.[35]

THE STRUCTURE OF MODERN FREEMASONRY

After taking the first three degrees of Masonry, Masons have a choice of "routes" they can take if they wish to advance; the Scottish Rite, or the York Rite.

SCOTTISH RITE

The Scottish Rite employs deism — basing religion on "reason rather than revelation" — as its philosophical structure. It is said to be the most powerful Masonic Order in the world.[36] That side of the Masonic ladder is composed of the more familiar thirty-three steps, and is the path usually chosen by those who seek worldly power, position, and wealth out of Masonry.

The twenty-nine steps up to the thirty-second degree of the Scottish Rite can be taken in as little time as a single weekend. When dignitaries are involved, even more corners can be cut if the Order wants them badly enough. For example, Teddy Roosevelt didn't join the lodge until he had become vice-president.

President Taft, General Marshall, and General Douglas MacArthur were all made Masons "at sight." That is, they had little idea what they were getting into. They did not have to undergo the regular initiation procedure. In other words they didn't have to take the blood oaths.

YORK RITE MASONRY

The York Rite, which is composed of thirteen steps, is supposedly for those of the Christian persuasion, although it differs very little in results. The York Rite branch of Masonry starts after the first three degrees. Masons make quite a show of Christian piety in the initial degrees of the York Rite to make it acceptable to newcomers who might have doubts. One of the maxims of the York Rite route of Masonry is: "Masonry, after all, is but a rule for orderly righteousness."[37]

ROYAL ARCH DEGREES

The first steps up the ladder on the York Rite side of Masonry are the four degrees that make up the Royal Arch degrees. These consist of the degrees of Mark Master (4th), Past Master (5th), Most Excellent Master (6th) and the Royal Arch, the seventh degree.[38] On the Scottish Rite side, the Royal Arch degree is the thirteenth.

It is at this point — the Royal Arch degree — that many members suffer a severe shock if their consciences are still active. In this degree, the candidate must swear to keep the secrets of a fellow Mason, "murder and treason not excepted ." With his hand on the Bible, the candidate for the Royal Arch degree must swear to the following:

> I will aid and assist a companion Royal Arch Mason when engaged in any difficulty, and espouse his cause so far as to extricate him from the same, if within my power, whether he be right or wrong.[39]

In other words, Royal Arch Masons are obligated under blood oaths to help extricate their fellows from any trouble legal, or illegal. Rev. Finney has observed that:

> Here, then, we have a class of men sworn, under most frightful penalties, to espouse the cause of a companion so far as to extricate him

from any difficulty, to the extent of their power, whether he is right or wrong. How can such a man be safely entrusted with any office connected with the administration of the law?[40]

This is why Masonry actively seeks members in the legal professions of every community, and raises them to the Royal Arch degree as soon as possible. In such communities then, Masonry is free to do whatever it pleases. According to British Masonic expert Stephen Knight:

The more Masons there are in any area or profession the more important it is to be a Mason if one is not to risk losing out, as a non-member of the club, in one's business, one's profession and one's preferment.

In many fields nowadays the disadvantages of being left out of the "club" are perceived as being too serious for a great many people to contemplate, whatever they may feel personally about the morality of joining a secret society, or about the misty tenets of speculative Freemasonry.[41]

In addition, Masons of the Royal Arch degree swear to promote and vote for any fellow Mason of that degree, "before any other of equal qualifications."[42] During the initiation into the Royal Arch degree, the candidate drinks wine from a cup made from the top half of a human skull.[43] This revolting rite is symbolic of the "blood oath" of the Royal Arch degree which demands that the candidate swears, "To have his skull struck off, and his brains exposed to the scorching rays of a meridian sun" should he divulge Masonic secrets.[44] In addition, he swears:

To keep in my heart all the secrets that shall be revealed to me. And in failure if this my oath, I consent to have my body opened perpendicularly, and to be exposed for eight hours in the open air that the venomous flies may eat of my intestines ... and I will always be ready to inflict the same punishment on those who shall disclose this degree and break this oath. So may God help and maintain me. Amen.[45]

In a desperate attempt to soften the impact, the Royal Arch oath blasphemously attempts to include Jesus. The candidate must swear:

As the sins of the world were laid upon the head of the Savior, so may all the sins committed by the person whose skull this was be heaped upon my head, in addition to my own, should I ever; knowingly or willfully, violate or transgress any obligation that I have heretofore taken....So help me God.[46]

Based on the overwhelming and uncontradicted evidence of dozens of authors over several centuries, there can be no excuse to allow anyone who is a Mason of the Royal Arch degree to become a local sheriff, judge, prosecutor, or police investigator. These men have all sworn with their lives to protect Masons of the same degree from the wheels of justice.

Perhaps the most shocking example of this comes with a quick review of the facts surrounding the Jack the Ripper murders in the East End of London in 1888. According to Knight, these murders of five prostitutes were perpetrated according to Masonic ritual, and then covered up by the Commissioner and Assistant Commissioner of the police, who were both Freemasons.

Four of the five prostitutes had learned a secret that only a handful of the most powerful men in Britain knew. It seems that in an age of intense anti-Catholic feeling, Prince Albert, grandson of Queen Victoria, and Heir Presumptive to the throne, had illegally married a Catholic commoner, and she had given birth to a son.

The Prime Minister, Lord Salisbury, was scared that the revelation of this scandal in the press might bring the downfall of the monarchy itself, and so issued secret orders that Albert's wife be hastily bundled off to a lunatic asylum, never to be seen or heard from again. He chose for the task a trusted friend, Queen Victoria's personal physician, Sir William Gull, and all without the Queen's knowledge.

Gull was a Freemason, and was said to be a relatively unstable one at that. When Prime Minister Salisbury discovered that word had leaked out to one prostitute, who had told three, and possibly four others, it was quickly apparent that they would have to be eliminated. Salisbury again turned to Sir William Gull.

Gull apparently justified the assigned killings in his own mind as a series of executions of traitors against the Crown and the nation. He conducted the murders in Masonic style and ritual.

What followed was an elaborate cover-up among the Masonic hierarchy of Scotland Yard. It started at the scene of the fourth murder, where Dr. Gull had scrawled a cryptic word in chalk on a wall nearby. The first policeman on the scene dutifully recorded the word—JUWES.

The policeman dutifully communicated the details of the murder scene to headquarters. Upon hearing the news, the Commissioner of London's Metropolitan Police, Sir Charles Warren, an eminent Freemason, rushed to the murder scene and quickly washed the message away before it could be photographed, despite the protestations of several senior policemen at the scene.

According to journalist Knight, this was the only real clue ever left by Jack the Ripper. *"Yet Warren washed it away"* even though a police photographic team had arrived at the scene with their bulky camera equipment.[47]

> This has never been explained. The truth was that Warren, who had been exalted to the Royal Arch in 1861, had realized that the writing on the wall was a masonic message.[48]

Warren impeded the investigation of the murders at every turn, caused endless confusion and delays, and personally destroyed the only clue the Ripper ever left.[49]

For years, "JUWES" was hypothesized to be an anti-Semetic misspelling of Jews. However, according to Knight, "the Juwes were the three apprentice Masons who killed Hiram Abiff and who are the basis of Masonic ritual."[50]

KNIGHTS TEMPLAR

After attaining the degree of "Royal Arch" in the York Rite, a Mason is eligible to continue up to the three degrees of the Order of Knights Templar. The history of the Templars is still shrouded in legend. Templars were the first Crusaders. Officially known as "Poor Knights of Christ and of the Temple of Solomon," they were founded in 1118 to conquer and maintain the Holy Sepulchre in Jerusalem and protect pilgrims to the Holy Land from marauding Muslim bands.

Initially they took vows of poverty, chastity, and obedience and are said to have built their quarters on the foundations of the ruined Temple of Solomon from which they took their name. Soon these warrior monks were known as the "militia of Christ" and wore white mantles bearing a splayed red cross. Their bravery was legendary and they vowed never to ask for mercy nor retreat unless outnumbered three-to-one. Ironically, this militancy has done nothing but serve as the foundation for one of the most damaging criticisms against Christianity—that is, the "first the cross, then the sword" aspect of colonization by "Christian" nations.

Mustafa El-Amin, a modern Muslim authority on Freemasonry, has written:

> During the period of the Crusades, many of the ideas and practices of the Muslim groups were adopted by the European Christian warriors. More specifically, it was through the Knight Templars that most of the Eastern secret societies' methods were introduced to Europe. The Templars were influenced by the Order of the Assassins.[51]

The Order of the Assassins was perhaps the most savage of the secret societies. They killed for pleasure while in a hashish stupor, with the idea that when you killed someone, you could steal their *gnosis*, or life force. A variation of one of their emblems, the scimitar, now graces the emblem of the "fun-loving," charitable organization, the Shriners.

As the fame of the Templars grew, so did their wealth. They received vast donations of money and land throughout Europe and adopted absolute secrecy to cover all their internal activities. Their goal was to become wealthy enough to "buy the world." In 1312 they possessed in Europe alone more than 9,000 feudal estates.[52]

As the Templars' treasury grew, so did their corruption. Eventually they became the object of widespread suspicion. They were rumored to engage in occult practices that included spitting and trampling on the Cross as initiation rites. Soon, the saying "to drink like a Templar" became commonplace.[53]

It is interesting to note that the Templars could be considered the first international bankers. They developed a sophisticated banking system whereby money could be deposited in one city and withdrawn in another. They were also the first to use checks instead of currency to pay debts.

Eventually, after the Templars were driven from the Holy Land, they set up their headquarters in France. But by 1306, Philip IV of France (Philip the Fair) grew fearful of them and sought to destroy them, hoping also to confiscate their treasures. On Friday the thirteenth of October, 1307, Philip had all the Templars in France—save thirteen—arrested. This is said to be the origin of the superstition that bad luck falls on every Friday-the-thirteenth.

Philip's fears were well founded. He discovered that the Templars were plotting against all the thrones of Europe and the Church as well. Apparently he had great difficulty convincing the populace that such a vast conspiracy was afoot, however. Albert Pike chuckled in *Morals and Dogma* at the dilemma of King Philip:

> It was impossible to unfold to the people the conspiracy of the Templars against the Thrones and the Tiara....[To do so] would have been to initiate the multitude into the secrets of the Masters, and to have uplifted the veil of Isis.[54]

Philip therefore chose to charge the Templars with magic, and, according to Pike, numerous "false witnesses" were found for this purpose. After extracting confessions of the nature of their secret rites from them by torture, he sent more than fifty Templars to the stake, including their Grand Master, Jacques de Molay, who is still venerated in Masonry as a martyr and whose name is enshrined as the young men's branch of modern Masonry. However, according to Albert Pike, before de Molay died he established what came to be called Scottish Masonry with lodges in four cities: Naples, Edinburgh, Stockholm, and Paris. These were the first lodges of modern Freemasonry.[55]

According to Pike, the Templars survived under a deep shroud of secrecy, and it was not long before they began taking their revenge — one that would extend some 400 years into the future.

> The Pope and the King [of France] soon after perished in a strange and sudden manner....The Order...lived, under other names and governed by unknown Chiefs, revealing itself only to those who, in passing through a series of Degrees, had proven themselves worthy to be entrusted with the dangerous secret.

The secret movers of the French Revolution had sworn to overturn the Throne and the Altar upon the Tomb of Jacques de Molai. When Louis XVI was executed, half the work was done; and thenceforth the Army of the Temple was to direct all its efforts against the Pope.[56]

Philip's desire to confiscate the vast wealth of the Templars was thwarted. On the same day of the group's mass arrest, their treasure — said to contain the legendary riches of the Temple of Solomon, including the mysterious Holy Lance of Longinus (the spear which reputedly pierced the side of Christ on the cross) — and all their documents disappeared and have never been found.

> Those who had escaped the storm afterwards met in obscurity so as to re-knit the ties that had united them, and in order to avoid fresh denunciations they made use of allegorical methods which indicated the basis of their association in a manner unintelligible to the eyes of the vulgar: that is the origin of the Free Masons.[57]

To Masons, the Templars are considered to be the Christian branch of Freemasonry. According to the 1957 edition of the *Masonic Bible*:

> The world is today in greater need of the Order of Knights Templar than [it was during] the heroic crusaders of the Twelfth century. There is more at stake, more to save. You will find in the precepts of this institution a renewed conviction that right must prevail, that oppression, by any class whatsoever, is wrong and incompatible with Christian thought. It still combines a religious and militant spirit, and is pledged to defend those principles and ideals upon which civilization is based.[58]

Many a good man has been deceived by this totally non-biblical line of purely Luciferan thought. It is nothing more than the philosophy of the ends-justify-the-means. In today's world, the Templars combine this ill-conceived "Christian" militancy with a commendable nationalistic spirit, the combination of which only the most informed student could resist. According to the *Masonic Bible*:

> To be a Knight Templar you must be right with God and country, honest with yourself and with others, ever ready to lay down your life, if need be, in the service of truth, righteousness and justice.[59]

SHRINE

After the thirty-second degree in the Scottish Rite, or the thirteenth, or Knights Templar degree in the York Rite, a Mason may become a member of the Ancient Arabic Order Nobles of the Mystic Shrine — a Shriner. Shriners are best known for wearing red fezzes with tassels and driving those little orange go-carts in parades, as well as sponsoring numerous fund-raising events including circuses, football games, and horse shows.

They are also well known for their nineteen high-profile, well-endowed children's hospitals, and three burn centers which treat children free of charge. The 880,000 U.S. Shriners operate out of 175 Shrine temples. Notable Shriners have been J. Edgar Hoover, General Douglas MacArthur, presidents Warren Harding, Franklin Roosevelt, Harry Truman and Gerald Ford, and senators Henry "Scoop" Jackson and Hubert Humphrey.[60]

The Shrine is the wealthiest "charity" in America. Its assets for 1984 were estimated by the Internal Revenue Service at $1.979 billion. That's almost twice as much as the second-richest charity, the American Red Cross, with assets of 1.07 billion, and four times as much as the American Cancer Society which takes third place, with $446.8 million in assets.

Evidence suggests, however, that the charitable nature of the Shrine is a mere facade when the expenditures of the various charities are compared. The American Red Cross, for example, spent four times as much money on its charitable programs in 1984 as the Shrine did—$781.9 million compared to the $189.2 million spent by the Shrine.[61]

In fact, the Shrine spent only 29.8 percent of its 1984 income on its program services, compared with 84 percent by the American Red Cross, 67.2 percent by the American Cancer Society, 70.6 percent by the American Heart Association and 73 percent by National Easter Seals. In fact, no other charity in the top fourteen listed by the IRS gave less than 57 percent of their total income to their program services—almost twice as much as the Shrine.

In other words, no other U.S. charity had nearly as much money to give and gave less of it than the Shrine. Unfortunately, this has been the history of Masonic charities in general.

What are the origins of the Shriner branch of Masonry? If you were to visit the George Washington Masonic National Memorial, you would be told that the Shrine has nothing whatsoever to do with eastern mysticism. You would be told that the Shrine and its ceremonies and rituals were dreamed up by a fun-loving group of New York professionals in 1870.

Unfortunately, a little digging in the Order's own literature shows that this fabrication is designed to mislead the general public. In reality, the Shrine was started when a Mason named William J. Florence was initiated into an eastern "secret society" by an "Arabian diplomat."[62] Although newspaper reports on the Shrine gladly repeat that Florence and his friends made up the rituals, drawing from "a smattering of biblical and Middle Eastern themes,"[63] the truth is that the Shrine ritual is really nothing more than occult, Middle-Eastern Masonry.

Florence went on to Algiers and Cairo and "made copious notes and drawings" of the Masonic ceremonies demonstrated there.[64] When he returned to New York, he teamed up with a friend, New York physician Walter M. Fleming, who was also a thirty-third degree Mason; Charles T. McClenachan, lawyer and expert of Masonic ritual; William Sleigh Paterson, printer, linguist, and ritualist; and Albert L. Rawson, a prominent scholar and Mason who provided much of the Arabic background.[65]

In the Masonic ritual, Masons travel from the west to the east in search of "light," "wisdom," or the "lost word." The Shriners' ritual states that certain individuals from the west went to Makkah [Mecca, Saudi Arabia] and received "the secret work" and brought it back to America and established Shriners' Temples throughout the Western Hemisphere.[66]

Masonry in general, and the Shriners in particular, worship the East for a reason: despite all their protestations to the contrary, theirs is nothing more than an American adaptation of Middle-Eastern Masonry. The mystical references to the "East" that run through not only the Shrine, but through the rituals of Masonry and its relatively benign women's division, the Order of the Eastern Star, refer to this Middle-Eastern tradition which looks toward Mecca, as a Catholic looks toward Rome.

Many visitors to Washington wonder why the female "Statue of Freedom," which stands high atop the Capitol dome is facing east. This is the sword-wielding, Grecian-clad, 19-1/2 feet-tall woman above whose head no building in Washington is allowed to rise, other than the 555-feet-tall Washington Monument. Why would she have her back on the entire nation? Perhaps she is beckoning the hapless wretches from Bowie, Maryland welcome.

MASONRY AND CURRENT BRITISH MONARCHY

Although most American Masons will devoutly argue that Anglo/American Masonry is entirely different from the more occult, conspiratorial Continental version, there is little, if any significant evidence to support this supposition. The blood oaths, symbols, grips, signs, postures, and even the apron, have remained virtually unchanged for thousands of years.

Perhaps the greatest difference between the two versions of the craft is that in Continental Masonry, the emphasis has been shifted towards world domination by violent revolution, whereas the more gentile Anglo/American version inspired by Lord Bacon stresses a revolution of enlightenment designed to establish their New World Order.

Currently, the controversy in Great Britain over Masonry is much more heated, and much more visible than in the United States with the British royal family divided over the matter. At the center of the controversy is Prince Charles, the heir to the British throne. When he becomes King, he will be the first British monarch in centuries who has not served as the titular head of British Masonry.

To British Masonry, the approval and participation of the British Royal Family is a vital badge of respectability. The father of the current Queen Elizabeth, King George VI was a devoted Mason. When Philip Mountbatten, Prince Philip of Greece, asked the King for the hand of his daughter, Elizabeth, in marriage in the summer of 1947, the King made it plain that he expected any husband of his daughter to maintain the tradition of patronage of Freemasonry. Philip promised the King that he would join the Order. [67]

He and the future British monarch, Princess Elizabeth;, were married in 1947 in Westminster Abbey, but he still had not become a Mason. Philip's favorite uncle, Earl Mountbatten of Burma fiercely opposed to Freemasonry, and had strongly advised Philip to have nothing to do with it.

King George died on February 6, 1952. Philip, despite his own reservations, felt honor bound to fulfill his pledge to the deceased King, and on December 5, 1952, he was initiated into the secrets of Freemasonry at Navy Lodge #2612. Queen Elizabeth II was crowned six months later, on June 2, 1953. [68]

Philip, however, never even took the customary first three degrees of Masonry. He stopped at the first degree of Entered Apprentice, a very unusual step — perhaps unique in the history of the craft. While he is still technically a member of the Order, he has snubbed it ever since, despite all invitations to ascend the Masonic ladder. [69]

Philip's son, Prince Charles, the current heir to the British throne, has inherited his father's and his favorite uncle's distaste for Masonry, and is adamant that he will never join any secret society. Adding to the anti-Masonic influence which has surrounded him, is King George's wife, Queen Elizabeth's mother, and Charles' grandmother, the venerable and beloved Queen Mother:

> The Queen Mother, despite - perhaps because of - being the wife of a devoted Freemason, does not approve of the Brotherhood. She is a committed Bible-believing Christian and, largely due to her influence, Prince Charles too is a committed (as opposed to nominal) Christian.[70]

NINE

ALBERT PIKE, MAZZINI, AND
THE ITALIAN REVOLUTION

No study of the New World Order would be complete without including some of the fascinating stories that surround Albert Pike and Giuseppe Mazzini, the American and Italian heads of the most occult forms of Masonry in the nineteenth century.

The furor over the murder of William Morgan in 1826 had caused American Masonry to almost cease to exist, and European Masonry was in turmoil as well. Bavaria had forbidden Masonry as a danger to the state in 1784, then again in 1845. In 1814, the Regency of Milan and the Governor of Venice had acted in a similar manner. King John VI of Portugal prohibited Freemasonry in 1816, and renewed it in 1824. In 1820 several lodges were closed in Prussia for political intrigues, and in the same year Alexander I banished the order from the whole Russian Empire. A similar occurrence took place four years later in Spain.[1]

In 1876, anti-Masonic author Richard Carlile wrote of his fears for Britain:

> Let them not wait to be disbanded by the Legislation, as a useless and mischievous association....The deluge of mystery has not only overwhelmed Babylon but Egypt, Greece, Rome, and will, if we do not light up the spirit of revelation in time, most assuredly overthrow this British nation.[2]

In Italy in the early 1800s some supporters of the Italian monarchy, along with a Catholic group, formed a secret fraternal association called the Carbonari. This was a perfect cover for the Illuminati, who soon controlled it. The Carbonari had apparently fallen for Weishaupt's ploy of making Christ the Grand Master of their lodge. This pseudo-Christian pattern was so successful that it has been followed throughout the lower degrees of Masonry ever since.

The success of the Carbonari in seducing both members of royalty and the Church quickly brought it, and its mother lodge, the feared Alta

Vendita, to the pinnacle of power among the Mystery Schools.

Upon the death of Weishaupt in 1830, at age eighty-two, control of the Illuminati fell to the Italians. This was probably because they showed a considerably greater natural proclivity for the black arts than did Weishaupt's Germans. According to Monsignor George Dillon:

> Italian genius soon outstripped the Germans in astuteness, and as soon as, perhaps sooner than, Weishaupt had passed away, the supreme government of all the Secret Societies of the world was exercised by the Alta Vendita or highest lodge of the Italian Carbonari. The Alta Vendita ruled the blackest Freemasonry of France, Germany, and England; and until Mazzini wrenched the sceptre of the dark Empire from that body, it continued with consummate ability to direct the revolutions of Europe.[3]

MAZZINI

Thus, it fell to the head of Italian Masonry, Giuseppe Mazzini, to try to make something of the shambles the recent European and American revelations had made of Masonry. He wasted no time, building on the Christian theme, but all the while pursued Masonry's unchanging anti-Christian goals with a bloody vengeance: the complete destruction of the Church, and all the remaining European monarchies. In the permanent instructions to the Alta Vendita we find the following, probably authored by Mazzini:

> Our final end is that of Voltaire and of the French Revolution, the destruction for ever of Catholicism and even of the Christian idea which, if left standing on the ruins of Rome, would be the resuscitation of Christianity later on.[4]

> The work which we have undertaken is not the work of a day, nor a month, nor of a year. It may last many years, a century perhaps, but in our ranks the soldier dies and the fight continues.[5]

The usual rules of secrecy were to apply, including compartmentalization. They were advised to be "as simple as doves," but "prudent as the serpent." They were told to never reveal the secrets of the Order, even to their immediate families.[6]

The deception of churchmen was encouraged. "Let the clergy march under your banner in the belief always that they march under the banner of the Apostolic Keys."[7]

Mazzini's goals for Masonry turned out to be identical to what we would call revolutionary Marxism. For example, in 1846, two years before Marx and Engels published the *Communist Manifesto*, Mazzini spoke boldly of additional revolutions in France and Italy. He advised that revolution making called for action, not learned debate. He felt that rhetoric should be limited to a few key "mottos":

> Learned discussions are neither necessary nor opportune. There are regenerative words which contain all that need be often repeated to the public. Liberty, rights of man, progress, equality, fraternity, are what the people will understand above all.[8]

Although Masonry is designed to look like a harmless fraternal society promoting high moral values, there can be no doubt that even the members of the first three degrees are being used by their secret masters in ways the average member cannot fathom. According to Monsignor Dillon, the secret chiefs of World Masonry were ever anxious to:

> ... make use of the most common form of Masonry notwithstanding the contempt they had for the bons vivants who only learned from the craft how to become drunkards and liberals. Beyond the Masons, and unknown to them, though formed generally from them, lay the deadly secret conclave which, nevertheless, used and directed them for the ruin of the world and of their own selves.[9]

These secret conclaves would provide the various lodges with "instructions," from which their leaders would take their guidance. Another such directive came from a member named Piccolo Tiger and was addressed to the Piedmontese lodges of the Carbonari in 1822. It suggested that the membership should infiltrate religious fraternal organizations and observe which members would be useful to their purposes:

> All Italy is covered with religious confraternities....Do not fear to slip in some of your people into the very midst of these flocks, led as they are by a stupid devotion. Let our agents study with care the personnel of these confraternity men, and they will see that little by little, they will not be wanting in a harvest.[10]

Organizations were to be formed that had nothing to do with Masonry on the surface, but which would be under its control:

> Create by yourselves, or, better yet, cause to be created by others, associations, having commerce, industry, music, the fine arts, etc., for object. Reunite in one place or another...these tribes of yours as yet ignorant: put them under the pastoral staff of some virtuous priest, well known, but credulous and easy to be deceived. Then infiltrate the poison into those chosen hearts; infiltrate it in little doses....Afterwards, upon reflection, you will yourselves be astonished at your success.[11]

THE FORMULA FOR HUMAN CORRUPTION

Tiger's instructions explained that the lodges should form a "relative evil," one tempered by "false philanthropy," and that once the new initiate is "ripe," he will be admitted into a "secret society of which Freemasonry can be no more than the antechamber."[12]

Masonry is disguised as a movement to free the common man from the corruption and tyranny of the Church and dictatorial monarchies, but behind the scenes, Masonry has another goal in mind. In a letter from Alta Vendita member Vindex, to fellow member Nubius, their real purpose is revealed for all to see:

> It is corruption en masse that we have undertaken; the corruption of the people by the clergy, and the corruption of the clergy by ourselves; the corruption which ought, one day, to enable us to put the Church in her tomb.[13]

The plan engineered and implemented by the Alta Vendita in the 1830s looks quite similar to the path trod by the United States in the late twentieth century. First of all, prostitution was legitimized, licensed, inspected, and protected. Then morality was systematically eliminated from literature. Education took on an Atheistic tone and became otherwise hostile to religion.[14]

The plan was wildly successful, but Mazzini wanted still more control, and seized it after the mysterious death of Nubius, one of the chiefs of Italian Masonry. The death of Nubius, however, may have been the reason we have these incriminating documents to examine today. It was the custom of many of the chiefs of Italian Masonry to gather incriminating evidence against their enemies, then leave it behind with the papal government of the Catholic Church in case they met an untimely death. Monseigneur Dillon says that this is probably how the archives of the Alta Vendita came to light.

Once again, the best laid plans of Illuminism had unravelled, this time at the hands of the internal paranoia of its chiefs. Without this self-destructive paranoia, we would know little about the Illuminati of the post-Weishaupt period.

Even though Mazzini was able to take control of Italian Masonry, the task of uniting World Masonry was still formidable. Italian Masons in particular, and World Masonry in general, were divided into numerous rival sub-groups, frequently hostile to one another. Around 1860, after many years of struggling to unite European Masonry, Mazzini wrote to Albert Pike, the recognized leader of Scottish Rite Masonry in the United States, to discuss the possibility of including the United States in an international group.

After the 1826 murder of Captain William Morgan, Pike tried to regroup American Masonry, which had been all but eliminated between 1830 and 1840. Many American lodges were forced to disband until the storm of public criticism abated.

ODDFELLOWS

During those years, a Masonic splinter group called the "Oddfellows" spread quickly in the U.S., having managed to avoid being associated with Masonry. Oddfellow is the name adopted by members of a Masonic society founded in London in 1788. Many of the Oddfellow lodges were disbanded in England around the turn of the century because of suspicions that their nature was subversive, though the stated purpose of the society was merely "mutual help and diversion."

A split among the British Oddfellows in 1813 caused some members to form the Independent Order of Oddfellows (I.O.O.F.). In 1819, they were introduced to America with their headquarters in Baltimore. In the 1840s, Albert Pike began his involvement with secret societies as an Oddfellow. When the anti-Masonic fervor abated, he joined the Masons in 1850. In 1856, he was admitted to the A.A. (Ancient and Accepted Scottish Rite) and by 1859 had risen to the title of M.P. Sovereign Grand Commander of the Supreme Council for the Southern Jurisdiction of the United States, headquartered then, as now, in Charleston, South Carolina.

In 1857, when the poet Henry Wadsworth Longfellow became an A.A., he visited Pike in Charleston. Longfellow told Pike that he had an innovation for the Order. The "innovation" turned out to be a way to secretly introduce Satanism into the Order.[15]

Again, the difference between Satanism and Luciferianism is very simple and easy to understand, and it is very necessary to this study. Briefly, Satanism is what we today refer to as "black magic," while Luciferianism is ironically known as "Theurgy" or "white magic." Occult expert Edith Starr Miller explained, "Luciferians never call their infernal master, 'Spirit of Evil' or 'Father and Creator of Crime,' as a Satanist would. Albert Pike even forbade the use of the word *Satan* under any circumstances."[16]

There is certainly no doubt that all the mystery schools espouse this Luciferian philosophy. Edith Starr Miller wrote in 1933 that:

> Luciferian Occultism controls Freemasonry....Luciferian Occultism...is therefore not a novelty, but it bore a different name in the early days of Christianity. It was called Gnosticism and its founder was Simon the Magician.[17]

In any case, Pike apparently thought any change unnecessary, and so would not take a definite stand. Finally, a compromise was worked out so that Longfellow could secretly use the Oddfellows for his experiments. Whether this "improvement" in the Oddfellow system remains to the present day is unknown.

Satanist or Luciferian, there is no doubt that Pike was bloodthirsty. During the American Civil War, Pike was a brigadier general, fighting on the side of the Confederacy. He was sent to Oklahoma and given the title of Indian Commissioner by the South. His mission was to raise an army of the most savage of the Western tribes. His band became so barbarous, however, that Jefferson Davis disbanded the unit.[18]

After the Civil War, Pike was tried and found guilty of treason and sent to jail. Masons went to bat for him to President Andrew Johnson, himself a Mason. By April 22, 1866, President Johnson pardoned him. The following day, Pike visited the president at the White House. The press was not informed of all this for nine months.[19]

So pronounced was anti-Masonic sentiment that it was an issue when Congress tried to impeach President Johnson in March 1867. Shortly after the impeachment investigation began, Pike and General Gordon Granger met with Johnson at the White House for approximately three hours. Later, Granger was summoned before the House Judiciary Committee in its impeachment investigation and asked about the latter meeting. The general told the committee:

> They [President Johnson and Pike] talked a great deal about Masonry. More about that than anything else. And from what they talked about between them...I understood from the conversation that the President was [Pike's] subordinate in Masonry.[20]

Shortly thereafter, on June 20, 1867, the president received the fourth through the thirty-second degrees of Masonry of the Scottish Rite in his bedroom at the White House by a delegation of Scottish Rite officials.[21] Later that month, President Johnson journeyed to Boston to dedicate a Masonic temple, accompanied by General Granger and a delegation of the Knights Templar.[22]

On June 25, *The New York Times* ran a page-one lead story concerning the Massachusetts celebration and extolled the virtues of Masonry in four of its seven front page columns. It failed to mention that in 1834, the Massachusetts Legislature investigated the Order and found it to be "a distinct Independent Government within our own Government, and beyond the control of the laws of the land by means of its secrecy, and the oaths and regulations which its subjects are bound to obey, under penalty of death."[23]

In 1870, Mazzini and Pike reached an agreement for the creation of the new supreme rite, to be called the New and Reformed Palladian Rite. Pike was to be called the Sovereign Pontiff of Universal Freemasonry, and Mazzini was to be called Sovereign Chief of Political Action. Pike was to draw up the statutes and grades.[24]

Membership in the "Palladium" was very limited, and its deliberations were shrouded in the strictest secrecy:

> No mention of it would ever be made in the assemblies of the Lodges and Inner Shrines of other rites...for the secret of the new institution was only to be divulged with the greatest caution to a chosen few belonging to the ordinary high grades.

> Palladism is essentially a Luciferian rite. Its religion is Manichean neo-gnosticism, teaching that the divinity is dual and that Lucifer is the equal of Adonay.

The whole masonic world was set up at Charleston, the sacred city of the Palladium.[25]

By 1889, Pike simultaneously occupied the positions of Grand Master of the Central Directory of Washington, D.C. (the head of D.C. Masonry), Grand Commander of the Supreme Council of Charleston (head of American Masonry), and Sovereign Pontiff of Universal Freemasonry (head of world Masonry).[26]

On July 14, 1889, he issued formal written instructions to the "23 Supreme Councils of the world." Therein he gives us our best look at the real inner workings of Masonry in general. If any Mason still believes that Masonry is based on good, or even Christian principles, he should read the following words of their former leader, Albert Pike, a man whose name is still highly respected by all Masons:

> That which we must say to the crowd is—We worship a God, but it is the God that one adores without superstition. To you, Sovereign Grand Inspectors General, we say this, that you may repeat it to the Brethren of the 32nd, 31st, and 30th degrees—The Masonic religion should be, by all of us initiates of the high degrees, maintained in the purity of the Luciferian doctrine.

> If Lucifer were not God, would Adonay (The God of the Christians) whose deeds prove his cruelty...and hatred of man, barbarism and repulsion for science, would Adonay and his priests calumniate him? Yes, Lucifer is God, and unfortunately Adonay is also God. For the eternal law is that there is no light without shade, no beauty without ugliness, no white without black .

> That is why the intelligent disciples of Zoroaster, as well as, after them, the Gnostics, the Manicheans and the Templars have admitted, as the only logical metaphysical conception, the system of the two divine principles fighting eternally, and one cannot believe the one inferior in power to the other. Thus, the doctrine of Satanism is heresy; and the true and pure philosophic religion is the belief in Lucifer, the equal of Adonay; but Lucifer, God of Light and God of Good, is struggling for humanity against Adonay, the God of Darkness and Evil.[27]

How do secret societies control dissenting members? How is it possible these vast conspiracies have existed for hundreds and even thousands of years, and yet so few initiates have divulged the awful truth of these fraternities?

The answer is fear. Secret societies have little control over a fearless man, or at least one who does not fear them. That is why the horrible blood oaths are still taken. Very few would have the courage to carry out such tortures, however. Even after the worst recorded breach of Masonic secrecy in history—that of Captain Morgan—the full penalties were not exacted. In fact, according to the dying words of one of Morgan's murderers, those who wrapped him in weights and pushed him into Lake Erie could hardly stand to do the deed and were conscience-stricken the rest of their lives.

No, it is fear that drives the engines of Satanism/Luciferianism/ Masonry. This is illustrated by the account of the poisoning of Italian revolutionary politician and Mason, Francesco Crispi. Crispi, who eventually rose to be Premier of the newly united Italy in 1877, started his climb as a close friend of Mazzini.

Crispi served the Masonic cause faithfully and was instrumental in the unification of Italy in the mid-1800s. It was he who talked the reluctant hero of Italian unification, General Giuseppe Garibaldi, into invading Sicily with his band of volunteers to aid the revolt instigated in 1860 by Masons. Garibaldi, known to be a Mason, himself, proclaimed himself dictator of Sicily, and named Crispi minister of the interior.[28] The King of Sardinia, Victor Emmanuel II was declared King of Italy.

At that point Crispi decided it might be more to his personal advantage to serve the new King of Italy, rather than Mazzini. However, his change in allegiance was soon discovered by Mazzini's spies and in 1862 Mazzini planned a surprise for him at a Masonic dinner in Turin.

During dinner, Crispi suddenly felt ill. His illness quickly worsened. A fire seemed to be burning within him. Soon he fell to the floor, obviously in the throes of a most appalling agony. Instead of offering assistance, the other guests began to laugh, then one of them stood and told him that they had discovered that he had switched his allegiance from their Order to the King, and that they had therefore invited him to the dinner to be publicly poisoned as an example to others. In her book, *Occult Theocracy*, Edith Starr Miller described the nightmarish evening:

> Crispi realized full well that he was lost. He knew there was no escape....he awaited a lingering death.
>
> The others surrounded him, watching him in silence with profound contempt. Suddenly, a door opened, a curtain was raised and a man appeared. He advanced slowly. It was Mazzini.
>
> "Poor wretch!" said he to the dying man. "I pity you."
>
> "Yes, ambition made me betray...It is true...I was going to sell myself...But I die...Do not mock me...I suffer too much!"
>
> "I do not speak to you in derision," said Mazzini. "Francesco Crispi, I forgive you.. Drink this and you are saved. You will be reborn..."[29]

As Crispi began to come around from the effects of the antidote, Mazzini warned:

You live, yes, Francesco; but henceforth you are more completely enslaved than the last of the negroes for whose freedom they are fighting over there in America..You live again and your ambition will be gratified...You will be minister, minister of the Monarchy. You will hold in your hands the reins of government but...you will obey us in all things, even should the orders we give you seem contradictory, even should their execution cause you to pass for a madman in the eyes of Europe! Yes...from this day forward, you belong to us, for you must never forget that, should you place us in a position where it might be expedient to cut short your existence a second time, no power in the world could save you from the death, the sufferings of which you have known today. Live then for Masonry. Fight Royalty and the Church...[30]

What a lesson to those assembled! Crispi, of course, did have his ambitions met, but he was also regarded as erratic for the rest of his career because of the strange orders he received from his masters. In one elaborate plan to legitimize Crispi, he was ordered to openly denounce Masonry, and, in return, Masons denounced him. He was supposed to become the leader of the anti-Masonic cause among the European upper class. However, few trusted him because of his well-known associations with Masonic intrigues in past years.

Crispi, Mazzini, and his compatriots went on to do their work well, and by 1871, Italy was united under the banner of a Masonic "Republic." Vast holdings of the papacy had been shattered. Masonic expert Monsignor Dillon, D.D., explained in a lecture in 1884, the way Masons obtained "supreme power" in Italy:

[By] professing the strongest sympathy for the down-trodden millions whom they called slaves.

Were the millions of "slaves" served by the change? The whole property of the Church was seized upon. Were the burdens of taxation lightened? Very far from it. The change simply put hungry Freemasons...in possession of the Church lands and revenues. The consequence is this, that after a quarter of a century of vaunted "regenerated Masonic rule," during which "the liberators" were at perfect liberty to confer any blessings they pleased upon the people as such, the same people are at this moment more miserable than at any past period of their history, at least since Catholicity became predominant as the religion of the country.

To keep power in the hands of the Atheists, an army, ten times greater, and ten times more costly than before, had to be supported by the "liberated" people. A worthless but ruinously expensive navy has been created and must be kept by the same unfortunate "regenerated" people. These poor people, "regenerated and liberated," must man the fleets and supply the rank and file of the army and navy; they must give their sons, at the most useful period of their lives, to the "service" of Masonic "United Italy". But the officials in both army and navy— and their number is legion—supported by the taxes of the people, are

Freemasons or the sons of Freemasons. They vegetate in absolute uselessness, so far as the development of the country is concerned, living in comparative luxury upon its scanty resources.[31]

THE PLAN FOR THREE WORLD WARS

Although they had finally united Italy, Mazzini and Pike realized that the unification of all Europe under the banner of Illuminism would be extremely difficult, if not impossible. Nationalism runs strongly in the human spirit, and is very difficult to erase, especially on a continent divided by warfare for many centuries. Therefore, they set to work on their greatest plan, a plan so vast in scope that only a reader familiar with the great power wielded by the secret societies could begin to believe it.

In 1871, Mazzini issued a letter in which he outlined the final three-part plan of the Illuminati: their grand design for ridding not just Europe, but the entire world of Christianity, and bringing it under the "illuminated" dictatorship of Luciferianism. This remarkable letter was for many years on display in the British Museum Library in London.[32]

Mazzini proposed a series of world wars. These wars were to embroil every nation in a conflict so bloody and chaotic that eventually every nation would surrender its national sovereignty to an international government, like the League of Nations, or the second attempt—the current United Nations — in order to prevent subsequent global bloodletting. One Masonic scholar wrote in 1987:

> "The true birth of World Democracy from its prenatal national confinement is even now in progress. A war-torn, bleeding World is in the midst of labor-pains, preceding the ordeal of birth. Labor-pains in the birth of a New Age!"[33]

However, knowing that national sovereignty would certainly die hard, three of these world wars were proposed by Mazzini and Pike in their original plan. The first of these world wars, they hoped, would topple the Czarist government of Russia and establish an Illuminized dictatorship—a new level in the game of control of populations. This would give the Illuminists a secure base from which to operate, with a large population and vast natural resources to fuel the new engine of Illuminism.

The second World War would allow the new Soviet Russia to capture Europe — or as it turned out, half of it. The third World War would be in the Middle East between the Moslems and the Jews, and would bring about the biblical Armageddon. Certainly by the end of this Third World War, the battle-wearied nations would be ready to accept any proposal as long as it promised peace, uniting the entire world under the fatal banner of the Luciferian New World Order.[34] Pike wrote to Mazzini about consequences of the Third World War in 1871:

[It will] provoke a formidable social cataclysm...and the most bloody turmoil. Then everywhere, the citizens, obliged to defend themselves against the world minority of revolutionaries, will exterminate those destroyers of civilization, and the multitude, disillusioned with Christianity,...will be without a compass, anxious for an ideal, but without knowing where to render its adoration, will receive the true light through the universal manifestation of the pure doctrine of Lucifer, brought finally into public view, a manifestation which will result from the general reactionary movement which will follow the destruction of Christianity and atheism, both conquered and exterminated at the same time.[35]

Mazzini and Pike may have planned *three* World Wars in 1871, but the two authors of the *Communist Manifesto*, Marx and Engels, both spoke of the first world war twenty-three years before that. Karl Marx wrote in 1848 that the "Slavic riffraff," referring to the Russian people, as well as the Czechs, and Croats, were "retrograde" races whose only function in the world history of the future was to be cannon fodder. Marx said, "The coming world war will cause not only reactionary classes and dynasties, but entire reactionary peoples, to disappear from the face of the earth. And that will be progress.[36]

As though merely repeating Marx's lead, co-author Friedrich Engels wrote in the same year:

The next world war will make whole reactionary peoples disappear from the face of the earth. This, too, is progress. Obviously, this cannot be fulfilled without crushing some delicate national flower. But without violence and without pitilessness nothing can be obtained in history.[37]

How can this be misconstrued? What "next world war"? At this point in history, there had never been a "world war."

TEN

KARL MARX AND THE INTERNATIONALE

In our day, if Masonry does not found Jacobite or other clubs, it originates and cherishes movements fully as satanic and as dangerous. Communism, just like Carbonarism, is but a form of the illuminated Masonry of Weishaupt.

Monsignor George Dillon, D.D., 1885[1]

Probably never in history has such a deceptive folklore surrounded a political figure as that which continues to encircle the legend of German-born Karl Marx, co-author of the *Communist Manifesto*, and the much-celebrated "father" of Communism. Even if we read about Marx in a typical, modern encyclopedia we get a benign picture of him. He is usually painted in glowing terms, such as the "founder of democratic socialism." However, there is recent evidence that Marx was far less interested in the travails of the common man than he was in doing the bidding of secret societies.

Though not widely known, Marx was a Satanist. In his student years, Marx authored a little-known drama, *Oulanem*. Modern Communists and socialists have gone to great lengths to suppress this telling literary creation of the young Marx. Below are some revealing excerpts:

> If there is a Something which devours,
> I'll leap within it, though I bring the world to ruins—
> The world which bulks between me and the abyss
> I will smash to pieces with my enduring curses.
> I'll throw my arms around its harsh reality,
> Embracing me, the world will dumbly pass away,
> And then sink down to utter nothingness,
> Perished, with no existence—that would be really living."[2]

Unfortunately, this was not just Marx's portrayal of a demonic character. As we shall see, it is the young man portraying himself. The Romanian expert on Marx, Rev. Richard Wurmbrand, comments:

In Oulanem Marx...consigns the entire human race to damnation. Oulanem is probably the only drama in the world in which all the characters are aware of their own corruption, and flaunt it and celebrate it with conviction. In this drama there is no black and white....Here all are servants of darkness, all reveal aspects of Mephistopheles. All are Satanic, corrupt, doomed.[3]

Marx didn't get a bad start in life. He was born in 1818, of relatively well-to-do parents. His father was a Jewish lawyer, a descendent of a line of rabbis. But Marx was always in trouble; drinking, spending money, and frequenting coffee houses. He finally entered Berlin University and managed to get a degree in philosophy.[4]

Strangely enough, in his early days, Marx, like his predecessor Weishaupt, professed to be a Christian. In fact, in his first known written work he wrote:

Through love of Christ we turn our hearts at the same time toward our brethren who are inwardly bound to us and for whom He gave Himself in sacrifice.

Union with Christ could give an inner elevation, comfort in sorrow, calm trust, and a heart susceptible to human love, to everything noble and great, not for the sake of ambition and glory, but only for the sake of Christ.[5]

In a thesis called *Considerations of a Young Man on Choosing His Career* he said:

Religion itself teaches us that the Ideal toward which all strive, sacrificed Himself for humanity, and who shall dare contradict such claims? If we have chosen the position in which we can accomplish the most for Him, then we can never be crushed by burdens, because they are only sacrifices made for the sake of all.[6]

How did such a boy go wrong? Something happened to the young Marx in that last year of high school, and he became passionately anti-religious. Marx fell in with a mysterious character named Moses Hess, whom Marx named the "Communist Rabbi." Hess apparently initiated him directly into an advanced level of Satanism. Suddenly, Marx began to use the word "destroy" frequently in his writings, so much so that his friends, though apparently few in number, gave him "Destroy" as a nickname.

At an age when most well-off young men are filled with a boundless enthusiasm for life, Marx painted a black picture in his poem *Invocation of One in Despair*:

So a god has snatched from me my all,
In the curse and rack of destiny.
All his worlds are gone beyond recall.
Nothing but revenge is left to me.[7]

In another poem, he aptly demonstrated the Masonic man-becomes-god doctrine:

> Then I will be able to walk triumphantly,
> Like a god, through the ruins of their kingdom.
> Every word of mine is fire and action.
> *My breast is equal to that of the Creator.*[8]

We may never know why Marx turned against Christianity, but what is blatantly obvious is that the young Karl Marx had been initiated into a Satanist cult. In his poem called *The Player*, which was later downplayed by both himself and his followers, he wrote:

> The hellish vapors rise and fill the brain,
> Till I go mad and my heart is utterly changed.
> See the sword?
> The prince of darkness
> Sold it to me.
> For me he beats the time and gives the signs.
> Ever more boldly I play the dance of death.[9]

According to Rev. Wurmbrand, the significance of the sword is that it is used in the initiation ceremony of Satanic cults.[10] All this took place before Marx was nineteen. In a letter dated November 10, 1837, he wrote the following cryptic passage to his father, probably about his conversion from Christianity: "A curtain had fallen. My holy of holies was rent asunder and new gods had to be installed."[11] Marx's father lovingly answered his son on March 2, 1837:

> Your advancement, the dear hope of seeing your name someday of great repute, and your earthly well-being are not the only desires of my heart. These are illusions I had had a long time, but I assure you that their fulfillment would not have made me happy. Only if your heart remains pure and beats humanly and if no deamon is able to alienate your heart from better feelings, only then will I be happy.[12]

Why was his father growing concerned about his son's spiritual welfare? Here are some examples of the poetry Marx gave his father on the occasion of the latter's fifty-fifth birthday:

> Because I discovered the highest,
> And because I found the deepest through meditation,
> I am great like a God;
> I clothe myself in darkness like Him.[13]

Obviously, Marx had gone beyond the more innocuous-seeming Luciferan stages of initiation, and had already accepted the philosophies of full-blown Satanism. According to Wurmbrand, Marx had become an avowed enemy of all gods—to "draw all mankind into the abyss and to follow them laughing."[14]

The motto for Marx's doctoral thesis was the cry of Prometheus: "In one word—I hate all the gods." But Marx was not alone. His close friend, Bruno Bauer, wrote in 1840 in a book entitled *Historical Criticism of the Synoptic Gospels*, that the Bible was a forgery, Jesus never existed, and therefore Christianity was a fraud.[15]

Soon thereafter, Marx and Bauer tried to secure the necessary financial sponsorship to publish a journal entitled *Journal of Atheism*. They were unable to get a sponsor, so no editions were actually published.[16]

In 1841, Marx obtained his doctorate in philosophy. He tried to get a teaching position but was rejected because of his revolutionary activities as a student. He took to journalism and founded and edited several revolutionary newspapers and did very well until one was closed by the Prussian government.

In 1843 he married, and moved to Paris to "study French communism." There he met Friedrich Engels, a young German radical who was the wealthy son of a textile manufacturer. It is ironic that two relatively wealthy young radicals wrote the *Communist Manifesto*.

Engels, too, was the political product of the "Communist Rabbi," Moses Hess. Hess wrote after meeting Engels: "He parted from me as an overzealous Communist. This is how I produce ravages."[17]

Marx and Engels hoped to transform all of Europe into flaming revolution, from which would spring not representative government of, by, and for the people, but a dictatorship by Satanists. The rivals of Marx and Engels were aware of this and pointed it out during the course of struggling for power.

The Socialist Guillaume, Secretary of the First Internationale, described Engels as a rich manufacturer accustomed to regarding workers as cannon fodder, and Marx as someone who had never come into touch with the working classes. To Guillaume, they both merely used the wage earners as the raw material they needed for the construction of their revolutionary machine. "They felt no more for the workers than the iron master feels for the metal he welds into shape."[18]

Rev. Wurmbrand wrote of Marx's motivations: "He had no vision of serving mankind, the proletariat, or socialism. He merely wished to bring the world to ruin, to build for himself a throne whose bulwark would be human fear."[19]

Wurmbrand states that Marx was a Satanist before he became a Communist. In other words, the Communism he was later credited with, was simply the best way to dupe the rest of the population into abandoning the Church and following the course mapped out by Weishaupt more than sixty years earlier:

> There is no support for the view that Marx entertained lofty social ideals about helping mankind....On the contrary, Marx hated any notion of God or gods. He determined to be the man who would kick out God—all this before he had embraced socialism, which was only

the bait to entice proletarians and intellectuals to embrace this devilish ideal.[20]

Marx's political philosophy is so full of holes that it cannot stand much scrutiny. For example, the very foundation of Marx's Communist theory is that society is on an inevitable course of development from capitalism to Socialism to Communism. Marx and Engels said of capitalism in the *Communist Manifesto*: "Its fall and the victory of the proletariat are equally inevitable." If it is inevitable, why did he see violence as a necessity? According to Marx, "There is but one way of simplifying, shortening, concentrating the death agony of the old society as well as the bloody labor of the new world's birth—Revolutionary Terror."[21]

This is impossible to justify in any frame of reference other than an evil and purely selfish one. Marx was not the messiah of social equality which he pretended to be, but merely a revolutionary. But what is social equality anyway? Can any governmental system make men economically equal without destroying the incentives that fuel the engines of civilization? The answer is that the nature of Communism is not to advance civilization, but to destroy it.

Rev. Wurmbrand quite correctly pointed out how Marx's Satanic influence was later to be the pattern for Soviet Communism:

> Eventually, Marx [refused to] admit the existence of a Creator....When no Creator is acknowledged, there is no one to give us commandments, or to whom we are accountable. Marx confirms this by stating, "Communists preach absolutely no morals." When the Soviets in their early years adopted the slogan, "Let us drive out capitalists from earth and God from heaven," they were merely fulfilling the legacy of Karl Marx.[22]

According to W. Cleon Skousen, author of *The Naked Communist*, Marxists have even developed their own version of the Ten Commandments:

> They believe that "Honor thy Father and thy Mother" was created by the early Hebrews to emphasize to their children the fact that they were the private property of their parents. "Thou shalt not kill" was attributed to the belief of the dominant class that their bodies were private property and therefore they should be protected along with other property rights. "Thou shalt not commit adultery" and "Thou shalt not covet thy neighbor's wife" were said to have been created to implement the idea that a husband was the master of the home and the wife was strictly private property belonging to him.[23]

Those who advocate women's rights would be horrified at Marxist teachings if they only knew them. According to Skousen, some Communist leaders advocated complete "libertinism and promiscuity" to replace marriage and family. An example of this is seen in a Soviet decree issued in 1919:

> Beginning with March 1, 1919, the right to possess women between the ages of 17 and 32 is abolished....[Women can no] longer be considered private property and all women become the property of the nation....Any man who wishes to make use of a nationalized woman must hold a certificate issued by the administrative Council of a professional union, or by the Soviet...attesting that he belongs to the working class.[24]

It goes on to state that pregnant women will be given time off from their work for four months before, and three months after the birth of the child, but then one month after delivery, "children will be placed in an institution entrusted with their care and education." Furthermore, it goes on to obliterate the concept of rape:

> There is no such thing as a woman being violated by a man; he who says that a violation is wrong denies the October Communist Revolution. To defend a violated woman is to reveal oneself as a bourgeois and a partisan of private property.[25]

Of course, Marx was not the only Satanist of his day who professed Communism for political gain. In fact, many of his friends were of like mind. Mikhail Bakunin, the Russian anarchist, admitted the direct connection between Socialist revolutions and Satanism:

> The Evil One is the satanic revolt against divine authority, revolt in which we see the fecund germ of all human emancipations, the revolution. Satan [is] the eternal rebel, the first freethinker and the emancipator of worlds. He makes man ashamed of his bestial ignorance and obedience; he emancipates him, stamps upon his brow the seal of liberty and humanity, in urging him to disobey and eat of the fruit of knowledge.[26]

Bakunin, who was also a member of Russian nobility, goes on to explain that the true nature of revolutions is not to free the poor from exploitation, but to "awaken the Devil in the people, to stir up the basest passions. Our mission is to destroy, not to edify."[27]

Another early friend of Marx was the French Socialist Pierre Joseph Proudhon. Following the Masonic philosophy of Lord Bacon, Proudhon published a book entitled *What is Property?* in 1840, wherein he stated that "property is theft." But Bakunin gave a deeper insight into the motivations of their mutual friend, saying he also "worshipped Satan."[28]

In another of his books, *Philosophy of Misery*, Proudhon follows the Masonic line again. He wrote of God: "We reach knowledge in spite of him."[29] In the same tome, Proudhon gives an excellent example of the course French Masonry had set for itself in the post-revolutionary period:

> Come Satan, slandered by the small and by kings. God is stupidity and cowardice; God is hypocrisy and falsehood; God is tyranny and poverty; God is evil. Where humanity bows before an altar, humanity, the slave of kings and priests, will be condemned ...I swear, God, with my hand stretched out towards the heavens, that you are nothing

more than the executioner of my reason, the scepter of my conscience....God is essentially anticivilized, antiliberal, antihuman.[30]

Is it any wonder that Anglo/American Masons today try to distance themselves from their French brethren?

Although Marx went on to win worldly acclaim, the personal price for him was high. He suffered from frequent illnesses, and even when physically healthy, endured long periods of depression that he claimed prevented him from working. He drank heavily and taught his children to do likewise. In one letter to Engels begging for more money, he explained: "The children appear to have inherited a lust for drink from their father."[31]

Marx's daughter, Laura, and her husband, the Socialist Lafargue, committed suicide together. Marx's favorite daughter, Eleanor, married the Satanist Edward Eveling, who lectured on such subjects as "The Wickedness of God." They too made a suicide pact. She died; he backed out at the last minute.[32]

Years later, Marxian apologists tried to suppress many of the more sordid details of Marx's life, and replaced them with fanciful stories. An example of this are the fanciful comments made by Great Britain's first Socialist prime minister, Ramsay MacDonald. The English translations of Marx's correspondence were carefully cleaned up of offending passages which might embarrass the Socialist/Communist agenda, because the truth would:

> ... hardly accord with Mr. Ramsay MacDonald's description of Marx as "the kindliest of men" and "the tender man who never saw a poverty-stricken child on the road without patting its head and ministering to its wants." Nowhere do we find a record of any incident of this kind.[33]

The attempt to clean up the image of Marx has been widespread, yet impossible to achieve completely. Even Lenin hinted at a dark, vast, yet-to-be-told story surrounding Karl Marx. "After half a century, not one of the Marxists has comprehended Marx."[34]

What was Lenin talking about? There is an entire body of the writings of Marx and Engels that has never been published, at least in the West. Why not? Because they show Marx to be a Satanist. In *The Revolted Man*, Albert Camus (the French novelist who won the 1957 Nobel prize for literature) stated that thirty volumes of Marx and Engels had never been published and expressed the presumption that if they were, a new Marx would emerge in the eyes of the world.[35]

A modern Soviet historian goes even further. Professor M. Mtchedlov, vice-director of the Marx Institute in Moscow, wrote in a letter to Rev. Wurmbrand that indeed as many as 100 volumes of Marx's work are in his institute's collection, and yet only thirteen have been reprinted for the public. His letter goes on to make the lame excuse that the reason only thirteen volumes have appeared is that World War II forestalled the printing of the other volumes. According to Wurmbrand:

> The letter was written in 1980, thirty-five years after the end of the war. And the State Publishing House of the Soviet Union surely has sufficient funds....There is no other explanation than that most of Marx's ideas are deliberately being kept secret.[36]

THE ROTHSCHILD OMISSION

In *DasKapital*, Marx renounced the very foundation of capitalism, and yet never mentioned its leading proponents of his time, the Rothschilds. According to Nesta Webster, this omission is glaring because the era from 1820 onward was known as the "age of the Rothschilds."

This may have been due, in large part, to the fact that much of the wealth of France had been destroyed a few years earlier in the French Revolution at the instigation of the German Illuminati. The fact is that by the middle of the 1800s, when Marx and Engels wrote the *Communist Manifesto*, the common dictum of Europe was "There is only one power in Europe, and that is Rothschild."[37] However, the invisibility of the Rothschilds is not accidental; it has been carefully cultivated through the years. Though they control scores of industrial, commercial, mining, and tourist corporations, not one bears the name Rothschild.[38]

The question remains to be answered whether the Rothschilds were secret financiers behind the Illuminati, the consequent French Revolution, and the Jacobin incursion of Citizen Genêt into the United States. Certainly the Rothschilds' influence upon industrial America was profound. Working through the Wall Street firms Kuhn, Loeb & Co. and J.P. Morgan Co., the Rothschilds financed John D. Rockefeller so that he could create the Standard Oil empire. They also financed the activities of Edward Harriman (railroads) and Andrew Carnegie (steel).[39]

By the beginning of the 1900s, the wealth of the now invisible House of Rothschild had grown to such proportions that "it was estimated that they controlled half the wealth of the world."[40]

Historian Webster asked the natural question of Marx's omission:

> Now how is it conceivable that a man who set out honestly to denounce Capitalism should have avoided all reference to its principal authors?...How are we to explain this astounding omission? Only by recognizing that Marx was not sincere in his denunciations of the Capitalistic system, and that he had other ends in view.[41]

The answer is that Communism was a product of the secret societies, and Marx was a mere figurehead doing their bidding. This is perhaps nowhere better illustrated than in Marx's work with the International Working Man's Association — the Internationale.

THE INTERNATIONALE

The International Working Man's Association, or First Internationale, was formed at a meeting on September 28, 1864 at St. Martin's Hall in London. Although the name "Internationale" made the group appear to be an international labor union convention, it really was a Masonic mix of elitist Socialists, Communists, Atheists, and Satanists, all quite ready to philosophize on the disposition of the working man, but few with any real practical experience. This group, of course, was one into which Marx and Engels should have fit very well.

Marx approached the Internationale with the natural condescension a father has for his children. Marx, however, was in for a surprise. It was apparently only here that he discovered he was to take a back seat to the other, more powerful forces driving Communism. Marx complained about this in a letter to Engels. "I was present, only as a dumb personage on the platform."

Marx was placed on a subcommittee to propose the statutes for the Internationale along with several Masons, among whom was none other than the personal secretary of Italian Illuminist Mazzini's, a man named Wolff. At the first meeting of the committee, Wolff proposed that the identical statutes of Mazzini's working men's association be used, and after some wrangling, this was generally adopted. James Guillaume, a Swiss member of the Internationale and its principal chronicler, stated:

> It is not true that the Internationale was the creation of Karl Marx. He remained completely outside the preparatory work that took place from 1862 to 1864.... Like the cuckoo he came and laid his egg in a nest which was not his own.[42]

In fact, the Internationale can hardly be viewed as anything but Illuminated Masonry in a new disguise. French historian E.E. Fribourg wrote in 1871: "The Internationale everywhere found support in Freemasonry." Regardless of the cause for which the Internationale was called, the leading men of Europe's secret societies quickly poured in, and it was soon absorbed by existing secret organizations. According to Webster, the Internationale became nothing more than "the outer shell that covered a ramification of conspiracies."[43]

Webster commented that the Internationale "became permeated with the spirit of Illuminism." In fact, whenever positions which were even slightly more moderate were introduced before the group, they were soon withdrawn. Garibaldi, the general who "liberated" Italy from the monarchy, was unnerved when his proposal, that the assemblage should state that "faith in God should be adopted by the Congress," met with a stony silence. An embarrassed Garibaldi backtracked quickly, qualifying his suggestion with the explanation that by God he meant the religion of Reason—as was practiced in the

French Revolution.[44]

In truth, the Internationale was nothing more than a gathering of Europe's secret societies under the guise of a labor convention:

> All talk of conditions of labour, all discussions of the practical problems of industry had been abandoned and the Internationale became simply an engine of warfare against civilization. By its absorption of the secret societies and of the doctrines of Illuminism all the machinery of revolution passed into its keeping. Every move in the game devised by Weishaupt, every method for engineering disturbances and for spreading inflammatory propaganda, became part of its programme.

> So just as the Jacobin Club had openly executed the hidden plan of the Illuminati, the Internationale, holding within it the same terrible secrets, carried on the work of World Revolution in the full light of day.[45]

The philosophy that came out of the Internationale was an entirely new justification for evil. It now became publicly acceptable to be immoral, if done in the name of freeing the working man from his condition of capitalist servitude. W. Cleon Skousen maintained: "Marxist Man has convinced himself that nothing is evil which answers the call of expediency."[46]

Conflicts within the Internationale did occur. Marx claimed that all power should reside in the state, while rivals like Russian Mikhail Bakunin pushed the thesis that a permanent state of anarchy should exist and said his goal was "the destruction of all law and order and the unchaining of evil passions!"[47]

Although their methods were supposedly different, the source of their ideas was the same. Historian Nesta Webster stated that Bakunin was a zealot for the doctrines of Illuminism and "a disciple of Weishaupt."[48]

Marx, however, eventually became too radical even for the Italian head of the Illuminati. Mazzini was one of the few who maintained a friendship with Marx throughout his life. Mazzini, a murderer in his own right, said that Marx had "a destructive spirit. His heart bursts with hatred rather than with love toward men."[49]

It is interesting to note that during the last years of his life, Marx undertook to learn the Russian language, as though privy to the eventual direction Communism would take. He died on March 14, 1883 in London, and was buried in Highgate Cemetery, which has since become the center of British Satanism. Mysterious rites of black magic are still celebrated at Marx's tomb.[50]

ELEVEN

THE SOVIET REVOLUTION

The next great project of secret societies was to prepare the conquest of Europe via the creation of what would become the Soviet Union.

Revolution in Russia was germinating through the 1880s, but did not break out until the beginning of the 1900s. By 1905, a premature attempt at revolution broke out in the streets of St. Petersburg and Moscow. Although the revolution was soon crushed, Czar Nicholas II was forced to establish an elected parliament called the Duma. The Czar jailed or exiled an estimated 250,000 revolutionaries, including Lenin, who went to Switzerland.

Lenin's accomplice, Leon Trotsky, was arrested in 1905. By 1907, he had escaped from prison, and eventually made his way to France, where he was soon expelled for his revolutionary activities there. Before he left, he founded a Bolshevist newspaper called *The Voice*. He ended up in New York in January 1917, where he went to work as a reporter for a Communist newspaper, *The New World*.

It was in New York that Trotsky discovered that the "revolution" had powerful American friends. He soon discovered that there were wealthy Wall Street bankers who were willing to finance a revolution in Russia. Within two months, Trotsky left New York to return to Russia, but this time, he had with him a fortune in gold, and even an entourage of 275 dedicated revolutionaries—many of them Americans—to aid him.[1]

Trotsky left New York aboard the *S.S. Christiana* on March 27, 1917. All of Europe at this time was in the midst of World War I. Within days, Trotsky was in jail again. The ship had stopped in Nova Scotia and the Canadian government had impounded both Trotsky and his new-found wealth.[2]

Canada, it seems, had the nerve to take Trotsky at his word. He had proclaimed that when the Bolsheviks came to power in Russia he intended to make a separate peace with the Germans, therefore freeing up a lot of Germans from the Eastern front so they could go kill Canadian soldiers on the Western front. For some reason, the Canadian government took a dim view of this.[3]

Who intervened to free Trotsky and his gold from that Canadian jail? None other than President Woodrow Wilson's closest White House advisor, Colonel House, the man who later brought America a central banking system (the Federal Reserve), and was said to have the complete trust of the Rothschilds. Within only a few days, Trotsky was provided with an American passport, and sailed on to Russia.[4]

World War I had taken a terrible toll on Russia. She suffered approximately 1,700,000 deaths, sixteen times more than the United States. Desertions from the Russian Army were rampant. Food shortages among the populace were growing because Russian currency was practically worthless.[5]

By March 1917, the citizens were in revolt. The Czar abdicated, and a provisional government was set up. Soon, the fighting spirit of the Russian Army returned. Germany was desperate to stop the Russians on the Eastern front and they found their answer in a willing Lenin.

Lenin was aided by German agents in returning to Russia from his exile in Switzerland. He was put on the infamous "sealed train" in Switzerland along with at least five million dollars (U.S.).[6] Traveling along with Lenin were another 159 dedicated Bolshevik revolutionaries. Germany was quite willing to see the Bolsheviks come to power because Lenin had chosen as a primary political issue the cessation of the war with Germany, so they ushered the train right through their lines without question.

Winston Churchill saw these forces at work and spoke out on November 5, 1919 in the House of Commons:

> Lenin was sent to Russia by the Germans in the same way that you might send a phial containing a culture of typhoid or of cholera to be poured into the water supply of a great city and it worked with amazing accuracy.[7]

The evidence clearly shows that Europeans and Americans financed Lenin and Trotsky in their attempts to foment a revolution in Russia. But does that mean that they represented the secret societies? Churchill seemed to think so. He implied that Lenin had the help of secret societies, and charged that Lenin had gathered together "the leading spirits of a formidable sect, the most formidable sect in the world, of which he was the high priest and chief."[8]

Lenin and Trotsky re-entered Russia in the spring of 1917, both with large treasuries of gold to fuel their revolution. Certainly, this revolution was not a natural outburst of the indigenous population. It was only by a course of systematic deception, and finally by force of arms, that the party, the "red bureaucracy," succeeded in establishing its domination. Such popularity as it had achieved had been won by the old method of the conspiracy — promising one thing and doing precisely the opposite.[9]

By July of 1917, Lenin managed to incite a revolution, but the Russian Army was able to suppress the uprising. On July 19, the government ordered Lenin's arrest as a German agent and Lenin fled to Finland. By early October, he felt it was safe to return, and on November 7, he led another revolution which was successful.

Since the Bolsheviks had earlier called for elections, Lenin was forced to hold them on November 25. More than seventy-five percent of the population voted against him. On January 18, 1918, when the People's Congress met, it was filled with anti-Bolshevik representatives. Lenin demanded that the Congress dissolve. They refused. The next day, Lenin sent armed guards to the legislative body and dissolved it for them. The Communists summarily eliminated the nearest thing to a representative government Russia had ever known.[10]

Thus Lenin and Trotsky promised a Constitutional Assembly, yet their first act was to dissolve the Duma. In March 1918, the Bolsheviks did indeed make peace with Germany and sent millions of Germans streaming to the western fronts to kill Allied soldiers. For this, American banking houses, controlled by the Rothschilds, immediately rewarded them with massive infusions of cash to prop up the Bolshevik dictatorship.

In addition to fulfilling promises he made to the Germans, Lenin had another reason for this action. He believed that the chaos of the war would make it possible to set off a series of Communist revolutions in every major capitalist nation. According to Skousen:

> He wanted to disentangle Russia from the conflict in order to get her prepared for her role as the "Motherland of Communism." This would give him a chance to consolidate his power in Russia and then to supervise the revolutions in the war-weary capitalist nations so as to bring the whole world under the dictatorship of the proletariat within a very short time.[11]

After making peace with the Germans, Lenin then set off to completely communize Russia. His efforts only succeeded after a further economic collapse and a civil war. This war between the "Whites" and Lenin's "Reds" lasted until 1922, and cost twenty-eight million Russian lives, more than sixteen times the number of men Russia lost in all of World War I.[12]

Lenin set the pattern of revolutionary deception in this, his first triumph. Initially, he allowed the peasants to seize much farmland, for example. He also initially allowed workers to control the factories and play important roles in local government. Soon enough, however, as Lenin began tightening his control, he forced the peasants to surrender most of the produce from the seized lands, and he centralized control of production.

After Lenin took power, he slowly began to understand that he was not really pulling all the strings. Someone else was silently in control of the Soviet nation. Lenin lamented:

> The state does not function as we desired. How does it function? The car does not obey. A man is at the wheel and seems to lead it, but the car does not drive in the desired direction. It moves as another force wishes.[13]

By 1921, Lenin despondently remarked in a letter that "I hope we will be hanged on a stinking rope."[14] In fact, Lenin was one of the few who helped to install the Communist dictatorship who did not meet that fate.

In 1922, a terrible famine hit Russia, and in that year alone another five million Russians starved to death—almost three times as many as died in WWI. Lenin had to admit that Marxism as an economic system was a failure. He instituted a radical economic reform. He eliminated the Marxist barter system and returned currency and wages to the Russian people. In less than a year, three-quarters of all retail distribution was in private hands. Peasant farmers were allowed to sell most of their grain on the open market. In a matter of months, starvation began to disappear.[13]

In the end, Lenin finally understood the consequences of his actions. In 1924, from his deathbed, Lenin said:

> I committed a great error. My nightmare is to have the feeling that I'm lost in an ocean of blood from the innumerable victims. It is too late to return. To save our country, Russia, we would have needed men like Francis of Assisi. With ten men like him we would have saved Russia.[16]

By 1924, Lenin was dead and his assistant, Joseph Stalin, used his ruthless tactics to take control of the nation. Stalin began wiping out the prosperous independent businessmen and peasant farmers who had flourished under the later days of Lenin's rule. Again, Russia was plunged into starvation, now ruled by the most dictatorial and murderous tyrant the world had ever known. Whole cities were wiped out at the hint of rebellion to his iron fisted rule. It is now estimated by Soviet sources that Stalin's reign of terror killed 40,000,000 Russians, many times the number slaughtered by Hitler.

In 1933, Stalin sent his friend Litvinov to Washington and got the

United States to recognize the Soviet Union on the promise that Stalin would stop trying to overthrow the U.S. government. Within ten months after the U.S. recognized the Soviet Union and sent an ambassador, Stalin had broken his promise and again openly advocated the violent overthrow of the U.S. government.[17]

Stalin was initially enrolled in school to become a priest at the theological seminary at Tiflis, close to his hometown of Gori near the border of Turkey, in the Russian province of Georgia. He soon discovered that the seminary was honeycombed with secret societies.[18]

He became involved in some of the most radical of these, and in his third year of seminary was finally exposed. When he was finally expelled for "lack of religious vocation" in 1899, he became a full-time Marxist revolutionary.[19]

Who financed Lenin and Trotsky? The evidence points to a variety of European and American financiers. One German responsible for the financing of the Bolshevik revolution was Max Warburg, the brother of American Paul Warburg, the prime mover in establishing the U.S. Federal Reserve System. Max ran a Rothschild-allied family bank in Frankfurt, Germany, and was the head of the German Secret Police during World War I.

Paul Warburg had another brother named Felix. It was Felix's father-in-law, Jacob Schiff, who seems to have been the main conspirator in the United States. Schiff was senior partner in the Wall Street investing firm of Kuhn, Loeb & Co. According to the *New York Journal-American* of February 3, 1949, it was estimated by Jacob's grandson, John Schiff, that the "old man" sank about $20 million for the final triumph of Bolshevism in Russia.

Other Westerners who helped finance the Bolsheviks, were J.P. Morgan & Co., the Rockefeller oil family, and Alfred Milner Rothschild. The White Russian General Arsene de Goulevitch confirmed the Western financing of the Soviet revolution years later when he identified Jacob Schiff as a long-time supporter of "the Russian revolutionary cause."[20] The general also claimed that "over 21 million roubles" were donated to the cause by Lord Milner.[21]

De Goulevitch also reported that British agents distributed money to Russian soldiers in November of 1917 to induce them to mutiny against the provisional government set up after the czar had abdicated six months earlier. This was what we now call the Bolshevik, or Soviet revolution of 1917.

The conspirators apparently had a considerable financial reward for their investment. According to de Goulevitch:

> Mr. Bakhmetiev, the late Russian Imperial Ambassador to the United States, tells us that the Bolsheviks, after victory, transferred 600

million roubles in gold between the years 1918 and 1922 to Kuhn, Loeb & Company [Schiff's firm]. [22]

In the Bolshevik revolution, some of the world's richest and most powerful men financed a movement which purportedly advocated the elimination of huge personal fortunes. Obviously, however, these men had no fear of Communism. Gary Allen has written: "It is only logical to assume that if they financed it and do not fear it, it must be because they control it. Can there be any other explanation that makes sense?"[23]

Since then, American financiers have striven mightily to keep Communism alive. According to Allen, "virtually everything the Soviets possess has been acquired from the West. It is not much of an exaggeration to say that the U.S.S.R. was made in the U.S.A."[24]

And what was the cost to the Russian people? By 1920, industrial production had dropped to only thirteen percent of the 1913 figure. There was an almost complete lack of clothing, shoes, and agricultural products. The rouble became almost worthless. The Russian price index of that day rose more than 16,000 times between 1917 and 1920. Crop yields fell from seventy-four million tons in 1916, to thirty million tons in 1920. The situation was exacerbated in 1920 with a drought and subsequent famine. It is estimated that in 1920-21, five million died of famine alone.[25]

With the ascendency of Joseph Stalin as the leader of Communist Russia, barbarism reached new highs. In 1945, twelve years after the end of Stalin's first "Five-Year Plan," he told Winston Churchill that during that period, twelve million peasants died in the reorganization of agriculture alone.[26]

In the meantime, the privileged class and their favorites had the best of everything, including foods and wines, the use of vacation villas in the country or in the Crimea, or even the right to live in old czarist palaces and mansions. These privileges of the ruling group, however, were obtained at the cost of complete insecurity, for even the highest party officials were under constant surveillance by the secret police and were inevitably purged, exiled, or murdered.[27]

THE MODERN COMMUNIST STATE

Despite the media's depiction of the "destruction" of Soviet Communism, America would do well to be cautious before rushing once again to bail out the Bolsheviks. Communism is disintegrating because it is not a viable ideology, but merely a tool of repression. Although Communism may be dying, the hydra which spawned it will certainly manifest itself in other ways.

Of course, we know that it is not the legitimate demands of the working classes which drive revolutionary Communism, but the power of the millenia-old secret societies. The problem did not start with

Communism; it won't end with Communism. To view the problem as being invented a century or two ago, is to forfeit the ability to fully understand what it is that must be opposed. It was neither Marx, nor the philosopher Rousseau, who originated these theories. They have merely been two of its custodians:

> It is not then to the philosophers, but to the source whence they drew many of their inspirations, that the great dynamic force of the Revolution must be attributed. Rousseau and Voltaire were Freemasons....The organization of the Secret Societies was needed to transform the theorizings of the philosophers into a concrete and formidable system for the destruction of civilization.[30]

Although the eventual ascendency of the Antichrist to a position of global power is inevitable, the ascendency of Communism is certainly not. Every day that Communism's march toward global hegemony is retarded, is, in Christian terms, another day to rescue a few more souls from Satan's grasp and in political terms, another day to live in that uniquely gentle form of freedom found only in America.

TWELVE

CENTRAL BANKING, THE COUNCIL ON FOREIGN RELATIONS, AND FDR

So you see...the world is governed by very different personages from what is imagined by those who are not behind the scenes.

1844, Benjamin Disraeli, Prime Minister of Great Britain[1]

Throughout the twentieth century the implementation of the Great Plan became much more sophisticated, disguising itself behind a variety of advanced financial, political, and social engineering schemes. Protected from exposure by an increasingly subservient press, secret societies made dramatic strides toward establishing their New World Order.

In the United States, the political activities of these organizations were hidden under layer after layer of scholarly associations and foundations. Their domestic activities focused on gaining control of the American banking system and remaking the educational system.

On the financial front, the priority became the creation of a central banking system in America. The Rothschild banking family of Europe had learned hundreds of years earlier that once you control the credit of a nation, you control its economy. Carroll Quigley, professor of history at Georgetown, Princeton, and Harvard universities, wrote in 1966 in his book, *Tragedy and Hope*:

> The history of the last century shows...that the advice given to governments by bankers...was consistently good for bankers, but was often disastrous for governments, businessmen, and the people generally. Such advice could be enforced if necessary by manipulation

of exchanges, gold flows, discount rates, and even levels of business activity.[2]

Karl Marx certainly understood the importance of centralizing controls on credit and other monetary policies. The *Communist Manifesto* calls for "centralization of credit in the hands of the state, by means of a national bank with...an exclusive monopoly."[3]

Lenin said that the establishment of a central bank was ninety percent of communizing a country. These central banks are actually owned as private corporations. The Bank of England, Bank of France, and Bank of Germany were not owned by their respective governments, as almost everyone imagines, but by privately-owned monopolies granted by the heads of state, usually in return for loans.[4]

Certainly, the bankers involved in nationalization schemes were well aware of the power a central bank gave them and the outcry which would ensue if the public ever became aware of it. For example, Reginald McKenna, chancellor of the Exchequer of England in 1915-1916, and chairman of the board of the Midlands Bank of England, told his stockholders in January 1924:

> I am afraid the ordinary citizen will not like to be told that the banks can, and do, create money....And they who control credit of the nation direct the policy of Governments and hold in the hollow of their hands the destiny of the people.[5]

Unlike the European nations, America vigorously resisted the pressures to institute a central banking system. The nation was funded by thousands of completely independent, locally-owned banks, who valued their autonomy. Gaining control over these independent financiers was clearly a big job, but one that had to be undertaken if any group wanted to achieve effective financial control of the country.

In 1791, some fifty-six years before the writing of the *Communist Manifesto,* Congress established a central bank, the first Bank of the United States, and gave it a twenty-year charter. Twenty-five thousand shares were sold for $400 apiece. The federal government owned only twenty percent of these shares. Private individuals owned the rest. Rothschild interests owned such a substantial share that they were said to be "the power in the old Bank of the United States."

Interestingly, George Washington and Alexander Hamilton supported the Bank of the United States, but Thomas Jefferson opposed it. The bank's charter was not renewed in 1811 because state banks opposed central control. But, in 1816, Congress chartered the second Bank of the United States.[6]

Sixteen years later, in 1832, President Andrew Jackson killed the Bank of the United States by vetoing another renewal bill. The next year he withdrew U.S. funds from it completely, saying, "You are a den of thieves—vipers. I intend to rout you out and by the eternal God, I will rout you out." He stated that the Bank was a "money power," and a monopoly which "the rich and powerful" used to their exclusive advantage. In addition, he stated:

> Many of our rich men ... have besought us to make them richer by acts of Congress. By attempting to gratify their desires, we have [pitted] ... interest against interest, and man against man in a fearful commotion which threatens to shake the foundations of our Union.[7]

President Jackson openly accused the Bank of meddling in politics by granting loans to Congressmen to influence legislation,[8] and said that this amounted to a "bold effort" to control the government.[9] Supporters of the Bank were angered by Jackson's veto of a renewal of the Bank's charter after it passed both houses of Congress in the summer of 1832. They ran Henry Clay on the National-Republican ticket in the presidential election of that year to oppose Jackson and made the central bank a major issue. Jackson's decision had been a popular one, however, and he and Vice-President Martin Van Buren were swept to a stunning victory at the polls, and a decisive electoral college vote of 219 to 49.[10]

Jackson favored a "hard money" policy in which the country's currency would be backed by gold and silver. On January 8, 1835, Jackson paid off the final installment of the national debt. He was the only president ever to do so. For this, he is still recognized as a hero among fiscal conservatives.

Although Jackson killed the central bank and put the nation on a firm financial footing, the power of the international banking houses remained strong. Many sources believe that they financed the South's withdrawal from the Union, precipitating the Civil War some thirty years later. It has been suggested that Abraham Lincoln's death was the direct result of his refusal to accept the Rothschilds' offer to help finance the North during the war, as they were already doing for the South. One source even claims that the Rothschilds operated through Judah P. Benjamin, an agent to the South during the Civil War, to hire John Wilkes Booth to kill Lincoln.[11]

Lincoln perceived the corrupting influence of the international bankers and commented:

> I see in the near future a crisis approaching that unnerves me and causes me to tremble for the safety of my country; corporations have been enthroned, an era of corruption in high places will follow, and the money power of the country will endeavor to prolong its reign by working upon the prejudices of the people until the wealth is aggregated in a few hands, and the Republic destroyed.[12]

It is interesting to note that in 1925, the Ku Klux Klan announced that "Lincoln was assassinated by order of the Pope."[13] Equally interesting is that the Klan—according to Masonic researcher Paul A. Fisher in his treatise on the subject, *Behind the Lodge Door*—is tied directly to Freemasonry, the historic antagonist of Catholicism. In 1925, Klan Imperial Wizard Hiram W. Evans proclaimed in an article entitled "The Klan: Defender of Americanism" that the Catholic Church "has always opposed the fundamental principle of liberty."[14]

THE FEDERAL RESERVE SYSTEM

In early 1907, Jacob Schiff, the head of the New York investment firm Kuhn, Loeb & Co., sternly warned the New York Chamber of Commerce that if a central bank were not instituted, financial chaos would ensue. It is interesting to note that this was the same Jacob Schiff who had invested $20 million in the Bolshevik victory in Russia in 1917. Schiff said:

> Unless we have a Central Bank with adequate control of credit resources, this country is going to undergo the most severe and far reaching money panic in its history.

As researcher Des Griffen put it:

> the United States plunged into a monetary crisis that had all the earmarks of a skillfully planned Rothschild "job." The ensuing panic financially ruined tens of thousands of innocent people across the country—and made billions for the banking elite. The purpose for the "crisis" was two-fold: (1) To make a financial "killing" for the Insiders, and (2) To impress on the American people the "great need" for a central bank.[15]

Experts were sent to America from Europe to assist in the final push for the American central banking system. In 1907, Paul Warburg was sent from the Rothschild-allied German banking firm, The House of Warburg, to become a partner in America's most powerful banking firm, Kuhn, Loeb and Co. Warburg was paid the astronomical salary of $500,000 a year. One of Paul's brothers, Max, ran the family bank in Frankfurt, Germany, and was the head of the German Secret Police during World War I. Another brother, Felix, was married to the daughter of Jacob Schiff.

In the same year Paul Warburg came to the United States, a major banking panic struck the country. A bank run was started when J.P. Morgan spread rumors about the insolvency of a competitor bank. The 1907 panic caused Congress to establish a National Monetary Commission, headed by Senator Nelson Aldrich. Aldrich was known as the mouthpiece of the international bankers. His daughter married John D. Rockefeller, Jr., whose grandson, Nelson Aldrich Rockefeller, became vice-president in 1974.[17]

The Commission spent nearly two years studying the central banking system in Europe. According to researcher James Perloff, in 1910, Aldrich met secretly with Paul Warburg and top representatives of the Morgan and Rockefeller interests. This took place at Morgan's hunting club on Jekyll Island, off the coast of Georgia. There the plan was formulated for America's central bank ... the Federal Reserve.

Shortly thereafter, Aldrich introduced what was known as the Aldrich Bill to Congress, but it aroused enough suspicion to prevent the initial measure from passing. In 1913 it was re-introduced under a new name, the Federal Reserve Act. The Act created a new, privately owned central bank, and granted it complete control over interest rates and the size of the national money supply—an exclusive license to literally print money.

Shortly before Christmas, 1913, a weary Congress, anxious to adjourn, finally passed the Federal Reserve Act. Congressman Charles Lindbergh—the father of then eleven-year-old "Lucky Lindy" of *Spirit of St. Louis* fame—remarked that the act established the most gigantic trust on earth and legalized "the invisible government of the monetary power."[18]

Under its new name, America's central bank survived, and waxed ever stronger, despite continuing questions about its wisdom, or even legality. Even President Wilson acknowledged the dangers of the new banking system.

We have come to be one of the worst ruled, one of the most completely controlled governments in the civilized world—no longer a government of free opinion, no longer a government by...a vote of the majority, but a government by the opinion and duress of a small group of dominant men.[19]

But Wilson was also deeply troubled about an influence that was even more pervasive. In his book, *The New Freedom*, he wrote:

> Some of the biggest men in the United States, in the field of commerce and manufacture, are afraid of something. They know that there is a power somewhere so organized, so subtle, so watchful, so interlocked, so complete, so pervasive, that they had better not speak above their breath when they speak in condemnation of it.[20]

In 1971, *New York Times Magazine* reported that Congressman Louis McFadden, chairman of the House Committee on Banking and Currency from 1920 to 1931 remarked that the passage of the Federal Reserve Act brought about "a super-state controlled by international bankers and international industrialists acting together to enslave the world for their own pleasure."[21] In the 1960s, Congressman Wright Patman, former chairman of the House Banking Committee and a powerful critic of the central banking system agreed.

> In the United States today we have in effect two governments....We have the duly constituted Government....Then we have an independent, uncontrolled and uncoordinated government in the Federal Reserve System, operating the money powers which are reserved to Congress by the Constitution.[22]

Less than four years after its passage in 1913, with World War I in progress, the Federal Reserve loaned American dollars to the Soviet Communists immediately following the Russian revolution. As we will see, a similar injection of American cash occurred less than thirty years later during the next World War.

On June 15, 1933, Congressman McFadden explained to Congress what the Federal Reserve, along with the Rockefellers' Chase Bank (soon to merge with the Warburg's Manhattan Bank to form Chase-Manhattan Bank), had done on behalf of the fledgling Communist government.

The Soviet Government has been given United States Treasury funds by the Federal Reserve Board and the Federal Reserve Bank acting through the Chase Bank....you will be staggered to see how much American money has been taken from the United States Treasury for the benefit of Russia.[23]

At about the same time, Chase Bank began selling Bolshevik bonds in the U.S., but this outraged the American public. Patriotic organizations denounced the Chase Bank as an "international fence." Chase was called a "disgrace to America."[24]

The Federal Reserve System is now the United States' major creditor. Since 1835, when President Jackson paid off the national debt, it took 147 years for it to hit one trillion dollars. Then, it only took another four years to go to two trillion dollars.[25]

In 1989 the national debt hit three trillion dollars. The interest payments alone in fiscal 1989 amounted to more than $240 billion. The total amount collected from individual income taxes was only $445 billion.[27] In other words, more than half of what Americans pay in federal income taxes goes into the pockets of bankers. It is clear that the United States is literally at the mercy of a huge, private monopoly, controlled by a handful of unelected men.

ROUND TABLE GROUPS

This is all very interesting, but is there hard evidence linking international banking to secret societies? There seems to be. In the late 1800s, multi-millionaire diamond tycoon Cecil Rhodes and some of his wealthy British friends decided to form a secret society loosely based on the legends surrounding King Arthur and his Knights of the Round Table, but based on Masonic principles. The group, formed in 1891, consisted of an inner circle, including Rhodes, Lord Rothschild, and others, known as the "Circle of Initiates" and an outer circle which came to be known as the "Round Table."

What were the founding tenets of this exceedingly powerful new secret society? Rhodes took his cues from his mentor, John Ruskin, his professor of fine arts at Oxford University. Ruskin was a follower of the philosophies of Plato, and read Plato every day.

Of course Marx, Engels, Proudhon and Saint-Simon drank from that same fountain. Therefore, there is a remarkable parallel in the writings of Ruskin, Marx and other disciples of Plato. Plato wanted a ruling class with a powerful army to keep it in power and a society completely subordinate to the monolithic authority of the rulers. He also advocated using whatever force was necessary for the wiping out of all existing government and social structure so the new rulers could begin with a "clean canvas" on which to develop the portrait of their great new society.[28]

Plato's "ideal" society called for the elimination of marriage and the family so that all women would belong to all men, and vice-versa. Children were to be taken by the state and raised anonymously. He envisioned a society built of three classes: the ruling class, the military class, and the worker class. Private property would be eliminated and the ruling class would devote their intellectual energy to determining what was good for the masses in the working class.

Between 1909 and 1913, the Round Table group became international in scope. Semi-secret Round Table groups were established in America and in all the chief British dependencies to spread their gospel. These still function in eight countries.[29]

When Rhodes died in 1902, he left much of his fortune to the Rhodes Scholarship, a program he established to bring foreign students to Oxford and teach them his ruling class concepts. The rest of his fortune was left to his original Round Table group. Armed with this money and that of other loyal Rhodes supporters the Round Table formed an interlocking group in 1919 called the Royal Institute of International Affairs, as part of an ambitious program of international expansion. In the U.S., this group was known—and is still known—as the Council on Foreign Relations (CFR).

In the United States, some of the wealthiest of these men set up well-endowed foundations to study how to go about implementing the goals of the secret societies. These foundations have been extensively studied only once, in 1953-1954, as a direct outgrowth of the McCarthy hearings.

Professor Quigley was the Georgetown University history professor chosen by these secret societies—the twentieth-century inheritors of the Baconian/Atlantean concept—to write their view of history. But far from belittling the "anti-Communist" thrust of the McCarthy hearings, Quigley could see from his unique perspective that, if anything, they had not gone far enough. He wrote that the McCarthy hearings landed well short of the mark. Quigley gloated that the important revelation of the McCarthy hearings was not the exposure of a few "Red sympathizers," but the uncovering of the very heart of the problem.

Following backward to their source the threads which led from admitted Communists like Whittaker Chambers, through Alger Hiss, and the Carnegie Endowment to Thomas Lamont and the Morgan Bank, [a Congressional Committee] fell into the whole complicated network of the interlocking tax-exempt foundations.[30]

The McCarthy hearings led in July 1953 to the Special Committee to Investigate Tax-Exempt Foundations. Headed by Tennessee Representative B. Carroll Reece, this group made some truly shocking discoveries concerning the connections between Communism and American tax-exempt foundations, although they were virtually unreported in the nation's press. Professor Quigley explained:

> It soon became clear that people of immense wealth would be unhappy if the investigation went too far and that the "most respected" newspapers in the country, closely allied with these men of wealth, would not get excited enough about any revelations to make the publicity worth while....An interesting report showing the Left-wing associations of the interlocking nexus of tax-exempt foundations was issued in 1954 rather quietly.[31]

The Committee appointed Norman Dodd as its research director. Dodd was never pleased with the coverage of the story by the press and devoted much of his life to studying these foundations, trying in vain to bring the story to the attention of the public. Late in life he finally started making headway. In a radio interview on May 30, 1977 he explained that he studied foundations over a fifty-year span and discovered what their real purposes are:

> The oldest of the tax exempt foundations came into existence long before the income tax and the estate tax, therefore they had come into existence, not motivated as foundations subsequently were motivated, by tax savings. These foundations had a purpose unrelated to tax savings incentives.[32]

He found that these oldest foundations represented eighty-five percent of the total amount of capital in the nation's foundations. One of the oldest of these is the Carnegie Endowment for International Peace, set up in 1908. Dodd was allowed to examine the minutes of the Board of Trustees and found that for the first year the members concentrated on an academic discussion of whether there was any means more effective than war to alter the life of the people of a nation.

Obviously, altering the course of life in America was their goal. It is only natural to ask: Why? For what purpose? Apparently, this was in accordance with some larger plan that required a different America than was currently constituted. As we have seen, the chaos surrounding war is an ideal growth media for rapid change—malevolent change. Dodd wrote:

> That leads to question number two, which is "how do we involve the United States in a war?" This occurred around the beginning of 1909, and I doubt if there was any subject more removed from the minds of the American people at that time than the possibility of being involved in a war.[33]

According to Dodd, the members of the Carnegie group concluded that in order to get America into an upcoming war, they had to control the diplomatic machinery of the State Department. This agreed with information Dodd had already developed from other sources, which revealed that all high appointments in the State Department took place only after they had been cleared through something called the Council of Learned Societies, which was set up by the Carnegie Endowment for International Peace.[34]

It is interesting to note that Masons, writing in their journal, *New Age*, claimed that the cause of World War I was "a secret treaty" between the Vatican and Serbia. Then, when the treaty became known, Gavrilo Princep assassinated the Roman Catholic heir to the Austro-Hungarian throne, Archduke Franz Ferdinand.[35]

It was later shown that the assassin, Princep, and others of the plotters were Freemasons and members of the "Black Hand," a revolutionary organization affiliated with Freemasonry.[36]

Once World War I was underway, Dodd saw in the minutes of the Carnegie Board a note to President Wilson requesting that he "see to it that the War does not end too quickly."[37] Wilson campaign backer Bernard Baruch was appointed to head up the War Industries Board. He, like the Rockefellers, reaped profits of $200 million from the war.[38]

Dodd then saw memos in which Carnegie Foundation members were congratulating themselves on their success, in that the war had brought about a change in the American psyche. Syndicated columnist Joseph Kraft, writing in *Harper's* in July, 1958, says that records from the Carnegie Endowment for International Peace showed that their trustees hoped to involve the United States in a world war to set the stage for world government.[39]

Dodd also learned the truth for himself:

> This is where the power comes from—to bring the idea of "one-world [government]" to the point where it is acceptable to the people of this country. That is the primary aim, and everything that has happened since then is a means to that one end.[40]

Eventually, during his investigation for Congress, Dodd was asked by the president of the Ford Foundation, Rowan Gather, to come and visit. Gather said:

> Mr. Dodd, you were invited because we thought you would tell us why Congress was interested in the operations of foundations like ourselves. All of us at the executive and policy-making [level] here at the Foundation have had experience with the O.S.S. or the European Economic Administration. We operate here from directives which are issued from the White House. The substance of these directives is as follows: We shall use our grant-making power...to alter life in the United States so that we can be comfortably merged with the Soviet Union.[41]

Dodd was stunned. "I almost fell off my chair," he said. After the end of World War I, the Federal Reserve was lending millions to the new revolutionary Communist dictatorship in Russia which had recently taken power.

Why would some of the richest men in the world financially back Communism, the system that was openly vowing to destroy the so-called capitalism that made them wealthy? According to Gary Allen:

> If one understands that socialism is not a share-the-wealth program, but is in reality a method to consolidate and control the wealth, then the seeming paradox of super-rich men promoting socialism becomes no paradox at all. Instead, it becomes logical, even the perfect tool of power-seeking megalomaniacs. Communism, or more accurately, socialism, is not a movement of the downtrodden masses, but of the economic elite.[42]

In 1970 researcher W. Cleon Skousen wrote in his book *The Naked Capitalist*:

> Power from any source tends to create an appetite for additional power....It was almost inevitable that the super-rich would one day aspire to control not only their own wealth, but the wealth of the whole world. To achieve this, they were perfectly willing to feed the ambitions of the power-hungry political conspirators who were committed to the overthrow of all existing governments and the establishment of a central world-wide dictatorship.[43]

Skousen then asks a common-sense question. What if these revolutionaries get out of control and try to seize power from the super-rich? After all, it was Mao Tse-tung who in 1938 stated his position concerning power: "Political power grows out of the barrel of a gun."[44]

The secret society of the London-Wall Street axis elected to take the risk. The master-planners attempted to control revolutionary Communist groups by feeding them vast quantities of money when they obeyed, and then financing their opposition if they seemed to be getting out of control.[45]

LEAGUE OF NATIONS

During World War I, "influencial groups in the United States and Britain" decided at the war's end to push for the world's first international government, the League of Nations. The League's Covenant was given top priority at the post-World War I Paris Peace conference, which opened on January 18, 1919. Led by President Woodrow Wilson and his most trusted advisor, the mysterious Colonel House, conference organizers worked to ensure that the League would be powerful.

The peace treaty that came out of the Paris conference not only contained the League of Nations' Covenant, but gave the League responsibility for enforcing all its provisions. The world, however, was not yet ready for the notion of a world government.

Though the French tried to establish a League with its own army, completely led by generals who could move "against aggressors without the permission of the member states," and it was the stated policy of Great Britain to support the League, Lord Curzon, the foreign secretary, called the League of Nations "a good joke."[46]

To the humiliation of President Wilson, Colonel House, and the secret societies, the U.S. Congress wouldn't ratify U.S. membership in the League. From that point on, the League became virtually powerless and gradually atrophied until it was replaced by the United Nations in 1946.

In 1912 Colonel House published a novel entitled *Philip Dru: Administrator: A Story of Tomorrow*. Within its covers, we get an interesting view of what House's—and President Woodrow Wilson's—plans for America might have been. Of America, House wrote:

> America is the most undemocratic of democratic countries....Our Constitution and our laws served us well for the first hundred years of our existence, but under the conditions of to-day they are not only obsolete, but even grotesque.[47]

> Nowhere in the world is wealth more defiant, and monopoly more insistent than in this mighty republic...and it is here that the next great battle for human emancipation will be fought and won.[48]

House's solution for these vexing problems of capitalism was a revolution, which would install an omnipotent dictator after a bloody civil war. By these means alone, according to Colonel House's character, Philip Dru, could "Socialism as dreamed of by Karl Marx" be established in the United States.[49] House wished the same for Russia, which would see a Communist revolution only five years after his book was published.

There can be no doubt that Colonel House had the complete confidence of the international bankers. In fact, according to Professor Charles Seymour, who edited *The Intimate Papers of Colonel House*, it was said of House that he was the "unseen guardian angel" of the Federal Reserve Act. "The Schiffs, the Warburgs, the Kahns, the Rockefellers, and the Morgans had faith in House."[50]

THE COUNCIL ON FOREIGN RELATIONS

During the Paris Peace Conference, and less than six months after the end of World War I, the representatives of the major international banking groups met at the Majestic Hotel in Paris, France on May 19, 1919.[51] Central banks had been created in all the financially important nations, and now that Russia had been made safe for totalitarianism, the next important steps toward the implementation of the New World Order had to be decided upon.

The group agreed to set up something called the Institute of International Affairs, off shoots of which still exist throughout the world.

Disguised in this way, secret societies could work undetected. The Round Table Group and the Royal Institute of International Affairs existed on an interlocking basis.[52]

By 1921, Colonel House had written the charter for the American branch of the Round Table, which would be officially incorporated as "The Council on Foreign Relations," or CFR. The CFR has made no great attempt to hide its power-consolidating intentions, either domestically or internationally. In the second edition of their prestigious quarterly journal *Foreign Affairs*, published in September 1922, the Council stated:

> Obviously there is going to be no peace or prosperity for mankind as long as [America] remains divided into fifty or sixty independent states....Equally obviously there is going to be no steady progress in civilization...until some kind of international system is created which will put an end to the diplomatic struggles incident to the attempt of every nation to make itself secure....The real problem today is that of world government.[53]

Lenin was an admirer of *Foreign Affairs*. The CFR is now in possession of Lenin's original copy of the journal containing underscored passages in which he was particularly interested.[54]

In 1959, the CFR prepared a position paper entitled *Study No. 7, Basic Aims of U.S. Foreign Policy*, in which the United States is urged to "build a new international order," and to "maintain and gradually increase the authority of the U.N."[55] On December 23, 1961, columnist Edith Kermit Roosevelt, the granddaughter of President Theodore Roosevelt, wrote in the *Indianapolis News* about the CFR point of view:

> The best way to fight Communism is by a One World Socialist state governed by "experts" like themselves. The result has been policies which favor...gradual surrender of United States sovereignty to the United Nations.[56]

Admiral Chester Ward, former Judge Advocate General of the U.S. Navy, and former CFR member, wrote in 1975 that the goal of CFR was the "submergence of U.S. sovereignty and national independence into an all-powerful one-world government."[57] He also explained how the organization works:

> Once the ruling members of the CFR have decided that the U.S. Government should adopt a particular policy, the very substantial research facilities of CFR are put to work to develop arguments, intellectual and emotional, to support the new policy, and to confound and discredit, intellectually and politically, any opposition.[58]

The CFR is still the preeminent non-governmental foreign affairs organization in the United States. Its membership list is a virtual "Who's Who" in American politics. In 1987, by its own account, 318 of the 2,440 members of the CFR were current U.S. government officials.[59] In 1988 researcher James Perloff wrote in his book, *The Shadows of Power*, that since the founding of the CFR in 1921, no less than fourteen secretaries of state, fourteen treasury secretaries, and eleven defense secretaries have been CFR members.[60] Membership in the semi-secret group is extremely important—if not a mandatory credential for success in national politics, just as its progenitor, Masonry, was in the preceding centuries.

During the post-World-War I period, Masonry's power was at its zenith. In 1923, sixty-nine percent of the U.S. House of Representatives, and sixty-three percent of the U.S. Senate were Masons. By 1948, the number of Masons in Congress had dropped to fifty-four and fifty-three percent respectively.[61]

Today, Congressmen and Senators are getting more wary of Masonic connections. By 1984, the percentages had dropped to twelve and fourteen percent respectively, but those figures can no longer be trusted. One Congressman was awarded the thirty-third degree of Masonry in September 1987 in Boston, although neither his official biographical sketch for the *Congressional Directory*, nor the routine *curriculum vitae* handed out by his office mentions Masonic connections.[62]

After World War I, the American public had grown tired of the internationalist policies of Democrat Woodrow Wilson. In the presidential election of 1920, Republican Warren Harding won a landslide victory with sixty percent of the vote. Harding was an ardent foe of both Bolshevism and the League of Nations. His election opened a twelve-year run of Republican presidents in the White House that led to an era of unprecedented prosperity.[63]

Through the Roaring Twenties some eight billion dollars was sliced off the federal deficit incurred during the Wilson administration. James Perloff observed: "This atmosphere was apparently not to the liking of the Money Trust."[64]

In 1929, only nine months after the inauguration of Herbert Hoover, the third consecutive Republican president, the leaders of America's new secret society, the Council on Foreign Relations, engineered the Great Crash of 1929. The Crash was the most significant fruit of the new Federal Reserve—the system initiated to prevent such occurrences. Between 1923 and 1929, the Federal Reserve inflated the nation's money supply by sixty-two percent.[65] In the year before the crash, more than 500 banks failed nationwide. The stage was now set for disaster.

Louis McFadden, chairman of the House Banking Committee blamed the international bankers for the Crash:

> It was not accidental. It was a carefully contrived occurrence....The international bankers sought to bring about a condition of despair here so that they might emerge as rulers of us all.[66]

Curtis Dall, a broker for Lehman Brothers, later to head up the ultra-right wing Liberty Lobby in the 1970s, was on the floor of the New York Stock Exchange the day of the Crash. As he explained in *FDR: My*

Exploited Father-In-Law, published in 1970, the Crash was triggered by the planned sudden shortage of call money in the New York money market.[67]

Plummeting stock prices ruined many small investors, but the top "insiders," like John D. Rockefeller, Bernard Baruch, and Joseph P. Kennedy, made vast fortunes by getting out just before the Crash, then buying back in at wholesale prices afterwards. It is said that Kennedy's wealth grew twenty-five fold in the six years following the Crash. Paul Warburg had issued a tip in March 1929—seven months before the disaster—that the Crash was coming, and even brought Winston Churchill to the visitors' gallery on the day of the panic, perhaps to impress him with his power.[68]

Also in 1929, the Council on Foreign Relations moved into their new headquarters in New York City, at 45 East 65th Street, right next to the home of Franklin D. Roosevelt, the new governor of New York.[69]

Between 1929 and 1933, the Federal Reserve cut the money supply of the United States by one-third, thereby prolonging the depression which followed the Crash, through the balance of the Hoover administration. The Crash was widely blamed on Hoover, and so Roosevelt was swept into office in the 1932 presidential election.[70]

Roosevelt wasted no time in coming to the aid of the Bolsheviks. He was the first U.S. president to officially recognize the Soviet Union. In 1934, he took the U.S. off the gold standard, making America even more reliant on its blatantly political Federal Reserve System. By arbitrarily jacking up the price of gold from $20 per ounce to $35 per ounce he made huge profits for the international banking community.

To pull the nation out of the depression, Roosevelt immediately turned to the Federal Reserve to borrow the money needed from the same bankers who engineered it in the first place. A huge variety of social programs soon emerged, making Roosevelt a hero to the common man. The price was that Roosevelt's socialistic government gained unprecedented control over American life. The vilified Hoover bitterly wrote in his memoirs that Roosevelt's programs were "pure fascism."[71]

With the Democratic Party firmly in hand, and war looming in Europe, the Money Trust, as it was called at the time, were taking no chances. They wanted their candidate nominated to oppose Roosevelt from the Republican side. The unknown Wendell Willkie, a former Democrat with no previous political experience, was steamrolled into the Republican presidential nomination. A fuming Republican Congressman, Usher Burdick, said on the floor of the House a few months before the November 1940 election:

> We Republicans in the West want to know if Wall Street...and the international bankers control our party and can select our candidate?...There is nothing to the Willkie boom for President except

the artificial public opinion being created by newspapers, magazines, and the radio. The reason back of all this is money. Money is being spent by someone, and lots of it.[72]

After Willkie's loss in the election, Roosevelt was most gracious toward his former opponent. He sent him on an around-the-world trip as his unofficial envoy in 1942. After his return, he wrote his infamous book, *One World*, which, of course, stressed international cooperation and denounced the American isolationism which had for so long kept the United States out of World War II.[73]

In a 1940 Gallup poll, eighty-three percent of Americans were against entering into World War II. It was President Roosevelt's task to somehow get America interested.

At this point there can be little doubt that both FDR and his military chief of staff, General George Marshall, were aware that a huge Japanese armada was headed to attack Pearl Harbor in December 1941. A growing body of evidence now shows that numerous warnings were given to both FDR and General Marshall by many credible, official sources that the attack was imminent. Perhaps most damning of these was the warning from U.S. Naval Intelligence the day before the attack that an armada of Japanese carriers was sighted only 400 miles northwest of Honolulu.[74]

Despite all this, no warning was sent to our armed forces stationed at Pearl Harbor. Not only did FDR and Marshall allow the attack to happen, they took steps to increase its effectiveness, such as stripping the island of most of its air defenses shortly before the raid, and allotting only one-third the surveillance planes needed to have detected it in advance.[75]

THIRTEEN

WORLD WAR II AND THE
COMMUNIST AFTERMATH

Adolph Hitler was directly connected to both the darkest aspects of German occult secret societies and the more refined, financier-oriented groups. Virtually all writers on Hitler mention his fondness for the occult. According to author Joseph Carr, "We know that Hitler and his top luminaries were either dabblers in the occult, or, outright satanists."[1]

According to Carr, as a youth Hitler was influenced by at least two Austrian magicians. The first, George Lanz von Liebenfels, lived in Vienna, Austria at the same time that the youthful Hitler did. Liebenfels founded an organization called "The Order of the New Templars" in Vienna around 1907, and chose the swastika as the emblem for his new organization. This group was nothing more than a modern German version of the Knights Templar.[2]

In a 1932 letter to a new initiate of his New Templars lodge, Liebenfels wrote that Hitler was one of his pupils, and one day he would "develop a movement that will make the world tremble."[3] But once Hitler ascended to power, he became fearful of his former occult friends and teachers. After 1938, when the Nazis invaded Austria, Liebenfels was forbidden to write anything for publication. It seems that Hitler felt particularly vulnerable to those from whom he had gained his own occult knowledge.

When the concentration camps opened after 1933, Freemasons and other occultists were found to have been imprisoned along with Jews.[4] In Germany alone, the number of Masons plummeted from 80,000 at the ascent of Hitler to power in 1933, to only 4,000 left alive at the end of World War II.[5] Fifty years later, Masons still see this atrocity as a badge of martyrdom, and offer it as proof of their righteousness.

Hitler feared and persecuted Masons just as any dictator would persecute any other secretive center of power. But Hitler's personal occultism continued. He practiced ritual magic, and held massive rallies filled with repetitive Nazi chants to invoke the gods of war. He knew the power of ritual. Like the "meaningless repetitions" of prayer warned of in Scripture, or the mantras of the Eastern occultists, rote repetitions will "become truths in themselves with little process of thought."[6]

Hitler's rise to power was financed by a curious combination of major German, British, and American banks and steel companies, including U.S. Steel. This is well documented in the book *I Paid Hitler*, published in 1941 and written by Germany's leading industrialist Fritz Thyssen. Thyssen, chairman of Germany's United Steel Works, was a German nationalist. He saw the Bolsheviks as a threat to Germany and sincerely believed that Hitler was the answer to their defeat.

He broke from Hitler and fled Germany in 1939 after Hitler's pact with Stalin allowed the invasion of Poland that September. It was no surprise to Thyssen that the West wanted Hitler to come to power. He stated in his book:

> Hitler rearmed Germany to an incredible degree and at an unheard-of-speed. The Great Powers closed their eyes to this fact. Did they really not recognize the danger, or did they wish to ignore it?[7]

The German chemical giant, I.G. Farben, received, after World War I, a $30 million loan from the Rockefellers' National City Bank. They quickly grew to be the largest chemical concern in the world. After World War II, a U.S. War Department investigation revealed that without I.G. Farben's immense resources, "Germany's prosecution of the war would have been unthinkable and impossible."[8]

In 1939, as the Nazis were poised to attack Western Europe, the Rockefellers' Standard Oil of New Jersey sold $20 million in aviation fuel to I.G. Farben. James Perloff points out that among the board of directors of I.G. Farben's American subsidiary, American I.G., was CFR founder Paul Warburg. According to Perloff:

> There were also several Germans on the board of American I.G.; after the war, three of them were found guilty of war crimes at the Nuremburg trials, but none of the Americans were ever prosecuted.[9]

Hitler was rabidly anti-Semitic. Although I will not attempt to explain that here, I wish to divest this book of any hint of anti-Semitism. Many in "conservative" circles today persist in their dogmatic claims that Jews are the source of evil in the world. Others claim that it is not the Jews, in general, who are evil, but only the Zionists. In any case, many still attribute the evils committed by international banking interests in particular, and secret societies in general, to a "Jewish conspiracy," using the discredited *Protocols of the Learned Elders of Zion* as source material. But W. Cleon Skousen, writing in *The Naked Capitalist* in 1970, gave what is probably one of the most accurate assessments on the subject:

> While the Rothschilds and certain other Jewish families cooperated together in these ventures, this was by no means a Jewish monopoly as some have alleged. Neither was it a "Jewish conspiracy." As we shall see, men of finance of many nationalities and many religious or non-religious backgrounds collaborated together to create the super-structure of economic and political power [under discussion].
>
> No student of the global conspiracy should fall for the Hitlerian doctrine that the root of all evil is a super "Jewish conspiracy." Nor should they fall for that long-since-discredited document The Protocols of the Learned Elders of Zion, which Hitler palmed off on the German people as an authentic declaration of policy by an all-Jewish congress....this infiltration of the Jewish community is no more applicable to the Jewish people as a whole than the scurrilous left-wing activities of the National and World Councils of Churches is a reflection on all Protestants.[10]

Although Hitler lost the war, the goal of Illuminism to establish a world government remained. If Hitler had been able to win World War II, and achieve world domination, then the goal would have been realized much more quickly. But though Hitler lost, Russia was able to gobble up Eastern Europe, and half of Germany, thanks to the maneuvering of secret societies in the United States and England. Millions of innocent lives were lost, much of Europe was destroyed, but the international financiers and industrialists profited greatly.

LEND LEASE SCANDAL

President Franklin D. Roosevelt helped set the stage for the next war by building the Soviets into a "super-power." In what may someday be recognized as a significant spy scandal of World War II, Roosevelt administration officials gave the Soviets the secrets of, and apparently even the materials, to build the atomic bomb.

Unbelievable, you might say. But the fact remains that it was the active participation of top White House staffers of President Franklin D. Roosevelt, if not the president himself, which allowed the Soviets to get the atom bomb, years before American scientists predicted they would be able to develop it on their own.

A little-known book sheds new light on this incredible, yet virtually unknown case of high-level atomic espionage in the Roosevelt administration. Entitled *Major Jordan's Diaries*, it was written by Air Force Major George Racey Jordan, and published in 1952.

Jordan worked as a supply expediter and liaison officer from May 1942 to June 1944 at both Newark Airport in New Jersey, and the big air base at Great Falls, Montana, which was the primary staging area for the massive supply operation to the Soviet Union known as Lend-Lease.

Thanks to Major Jordan's book, it can be said with authority that during World War II, the United States built the war machine of the Soviet Union. So great was the magnitude of this "aid" to what was at best only our temporary ally, that it is impossible to believe that it was all just some sort of miscalculation, or mistake, on the part of the Roosevelt administration.

Major Jordan became suspicious of the magnitude of material being sent to the Soviets, and in his capacity as Liaison Officer began keeping a diary of what was being ferried to them via the Alaska-Siberia route.

Although Jordan knew nothing about atomic bombs, he knew that his counterpart, a Soviet colonel named Kotikov, kept a very special file on one corner of his desk in Great Falls, Montana, that he referred to as his "bomb powder" factory. Colonel Kotikov was known as the "Soviet Lindbergh" because he was the first to fly a seaplane from Moscow to Seattle along the polar cap.

Jordan kept meticulous records on the materials for the bomb powder factory, as he did on all materials shipped.

> These materials, which are necessary for the creation of an atomic pile, moved to Russia in 1942:
>
> Graphite: natural, flake, lump or chip...$812,43....Aluminum tubes (used in the atomic pile to "cook" or transmute the uranium into plutonium)...$13,041,152. We sent 834,989 pounds of cadmium metal for rods to control the intensity of an atomic pile; the cost was $781,472. The really secret material, thorium, finally showed up and started going through immediately. The amount during 1942 was 13,440 pounds at a cost of $22,848.[11]

Jordan reported that on January 30, 1943, 11,912 pounds of thorium nitrate was shipped to Russia from Philadelphia on the S.S. *John C. Fremont*.[12] A year later, General Groves, the security-conscious head of the U.S. A-bomb project, discovered the thorium shipments, and was able to stem the flow of this vital material.[13]

Another problem recounted by Major Jordan with the Lend-Lease "pipeline" was the entry of Soviet personnel into the United States.

Major General Follette Bradley, USAF (Ret.), winner of the Distinguished Service Medal, wrote about this incident to the *New York Times* which published his letter on Aug. 31, 1951:

> Of my own personal knowledge I know that beginning early in 1942 Russian civilian and military agents were in our country in huge numbers. They were free to move about without restraint or check and, in order to visit our arsenals, depots, factories and proving grounds, they had only to make known their desires. Their authorized visits to military establishments numbered in the thousands. I personally know that scores of Russians were permitted to enter

American territory in 1942 without visa. I believe that over the war years this number was augmented at least by hundreds.[14]

In early 1943, Major Jordan became suspicious of an unusual number of black patent-leather suitcases, bound with white window-sash cord and sealed with red wax, which were coming through on the route to Moscow. These suitcases were said to be of a diplomatic nature and so Jordan was not supposed to open them under any circumstances. One night in March, the Russians took Jordan out to dinner, and the sudden display of friendliness made him suspicious. He called back to the airfield to see if there was any unusual activity going on.

Sure enough, two Russian special couriers had just arrived from Washington and were demanding a plane for Russia with about fifty of the mysterious black leather suitcases in tow. Jordan gave his hosts the slip and drove at top speed for the airfield, only four miles away. With an armed sentry for protection, and against the will of the shrieking Soviet couriers, Jordan opened about one-third of the suitcases, and took a cursory look inside.

In the dim light of a single incandescent bulb, in the dome of the cabin of the requisitioned C-47, Jordan saw that the destination stamped on the cases read: "Director, Institute of Technical and Economic Information" in Moscow. The suitcases were filled with a wide assortment of items, such as common service-station road maps with industrial sites marked on them. Other documents related to classified military facilities, such as the Aberdeen Proving Grounds, one of the most sensitive areas in the war effort.

Another suitcase contained engineering and scientific papers, bristling with formulas, calculations, and professional jargon. Also in this case was a handwritten note on White House stationary addressed to "Mikoyan." Jordan wrote, "By questioning Colonel Kotikov later, I learned that A.I. Mikoyan at the moment was Russia's No. 3 man, after Premier Stalin and Foreign Commissar Molotov. He was Commissar of Foreign Trade and Soviet boss of Lend-Lease."[15]

The first word of the note was a person's first name, but it was not legible. The message, however was, "_____, had a hell of a time getting these away from Groves." The message was signed "H.H.," the frequently-used abbreviation for Harry Hopkins, the former Secretary of Commerce, and then head of President Roosevelt's Lend-Lease program.

Clipped to this note to Molotov from Harry Hopkins was a large map which bore the legend "Oak Ridge, Manhattan Engineering District," and a carbon copy of a report from Oak Ridge, with the name "Harry Hopkins" typed on it, as though it was a copy specifically prepared for Hopkins.

The text of the report contained words Major Jordan was unfamiliar with then, but which we all know today. Among them were "uranium," "cyclotron," "proton," and "deuteron."[16]

Of course, Colonel Kotikov was furious with Major Jordan, and Jordan assumed he would be fired. But surprisingly, he was allowed to stay on. Although Jordan reported everything that had transpired to the intelligence section of the Air Force, he heard nothing in return.

In April 1943, Colonel Kotikov asked if room could be made for an extra-special consignment of what he called "experimental chemicals." Major Jordan told him he could not because they were backlogged a quarter million pounds already. Jordan says Kotikov got on the telephone and rang up Harry Hopkins personally, to tell Major Jordan to expedite the shipments. "It was quite a moment. I was about to speak for the first time with a legendary figure of the day, the top man in the world of Lend-Lease in which I lived."[17]

After a few opening questions, Jordan recounts his conversation with Hopkins as follows:

> H.H. - "Now Jordan, there's a certain shipment of chemicals going through that I want you to expedite. This is something very special."

> Col. Jordan - "Shall I take it up with the Commanding Colonel?"

> H.H. - "I don't want you to discuss this with anyone, and it is not to go on the records. Don't make a big production of it, but just send it through quietly, in a hurry."[18]

After his conversation was terminated with the infamous Harry Hopkins, Jordan asked Colonel Kotikov what the name of this important chemical was. Colonel Kotikov went to his desk and pulled from a folder marked "Bomb Powder" a sheet of paper and showed Major Jordan a word he had first seen the previous month, in the black leather suitcase—"uranium." Jordan wrote:

> This shipment was the one and only cash item to pass through my hands, except for private Russian purchases of clothing and liquor. It was the only one, out of a tremendous multitude of consignments, that I was ordered not to enter on my tally sheets. It was the only one I was forbidden to discuss with my superiors, and the only one I was directed to keep secret from everybody.[19]

Despite the urgent requests of Mr. Hopkins, the shipment of uranium did not arrive from Canada for five weeks. When it did, it arrived by train in fifteen wooden cases. The cases were trucked to the airbase at Great Falls and took off for Fairbanks without a hitch.

But at Fairbanks, one box fell from the plane, smashing a corner and spilling a small quantity of chocolate-brown powder. Out of curiosity, a soldier there picked up a handful of the unfamiliar grains, with a notion of asking somebody what they were. A Soviet officer slapped the crystals from his palm and explained nervously, "No, no—burn hands!"

Totally, three consignments of uranium chemicals, 1,465 pounds, or nearly three-quarters of a ton were shipped to the Soviet Union. In addition, one kilogram, or 2.2 pounds, of uranium metal was shipped at a time when the total American stock was 4.5 pounds.[20] Major Jordan also documented in his meticulous style that even 1,000 grams of precious deuterium oxide, or "heavy water," was sold to the Soviets in November 1943. "If General Groves had been consulted, the heavy water would never have left this country. Had it been known at the time...that 1,000 grams were available, unquestionably he would have bought the treasure himself."[21]

Jordan says that he was shocked when he later discovered what uranium was used for. On September 23, 1949, President Truman announced that the Soviet Union had exploded an atomic device. Lamented Jordan, "There seemed to be no lengths to which some American officials would not go in aiding Russia to master the secret of nuclear fission."[22]

After the war, Major Jordan told his story to several congressional investigating committees, which led to a personal attack on him by Professor Harold C. Urey, an American scientist, who sat in the innermost circle of the Manhattan Project. On December 14, 1949, in a report of the Atlantic Union Committee, Dr. Urey said that Major Jordan should be court-martialed if he had removed anything from planes bound for Russia.

Although Julius and Ethel Rosenberg were convicted in 1951, and executed for the crime of passing atomic bomb secrets to a Soviet courier, there is substantial evidence that higher-level espionage was being conducted by President Roosevelt's assistant, Harry Hopkins.

In one final outrage, if our shipping the Soviets the uranium, and all the other materials to get their infant bomb production capacity off the ground weren't enough, Major Jordan revealed that even printing plates for the money the Americans printed for Germany after the war were sent to the Russians. Colonel Kotikov told Jordan during his last week on the job that a "money plane" had crashed in Siberia and had been replaced.

When Jordan asked what he meant by a "money plane," Kotikov told him that engraving plates and other materials had been shipped to Russia so the Soviets could print the same money, backed by the U.S. Treasury, that the Americans were. Jordan was incredulous:

> I was certain he was mistaken. I was quite sure that never in history had we let money plates go out of the country. How could there be any control over their use? "You must mean, Colonel, that we have printed German occupation money for Russia and shipped the currency itself."

> "No, no," he replied. He insisted that plates, colored inks, varnish, tint blocks, sample paper—these and similar materials had gone

through Great Falls in May in two shipments of five C-47s each. The shipments had been arranged on the highest level in Washington, and the planes had been loaded at the National Airport [near Washington, D.C.].[23]

The United States' taxpayers apparently lost, by the best figures available, approximately $250,000,000 until the U.S. Treasury stopped redeeming the German marks in September 1946, with no accountability whatsoever.

Some of the other items sent to the Soviets, and later described by an outraged General Groves as "purely post-war Russian supplies," were 121 merchant ships worth $123 million; 1,285 locomotives worth $103 million; motor trucks and buses worth $508 million; tractors worth $24 million; telephones worth $33 million; generators worth $222 million; and more than 2.5 million automobile inner tubes worth $6,659,880.

Professor Antony Sutton of Stanford University's Hoover Institution observed in his authoritative *Western Technology and Soviet Economic Development, 1917-1930*:

> Stalin paid tribute to the assistance rendered by the United States to Soviet industry before and during the war. He said that about two-thirds of all the large industrial enterprise in the Soviet Union had been built with United States help or technical assistance.[24]

The revelation by Major Jordan of these shipments to Russia sparked an investigation in June 1947 by Senator Styles Bridges, chairman of the Committee on Appropriations. At a closed hearing, Assistant Secretary of War Howard C. Peterson admitted that as far as he knew Russia still had the plates and was still printing currency:[25]

> The American people are bound to the people of the Soviet Union in the great alliance of the United Nations. We are determined that nothing shall stop us from sharing with you all that we have.[26]

As interesting and specific as all this information is, however, it is not all that President Roosevelt "did" for America.

In the twelve years during which he occupied the White House, FDR probably did more than any other single politician in history to bring to fruition the plans of the New World Order.

WORLD WAR II

With Lend-Lease, Roosevelt gave the Soviets as much as he could steal from the bounty of the American industrial and scientific community. In addition, he had the job of trying to insure that the Soviets would gain as much European territory as possible during the chaos at the end of World War II. To some this is an outrageous charge, but the facts speak for themselves.

By May of 1943, the Allies had pushed the Germans out of Africa. On June 11, they invaded Sicily, and on September 3, 1943, Allied forces swept into Italy. But suddenly and inexplicably, the brakes were applied to Allied troops only a few hundred miles from Germany's southern border. The "tremendous fighting machine," as General Mark Clark called the Allied army, headed north through Italy and was broken up, prolonging the war by many months. In his 1950 book, *Calculated Risk*, General Clark stated:

> A campaign that might have changed the whole history of relations between the Western World and Soviet Russia was permitted to fade away....These were decisions made at high level and for reasons beyond my field and my knowledge....Not only in my opinion, but in the opinion of a number of experts who were close to the problem, the weakening of the campaign in Italy...instead of pushing into the Balkins was one of the outstanding political mistakes of the war....

> It is incomprehensible why divisions were withdrawn from the front," according to one German general whom we interviewed after the war. "Whatever the reasons, it is sure they all accrued to the benefit of the German High Command. [27]

This delay, supposedly designed to save troops for a coming Allied invasion in northern France some nine months later, gave the Soviets time to push the German troops that had invaded Russia, as part of Operation Barbarossa two years earlier, out of Russia and back across Eastern Europe. After all, it was not until January 1945 that the Soviets entered Warsaw; February 13 that they entered Budapest, Hungary; and April 13, 1945 before they entered Vienna, Austria.

Other sources seem to bear this theory out. Apparently, the decision to withdraw fighting divisions from the Italian front, just as they were headed for the soft underbelly of Germany, was made at an Allied conference in Quebec in 1943. Here, Churchill wanted to drive right into Germany from the south, "and bring the Central European and Balkan countries under Allied control, before they were allowed to slip into Red slavery. This policy would have led to a genuine Allied victory and the fulfillment of the original declared aims of the war."[28]

But Churchill was overridden by the Americans who "insisted that troops be withdrawn from Italy and used in a secondary invasion of France ...."[29] After the June 1944 Normandy invasion of France, the Allied armies were placed under a fast-rising General Eisenhower, a soon-to-be member of the Council on Foreign Relations.[30] During the months that followed, the Allied armies, under the direction of Eisenhower, made a leisurely advance towards Germany on a sprawling front.[31]

On the Eastern front, the Soviets felt little hesitancy. Professor Quigley wrote:

> The Soviet advance became a race with the Western Powers, even though these Powers, by Eisenhower's orders, held back their advance at many points (such as Prague) to allow the Russians to occupy areas the Americans could easily have taken first."[32]

And what was the effect of this policy on the nations swallowed by the Soviet advance? The former ambassador to Hungary at that time, John F. Montgomery, wrote about the Russian occupation in his book entitled *Hungary, The Unwilling Satellite*:

> It was a period of calculated destruction. The Russian method of occupation follows a certain pattern necessitated by the difference between the East and West in standards of living.
>
> After a spearhead of disciplined troops which destroys any remaining opposition, propaganda shock troops arrive. Their job is to destroy all evidence of higher than Russian standards of living in enemy territory, before the ordinary soldier appears upon the scene. A man who eats at a table and sleeps on a bed is considered a bourgeois. Boxes are to be substituted for tables and straw for beds. In Hungary such a policy meant destruction of workers' and peasants' homes as well as those of the wealthy classes.[33]

Stories of Russian depravity were legion. Russian troops behaved with a frenzy that hasn't been surpassed in intensity since the commencement of human history. There will, of course, be those who will apologize for Eisenhower, saying that he was only following orders handed down by his superiors.

Although the new secret society of the Council on Foreign Relations was now in the driver's seat, the traditional secret societies still played some role. Rev. Jim Shaw, a thirty-third-degree Mason who left the organization in the 1970s and wrote *The Deadly Deception* made an interesting observation to a reporter who interviewed him in 1989. Concerning the famous picture of Roosevelt, Churchill, and Stalin at the Yalta conference, Rev. Shaw said: "And there they were, Roosevelt, Churchill and Stalin—all three Masons."[34]

French Masonry has honored Roosevelt by naming a lodge, to which the current French president belongs, after him. Roosevelt was a thirty-second degree Mason, a Knight Templar, and a member of the mystic Shrine. In 1933, FDR, dressed in the regalia of the Georgia Grand Lodge of Masons, raised his son, Elliot, to the degree of Master Mason at Architect Lodge 519 in New York City.[35]

Support for both secret societies and Marxism has run in FDR's family. His ancestor, Clinton B. Roosevelt, a New York assemblyman, was a noted American Socialist. He authored *The Science of Government Founded in Natural Law* wherein he outlined his plan for setting up a world government. He and his friend, Horace Greeley, founder and owner of *The New York Tribune* and *New Yorker* magazine, both participated in leftist social engineering schemes in America. One was called "Brook Farm."

Roosevelt was surrounded by members of the various Communist movements which were spread throughout America at the time of the Bolshevik Revolution. At the Yalta and the Tehran conference, where the acquisition of half of Europe by the Soviets was formalized by treaty after World War II, who was Roosevelt's top advisor? Alger Hiss, a member of the Council on Foreign Relations who was later convicted of espionage as a Soviet spy.[36]

Stalin, Roosevelt & Churchill: all three were Masons
(courtesy of the Library of Congress)

Roosevelt didn't seem to care about his Communist connections. On one occasion, he made the following statement to Martin Dies, chairman of a special House committee on un-American activities, and Dies testified to it before Congress:

> I do not believe in communism any more than you do, but there is nothing wrong with the communists in this country. Several of the best friends I have are communists.[37]

In February, 1953, the official publication of the Grand Lodge of New York entitled, "Empire State Mason," concluded that if the New World Order ever comes into being, then Franklin Delano Roosevelt should get much of the credit.[38] James Perloff noted:

> Only the Communists acquired something from World War II: Eastern Europe, and a foothold in Asia. The war had a commonly overlooked irony. It was begun to save Poland from conquest by Germany. Yet when it was over, Poland had been acquired anyway— by the Soviets.[39]

Did the secret societies lose the inside track after the death of Roosevelt? Hardly. It is well known that his successor, Harry Truman, was a Mason. A beautiful portrait of Truman dressed in full Masonic garb is still displayed in Masonic lodges throughout the United States.

When Roosevelt died unexpectedly, former Missouri senator and vice-president Harry S. Truman was thrust into the limelight. In the eyes of the CFR, Truman was more than a bit unprepared for the job, but under its watchful tutelege, he blossomed quickly and dependably.

Within six months, in late 1945, President Truman dispatched General Marshall to China on an emergency mission. The Nationalist regime of Chinese leader Chiang Kai-shek had been a faithful ally of the United States. Chiang had been fighting a bitter war with Chinese Communists, led by Mao Tse-tung, for four years. Stalin had secretly agreed with Roosevelt to redirect some of the Lend-Lease supplies sent by the United States to Mao, to help the Communist cause there. Despite this, Chiang had fought well and was about to deliver the Communists a crushing debacle.[40]

Marshall's job was to literally snatch victory from the jaws of defeat. Marshall, like Eisenhower, was an obscure colonel until FDR's presidency, when he rose past dozens of senior officers to become Chief of Staff.

Threatening to withdraw U.S. support, Marshall negotiated truces with the Communists against Chiang's will. He was then forced to accept Communists into his government. Finally, after Mao had time to regroup and began to seize more territory, Marshall slapped a weapons embargo on the faithful and bewildered Chiang.[41]

From that point on, the CFR propaganda line repeated ad-nauseum in the American press was that Chiang was a corrupt dictator, while Mao was an "agrarian reformer." This propaganda was disseminated by the CFR affiliate for Far Eastern affairs, the Institute of Pacific Relations (IPR).[42]

In 1952, the FBI raided the offices of their journal *Amerasia*, and later reported to the Senate Judiciary Committee:

> The Institute of Pacific Relations was a vehicle used by the Communists to orient American Far Eastern policies toward Communist objectives. Members of the small core of officials and staff members who controlled IPR were either Communist or pro-Communist.[43]

In 1948, Congress voted $125 million in military aid to Chiang, but the Truman administration managed to bog it down in red tape until Chiang's defeat. He fled to Taiwan where he made it a bastion of freedom that out-produced the entire Chinese mainland. Mao, on the other hand, instituted a Communist dictatorship and slaughtered tens of millions of victims in countless, bloody purges.

On January 25, 1949, Congressman John F. Kennedy made an impassioned speech on the floor of the House. He said the responsibility for the China debacle rested "squarely with the White House and the Department of State. The continued insistence that aid would not be forthcoming, unless a coalition government with the Communists were formed, was a crippling blow to the National Government."[44]

James Perloff stated in *Shadows of Power* that there would never have been a Korean War were it not for the machinations of Roosevelt and his CFR political ideologues that brought Russia into the Pacific theater.

When North Korea troops attacked across the thirty-eighth parallel, Truman and Marshall did whatever they could to aid their advance. Believe it or not, after General MacArthur drove the North Koreans back to the Yalu River, Truman actually ordered the U.S. Navy to prevent Chaing's military from attacking mainland China. This allowed China to send all its forces into battle across the Yalu River.

As if that weren't enough, to halt the Chinese advance, MacArthur ordered the Yalu's bridges bombed. Within hours, General Marshall countermanded that order! MacArthur was furious:

> I realized for the first time that I had actually been denied the use of my full military power to safeguard the lives of my soldiers and the safety of my army...it...left me with a sense of inexpressible shock.[45]

According to MacArthur's memoirs, General Lin Piao, commander of Chinese forces in Korea, would later comment:

> I never would have made the attack and risked my men and my military reputation if I had not been assured that Washington would restrain General MacArthur from taking adequate retaliatory measures against my lines of supply and communication.[46]

THE UNITED NATIONS

On April 25, 1945, just thirteen days after the death of Roosevelt, and twelve days before the surrender of Germany, fifty nations met in San Francisco to consider the new United Nations Charter. In attendance were at least forty-seven CFR members among the American delegates, including Alger Hiss and Harry Dexter White, both of whom would later be uncovered as Soviet spies. Also included in the entourage were such notables as Nelson Rockefeller and John Foster Dulles.[47]

The Communist Party USA strongly supported the United Nations idea. In the April 1945 edition of their official theoretical journal, *Political Affairs*, the marching orders were given:

> Great popular support and enthusiasm for the United Nations policies should be built up, well organized and fully articulate. But it is also necessary to do more than that. The opposition must be rendered so impotent that it will be unable to gather any significant support in the Senate against the United Nations Charter and the treaties which will follow.[48]

On June 26, 1945, President Harry Truman signed the new United Nations Charter. On December 14, 1946, the U.N. accepted a gift of $8.6 million from John D. Rockefeller, Jr., to buy the eighteen acres of land along the East River in New York City upon which their current building sits. The next year, the U.S. Congress approved a $65 million interest-free loan to finance the construction of the U.N. buildings.

As banker James Warburg, the son of Council on Foreign Relations' founder Paul Warburg, confidently told the United States Senate on February 17, 1950: "We shall have world government whether or not we like it. The only question is, whether world government will be achieved by conquest or consent."[49]

FOURTEEN

THE PRESENT

Although World War II ended in 1945 with the American public thoroughly tired of hostilities, conquest by force of arms did not. The Soviet Communists not only swept up half of Europe, but went after a substantial part of the rest of the world as well, many times under the banner of their newly created United Nations. With Roosevelt's stamp of approval, and Truman's tacit approval, Communism made great strides on many fronts. Obviously, Communists thought their New World Order was within relatively easy grasp if only they could move quickly enough before America woke up to the deception.

Few Americans had the political sophistication to see through the sham. Foremost among those who did was the brilliant American general George S. Patton, who at one point announced that he was fully prepared to drive his Third Army straight to the heart of Moscow to rout out the Bolsheviks. Unfortunately, General Patton died prematurely in 1945 in a freak automobile accident in Germany.

In 1950, a Republican Senator from Wisconsin, Joseph McCarthy, made allegations that the State Department was harboring Communists. President Truman, a Democrat, and Secretary of State Dean Acheson denied McCarthy's charges, but many Americans believed they were true.

By 1953, when General Dwight D. Eisenhower became president, McCarthy accused his administration of treason. By 1954, nationally televised hearings were underway to air the accusations. During these hearings, McCarthy, also claimed that there was a deep-penetration Soviet spy network at work in America.

As we have seen, calling the CFR's machinations a spy network is hardly appropriate. Some are probably spies in the traditional sense. Many are deluded idealists. But to view it in traditional terms of nation against nation is to play the game the way those who are the real enemies of America want it played. In 1966, Carroll Quigley of Georgetown University explained:

> There does exist, and has existed for a generation, an international Anglophile network which operates, to some extent, in the way the radical Right believes the Communists act. In fact, this network, which we may identify as the Round Table Groups, has no aversion to cooperating with the Communists, or any other groups, and frequently does so. I know of the operations of this network because I have studied it for twenty years and was permitted for two years, in the early 1960's, to examine its papers and secret records.[1]

Quigley apologized for the fact that although the members of these secret societies controlled Communism in the U.S., they were really "gracious and cultured gentlemen" who admittedly had made a mistake bringing Soviet Communism into a position of such dominance in world affairs, but still had nothing but the best of intentions for the world:

> It was this group of people, whose wealth and influence so exceeded their experience and understanding, who provided much of the framework of influence which the Communist sympathizers...[used] in the United States in the 1930s. It must be recognized that the power that these energetic Left-wingers exercised was never their own power or Communist power but was ultimately the power of the international financial coterie.[2]

THE C.I.A. MOLE THEORY

Roosevelt's left-leaning tendencies even influenced the American intelligence community. At the start of World War II, Roosevelt put General William (Wild Bill) Donovan in command of the nation's first full-fledged organization for intelligence and secret operations, the Office of Strategic Services, or OSS.

Donovan saw nothing particularly wrong with Communists. It is now known that Donovan, instead of screening out members of the Communist Party, actually recruited OSS personnel directly from Communist ranks.[3] When the FBI provided General Donovan with evidence that some of his OSS personnel were members of the Communist Party, he replied, "I know they're Communists. That's why I hired them."[4]

After World War II, the OSS became the CIA. Since that time, the Soviets have been very successful at stealing U.S. secrets. The head of the CIA, General Walter Bedell Smith, stated publicly in 1952 that he was sure there were Communist agents working inside the CIA.[5]

In fact, no less than three high-level Soviet KGB defectors—Anatoli

Golitsin, Yuri Nosenko, and Michal Goleniewski—have stated they believe there are high level spies working in U.S. intelligence. Despite these serious charges, there has never been an outside investigation of subversion in the CIA. One was attempted in the mid-1950s, but the vice-president of the United States, Richard M. Nixon, led the fight to prevent it.[6]

There are still many who perpetuate the theory that there is a deep-cover spy planted somewhere within our intelligence machinery—the "CIA mole" theory. The idea is that if we could somehow root this single, high-level mole out, then all our troubles would be over.

This same theory is prevalent in Great Britain where the general consensus is that if only the last spy in the infamous Kim Philby spy ring could be caught, then the UK would finally be secure from the Communist onslaught. This is the basis for a best-selling book *Spy Catcher*, by Peter Wright, former assistant director of Britain's agency for counter-intelligence.

Although the book is a very interesting account of Wright's relentless pursuit of this ring of spies, it seems a bit naive when you look at the history of the "world revolution" movement. Interestingly, Mr. Wright admits that he is not a Mason. He states therefore, that he was not privy to the real secrets of the great spy rings of post-war Britain.[7]

OTTO OTEPKA & CASTRO

Counterintelligence — the business of detecting spies — has been on a long, dismal slide ever since. When John F. Kennedy was President, for example, Otto Otepka was the Chief Security Evaluator for the State Department. Shortly after the election in 1960, Otepka was called into a meeting with Secretary of State Dean Rusk and Attorney General Robert Kennedy and was asked whether it would be possible for Walt Whitman Rostow to be employed by the State Department without a background security investigation.

Otepka replied that he could not issue a clearance for Rostow because he had already been investigated by the CIA and the Air Force, and that both had denied him a clearance. Bobby Kennedy was upset and told Otepka that "those Air Force generals who did this are a bunch of jerks."[8]

Shortly after this 1960 meeting, Rostow was appointed by President Kennedy to be his special assistant for National Security Affairs. In 1963, Otepka was called to testify before the Senate Internal Security Subcommittee concerning William Wieland, who had been a State Department officer in charge of Cuban affairs. Wieland had played a key role in shaping the disastrous policy that allowed Fidel Castro to seize power from right-wing dictator Fulgencio Batista.

Otepka had discovered that Wieland, at the time of obtaining employment in the State Department, had concealed information about his past, including an unresolved allegation that he had been connected with the Cuban Communist Party many years before. Otepka also discovered that Wieland had concealed evidence that Castro was a Communist. Otepka described the attitudes of some at the State Department:

> There was just a preponderance of evidence showing that Fidel Castro was a Communist. Yet, William Wieland was advising his superiors...that there was no evidence that Castro was a Communist, and that we should seek an accommodation with Castro, and get rid of...Batista.

> When all of this was brought out in my evaluation report, I found out that Wieland had his supporters upstairs who immediately came to his rescue, who didn't want these facts to come out.[9]

Otto Otepka was immediately reassigned, and the State Department tried to force his resignation. He was moved to a small office and given the tedious task of indexing the *Congressional Record*. In the end, Otepka was vindicated, but conditions at the State Department did not change. William Wieland was promoted, and Otto Otepka never again served as Security Evaluator and in fact, the job itself was abolished.[10]

Allowing Fidel Castro to transform Cuba into the first Soviet military foothold in the Western Hemisphere was the greatest outrage of the Eisenhower administration.

In 1957, when Castro was fighting a guerrilla war against military dictator Fulgencio Batista, he promised the Cuban people freedom. *New York Times* journalist Herbert L. Matthews, a CFR member, depicted Castro as the George Washington of Cuba in a series of articles. The media portrait painters repeated the same refrains they had used less than a decade earlier on Chiang Kai-shek. Batista was depicted as a corrupt tyrant, while Castro, according to Matthews, was "a man of ideals" with "strong ideas of liberty, democracy, social justice."[11]

However, to the newspaper's credit, it also published, in 1979, a letter from former U.S. Ambassador to Cuba Earl E.T. Smith in which Smith stated:

> Castro could not have seized power in Cuba without the aid of the United States. American government agencies and the United States press played a major role in bringing Castro to power....The State Department consistently intervened...to bring about the downfall of...Batista, thereby making it possible for Fidel Castro to take over the Government of Cuba.[12]

After being asked to abdicate by President Eisenhower, Batista left office on December 31, 1958. The next year, Castro, the new leader of Cuba, spoke to the CFR members in New York at their headquarters at Pratt House. Within three years, he had Soviet missiles pointed at the USA.[13]

AMERICAN EDUCATIONAL SYSTEM

As important and sensational as these political revelations are, the advocates of the New World Order have also been busy fighting equally important battles within the borders of the United States. Key to their long-range plans is the remaking of the American educational system.

Since religion, especially Christianity, is anathema to their plans, references to it have been removed from American public education on the grounds that religion must not be forced upon children. In the place of Christianity, however, the time-worn "religion of reason" of the secret societies, now known generally as "humanism," has been inserted. Piece by piece, the nation's educators are being convinced to teach a system that grows ever closer to the agenda set forth by Weishaupt and Marx.

Why highlight the religious aspect? Because that is the crux of the issue. If a man can be brought to accept atheism—that there is no God—then the need for morality totally disappears. Why should we be moral if there is no God to bring us to account for our actions in this life or the next?

Once this philosophical underpinning for morality is broken down, men can be convinced to justify any action because to them, the ends do justify any means. This is why the most effective opposition to Communism has been the Church. Certainly, that is the way Marxists view it. Karl Marx wrote, "We make war against all prevailing ideas of religion, of the state, of country, of patriotism. The idea of God is the keynote of a perverted civilization. It must be destroyed."[14] Lenin also proclaimed Atheism to be an integral part of Communism.[15]

Professor Paul Vitz of New York University has studied how traditional American values have been eliminated from American textbooks:

> Studies make it abundantly clear that public school textbooks commonly exclude the history, heritage, beliefs, and values of millions of Americans. Those who believe in the traditional family are not represented. Those who believe in free enterprise are not represented. Those whose politics are conservative are almost unrepresented. Above all, those who are committed to their religious tradition—at the very least as an important part of the historical record—are not represented.[16]

However, such was certainly not the case in years past. In eighteenth century America, *The New England Primer* and *McGuffey's Eclectic Reader* were the backbone of grammar school education. Even in that day, the latter sold 120 million copies. The Christian orientation of both these volumes was clear. McGuffey said in his *Eclectic Reader*, "The Ten Commandments and the teachings of Jesus Christ are not only basic but plenary."[17]

Dr. W.P. Shofstall, state superintendent for public schools in Arizona in 1973 said, "The Atheists have, for all practical purposes, taken over public education in this country. I cannot help but remember the words of the Scripture which says: The fool hath said in his heart, There is no God."[18]

Seizing the educational system of a nation is nothing new. Masonry began similar work a century ago in Italy. On April 20, 1884, Pope Leo XIII sent out an Encyclical Letter on Freemasonry to all "brethren, all Patriarchs, Primates, Archbishops, and Bishops of the Catholic world." A portion of the letter read:

> Masonry also attempts to control the education of youth, and mold it to its own godless pattern. So the Church is allowed no share in education, and in many places Masonry has succeeded in placing it entirely in the hands of laymen, and has banished from moral teaching all mention of man's duties to God.[19]

REWRITING U.S. HISTORY

In America, the task of Masonry to redefine the values which would be taught to the next generation was prodigious indeed, requiring a huge investment. The plan operated for many years, however, before being discovered.

In 1954, a special Congressional Committee investigated the interlocking web of tax-exempt foundations to see what impact their grants were having on the American psyche. The Committee stumbled onto the fact that some of these groups had embarked upon a gigantic project to rewrite American history and incorporate it into new school textbooks.

Norman Dodd, the Committee's Research Director, found in the archives of the Carnegie Endowment for International Peace the following remarkable statement of purpose:

> The only way to maintain control of the population was to obtain control of education in the U.S. They realized this was a prodigious task so they approached the Rockefeller Foundation with the suggestion that they go in tandem and that portion of education which could be considered as domestically oriented be taken over by the Rockefeller Foundation and that portion which was oriented to International matters be taken over be the Carnegie Endowment.[20]

The Rockefeller Foundation agreed to take on the domestic portion of the task. The purpose of all this interest in history, was of course, to rewrite it. Dodd explained:

> They decided that the success of this program lay in an alteration in the manner in which American history was to be presented. They then approached four of the then most-prominent historians — such as Mary and Charles Beard — with the suggestion that they alter the manner in which they were accustomed to presenting the subject. They [were] turned down flat, so...they decide they [had] to build a

coterie of historians of their own selection.[21]

The Guggenheim Foundation agreed to award fellowships to historians recommended by the Carnegie Endowment. Gradually, through the 1920s, they assembled a group of twenty promising young academics, and took them to London. There they briefed them on what was expected of them when they became professors of American history. That twenty were the nucleus of what was eventually to become the American Historical Association.[22]

In 1928, the American Historical Association was granted $400,000 by the Carnegie Endowment to write a seven-volume study on the direction the nation was to take. The thrust of these books, according to Dodd, was that "the future of this country belongs to collectivism and humanism."[23]

Dodd concluded from his study that these tax-exempt foundations — by virtue of the fact that they pay for these studies — lay at the heart of a group determined to destroy the United States.[24]

These educational changes were applied very gradually, so as not to alarm the general American populace, but they have been documented. This, in tandem with state and federal court decisions in the later half of the twentieth century, has proven very effective at achieving this goal. Masonry is still very active in the area of education. An excellent book on the subject is Paul A. Fisher's *Behind the Lodge Door*.

Perhaps the greatest advantage the forces of the New World Order possess is that they know they are at war. America, at best, only suspects it. How the New World Order will be manifested in the next century cannot be predicted, but one thing is clear: secret societies will continue to masquerade as benign, humanitarian organizations and to attack critics who penetrate their disguise.

Although Freemasonry has been reduced to a level of less importance in the twentieth century than it held in the seventeenth, eighteenth, and nineteenth centuries, it is still far from benign.

Anglo-American Masons are outraged by the implication that there is anything nefarious about their modern-day organization. They claim that Anglo-American Freemasonry, as currently constituted, was not founded until 1717, when four lodges united under the Grand Lodge of England. This may well be the case, and the British were merely trying to divest themselves of the debaucheries of Continental Masonry.

But why then, if they were trying to divest themselves of their past, did they keep the blood oaths, secret handshakes, passwords, symbolism, and even the name of their parent craft? In fact, it is difficult for the student to see just what was changed, other than the half-hearted inclusion of the Bible and a few references to God who they prefer to call the "Great Architect of the Universe." It strains credibility to believe that their ultimate goals have changed when little else has.

Those of us who criticize, however, must remember to never paint the members of these organizations with too broad a brush. Fortunately, there are very few completely evil men in this world. The vast majority of members in these groups are merely deceived. Their minds can be changed when presented with the truth. It's important to remember that the people best able of helping defeat the machinations of the secret societies are its members.

NIXON REVISITED

The theory that President Nixon did not deserve the image of the conservative anti-Communist he so carefully cultivated in the media has been outlined in chapter one. In light of the preceding material, this may not be as implausible a theory as it may have initially appeared to be.

Nixon, like Truman, was not part of the CFR insider crowd at the start of his political life. But like Eisenhower and Marshall before him, he too enjoyed a meteoric rise to power. He went from small-town lawyer in 1946 to vice-president-elect of the United States in 1952.

Nixon was propelled into a California congressional seat when the ten-year Democratic incumbent, Jerry Voorhis, had the courage to introduce a bill calling for the elimination of the Federal Reserve System, and then denounced deficit spending in his book, *Out of Debt, Out of Danger*. According to Voorhis, in October 1945, a representative for a large New York financial house flew to California to help assemble support for Nixon. Voorhis was vilified by this emissary as "one of the most dangerous men in Washington" thanks to his stand on the Federal Reserve and deficit spending.[25]

Nixon won the congressional seat in 1946. In 1947, he introduced a remarkable piece of legislation which called for the United Nations to be able to enact, interpret, and enforce world law to prevent war.[26]

In 1950, in a campaign so dirty that it gave him his nickname "Tricky Dick," Nixon won a seat in the U.S. Senate. Once there, he did play a minor role in exposing Alger Hiss as a Soviet spy, but exaggerated his role significantly, thereby creating an anti-Communist image which he later parlayed into the vice-presidential nomination on the Eisenhower ticket in 1952.

Many traditional Republicans were looking to support Senator Robert Taft of Ohio, son of the former President, who was considering running with General MacArthur in the V.P. slot. General MacArthur had rocketed to stardom due to his criticism of Truman's conduct of the Korean War, and had subsequently been fired by Truman. This action, however, was so unpopular that Truman did not seek reelection. Democratic contender Senator Adlai E. Stevenson was easily defeated by Eisenhower and Nixon, who then served as vice-president for eight years.

In 1961, after losing the presidential race to John Kennedy, Nixon joined the Council on Foreign Relations. He dropped his membership in 1965 to run for governor of California against Pat Brown, when that membership became a hot political issue in the race. After losing this race, most observers mistakenly thought Richard Nixon was washed up.

But not so. He moved in next door to Nelson Rockefeller in his apartment building at 810 Fifth Avenue in New York. Nixon took a prestigious job in a law firm working under Rockefeller's personal attorney, John Mitchell. In 1967, the CFR signaled that Nixon had its support in the upcoming 1968 elections by allowing him to publish an article in the October 1967 edition of its journal *Foreign Affairs*. Nixon wrote that after Vietnam, Asia needed "to evolve regional approaches...to the evolution of a new world order."[27]

Syndicated columnist Roscoe Drummond noted in 1969: "The most significant political fact of the hour is now so evident it can't be seriously disputed: President Richard M. Nixon is a 'secret liberal.'"[28]

Once elected, Nixon set a new record; he appointed 110 CFR members to government posts. In addition, he appointed Henry Kissinger, "the Council's most influential member," as his national security advisor because Nelson Rockefeller said he was "the smartest guy available."[29]

By 1970, Kissinger stood accused of having been a Soviet agent by the highest-ranking Polish agent ever to defect to the West, Michal Goleniewski. The CIA was made aware of these charges by British counterintelligence, but CIA counterintelligence chief James Jesus Angleton never pursued the accusations, and even tried to discredit Goleniewski as not being a genuine defector.[30] Angleton later died mysteriously in a boating accident. Some believe, however, that he merely faked his death and actually defected to the Soviet Union. In their 1989 book *Widows*, William R. Corson, Susan B. Trento, and Joseph J. Trento claimed:

> No follow-up investigation of Kissinger was done. Angleton discredited the Goleniewski report with the FBI. No one seemed willing to order an investigation into the President's National Security Adviser at a time when Kissinger seemed to be gaining Nixon's total confidence.[31]

In 1977, the most important American "mole" inside the Soviet government had been compromised, and CIA counterintelligence expert Leonard V. McCoy was assigned the task of investigating it by CIA director Admiral Stansfield Turner. During this investigation, McCoy, the number-two man in CIA counterintelligence, discovered that Henry Kissinger, then out of government, had been advising Soviet Ambassador Anatoly Dobrynin on how to deal with the new Carter administration in the ongoing SALT II negotiations.[32]

McCoy was shocked. "The idea that a former Secretary of State and National Security Adviser would meet alone, as a private citizen, with the Soviet Ambassador to discuss negotiating techniques seemed almost beyond belief to McCoy."[33] He later revealed to CIA analyst David S. Sullivan that "the only way to describe Kissinger's actions...was treason."[34] McCoy's report to Admiral Turner was sent on to the White House.

For his efforts, McCoy was dragged in front of Admiral Turner and his deputy, Frank Carlucci. He was summarily reduced one civil service grade, effectively putting an end to his CIA career.[35] Incidentally, Admiral Turner was widely considered by both McCoy and other intelligence professionals to be a pompous amateur. Carlucci, who was later to become Secretary of Defense under President Reagan, is widely considered by professionals in the field to be nothing more than a consummate bureaucrat, and therefore a poor choice for any defense/intelligence role. McCoy, on the other hand is still widely respected in intelligence circles.[36]

FIFTEEN

THE CONSTITUTIONAL ASSAULT

Though surprisingly few people are aware of it, one of the greatest dangers to American freedoms is the threat of a constitutional convention, and tax-exempt foundations have sponsored the attempt several times this century.

There are only two ways of changing the U.S. Constitution: (1) By a two-thirds vote of both houses of Congress, or (2) If two-thirds of the state legislatures pass resolutions for a constitutional convention.

After the resignation of President Nixon in August, 1974, the push began to have two-thirds of the state legislatures pass resolutions asking Congress to call a constitutional convention, as stipulated in Article Five of the U.S. Constitution. In 1975 the first six states did so.[1]

Only four years later, a total of thirty of the necessary thirty-four states passed resolutions calling for a constitutional convention, but getting the last four states proved to be difficult. By 1983, the total stood at thirty-two of the needed thirty-four. Since then, three states have rescinded their calls for a convention, but there is confusion over whether these withdrawals will be ignored or considered legally valid.

Legal scholars differ over whether there is a time limit restricting these resolutions. Some say the resolutions of the first six states to approve a Con-Con call will run out in 1991. Others say they are operative in perpetuity unless rescinded. Opponents fear that it is just a matter of time before the overwhelming financial, organizational, and political power of the Con-Con proponents convinces the additional states to pass Con-Con resolutions.

Although the battle rages every year in the remaining eighteen state legislatures which have yet to issue, calls, details of the Con-Con battle rarely appear in the media.

Even the legislators are frequently confused. Proponents of the Con-Con always fraudulently claim that the convention will be limited to a single issue. Of the thirty-two states which have passed Con-Con "budget" resolutions, however, twenty of them have also issued calls for a convention to consider a Right-To-Life amendment. You certainly can't have it both ways. Whatever the issue, all the legislators are incorrectly told that the entire Constitution would not be opened for massive change.

Former Chief Justice of the U.S. Supreme Court, Warren Burger, is outspoken in his criticism of the Con-Con. In a January 30, 1987 speech in Detroit, he said, "There is no way to put a muzzle on a constitutional convention."[2]

Less than nine months after the thirty-second state called for a Con-Con, former Secretary of Defense Melvin Laird was concerned enough to write an article in the *Washington Post* in which he outlined the dangers of a constitutional convention:

> There is no certainty that our nation would survive a modern-day convention with its basic structures intact and its citizen's traditional rights retained. The convening of a federal constitutional convention would be an act fraught with danger and recklessness...there is little or no historical or constitutional guidance as to its proper powers and scope.[3]

Those who think a Con-Con could be restricted to just one issue, would do well to consider Secretary Laird's analysis:

> The only precedent we have for a constitutional convention took place in Philadelphia in 1787. That convention, it must be remembered, broke every legal restraint designed to limit its power and agenda.[4]

The Dean of the William and Mary Law School, former U.S. Senator William B. Spong, Jr. wrote in 1987:

> It is doubtful that a modern convention could be limited to a single issue. There is no guarantee that, once the delegates are convened, Pandora's box would not be opened by groups concerned with a single interest, placing at risk all of the language of our Constitution, including the Bill of Rights.[5]

It must be pointed out that most state legislatures who have voted for a Con-Con have done so with the best intentions, but with little thought for the larger issues at hand. According to Laird:

> Ironically, while a constitutional convention could totally alter our way of life, the petitions for a convention...have often been acted upon hastily at the state legislature level in a cavalier manner. Over one-half of the states calling for a convention have done so without the benefit of public hearings, debate or recorded vote. This momentous decision,

in other words, is being made surreptitiously, as if it cannot withstand the scrutiny and discussion of a concerned and intelligent citizenry.[6]

Why a Con-Con? The idea is not new. President Woodrow Wilson's closest advisor, Colonel House, thought the U.S. Constitution was the product of eighteenth-century minds, and was so thoroughly outdated that it should be "scrapped and rewritten."[7]

In 1947, two prominent CFR members, Norman Cousins and James P. Warburg, formed something called the United World Federalists to try to merge the U.S. into the United Nations. Ronald Reagan was associated with the United World Federalists before he became a conservative in the early 1960s.[8] This group actually got twenty-seven state legislatures to pass resolutions demanding a Con-Con to "expedite and insure" U.S. participation in a world government. By the end of 1950, however, most states had repealed the resolutions once the consequences of a Con-Con became clear.

In 1954, Senator William Jenner warned that the Con-Con idea was not dead, but only sleeping:

> We have operating within our government and political system, another body representing another form of government, a bureaucratic elite which believes our Constitution is outmoded and is sure that it is the winning side...All the strange developments in foreign policy agreements may be traced to this group who are going to make us over to suit their pleasure.[9]

In 1974, the same year that President Nixon resigned his Presidency, Rexford Guy Tugwell, one of the "academic liberals" from the old FDR "brain trust" of the 1930s published a book called *The Emerging Constitution*. It claimed that our old Constitution was too cumbersome and needed drastic change. It proposed something called a "Constitution for the Newstates of America." The Newstates Constitution proposed to replace the fifty states with between ten and twenty regional Newstates "which would not be states at all but rather subservient departments of the national government. The government would be empowered to abridge freedom of expression, communication, movement and assembly in a 'declared emergency.' "[10]

In other words, the Bill of Rights would be discarded. In addition, private ownership of guns would be prohibited and "the bearing of arms or the possession of lethal weapons shall be confined to the police, members of the armed forces, and those licensed under law." Freedom of religion would no longer be considered a "right," but a revokable "privilege."

In addition, the Newstates Constitution would have given the president of the Newstates of America a nine-year term, and allow him to appoint most of the 100 Senators to lifetime terms. The House of Representatives would have 100 members elected at-large as a single ticket with the president and vice-president (for nine-year terms).[11]

In the 1970s the Ford Foundation spent $25 million over ten years to produce and promote the Newstates Constitution. In late 1975, something called the World Affairs Council sponsored the preparation of a new founding document which was called "A Declaration Of INTERdependence." Written by CFR member Henry Steele Comsmager, it was meant to replace the Declaration of Independence in time for it's 200th birthday at a ceremony in Philadelphia in 1976. The declaration includes the following:

> Two centuries ago our forefathers brought forth a new nation; now we must join with others to bring forth a new world order...To establish a new world order of compassion, peace, justice and security, it is essential that mankind free itself from the limitations of national prejudice and acknowledge that...all people are part of one global community.

We call upon all nations to strengthen and to sustain the United Nations and its specialized agencies, and other institutions of world order...that we may preside over a reign of law that will not only end wars but end as well that mindless violence which terrorizes our society even in times of peace.[12]

This was signed by more than 100 U.S. Senators and Congressmen, including Senator Charles Mathias, also a member of both CCS and the CFR; Senator Alan Cranston, CFR; and Senator Clairborne Pell, CFR. Also signing were House members Paul Simon, Patricia Schroeder, Louis Stokes, Edward Boland, and Les Aspin.[13]

After the Declaration of INTERdependence became a subject of controversy, many withdrew their support. But we shouldn't be too hard on those who did support it. The world *is* emerging as a global electronic community, and as the years go by the pressure to blurr all national distinctions will grow increasingly great in response to world-wide environmental concerns, such as the destruction of the ozone layer of the earth's atmosphere.

The error in logic, though, is subtle and worth repeating. As predicted in biblical prophesy, once the *power* vested in nations is transferred to a single worldly authority, we can be sure that the reign of the Antichrist will begin. Without a system of checks and balances, no earthly authority is "corruption-proof."

Since 1975, as many as forty draft versions of the revised constitution have been prepared. [14] By 1984, a more toned-down version was presented by a group known as the Committee on the Constitutional System (CCS). This has been the group anticipating the results of the Con-Con drive, spearheaded by with the National Taxpayer's Association since 1980. The CCS proposal includes the following:

- Permit the President to dissolve Congress (when he thinks Congress is intractable')

- Eliminate the 22nd Amendment which limits a President to two terms.

- Reduce the cost of Presidential and Congressional elections by holding them at irregular intervals so that the date would not be known very far in advance.[15]

The true intentions of this group, however may be revealed by one of its board members, James MacGregor Burns, a professor and historian who in 1984 wrote the following analysis of the situation for CCS members:

> Let us face reality. The framers [of the Constitution] have simply been too shrewd for us. They have outwitted us. They designed separate institutions that cannot be unified by mechanical linkages, frail bridges, [or] tinkering. If we are to turn the founders upside down...we must directly confront the Constitutional structure they erected.[16]

What are they after? Basically, they want power centralized. They would like to see the concept of the separation of powers as manifested in the current Constitution eliminated in the future. Certainly, once power was centralized, the federal government would be more stream-lined, just as would world affairs under an empowered United Nations, but the result would be dictatorship in either scenario.

Regardless of the level at which it exists—from personal relations, to the realm of the international—unchecked power leads inevitably to tyranny. According to professor Alexander DeConde, this was the feeling of second U.S. President John Adams, who asserted that "the idea of government by a single legislative assembly...was the frame-work of despotism."[17]

The separation of powers concept is that the judicial, the executive, and the legislative branches of the federal government are separate yet equal, and therefore it is difficult to bring to a state of dictatorship. The U.S. Constitution even separates the Congress into two bodies. The debate over the utility of the separation of powers is, of course, nothing new. It has raged throughout the history of the United States. To John Adams, a government without checks and balances was unworkable and, according to professor DeConde, "the first step toward anarchy." On the other hand, to Thomas Jefferson, the concept of separation of powers was like having "a red rag waved before an enraged bull."[18]

Realizing that the separation of powers concept will be difficult to eliminate, the planners of the New World Order have only two options: A Con-Con, where the changes can be done in wholesale fashion; or a gradual approach where changes are made slowly enough so that no effective opposition to them can form. Henry Hazlitt, a chief Con-Con proponent and advisor to the National Taxpayer's Union, addressed this vexing problem in his 1974 book A *New Constitution Now*:

> The very minimum change necessary, if our Constitution is to have

> any real flexibility...is a change from our present method of constitutional amendment itself....Conceivably Congress could frame a lengthy amendment providing for a parliamentary form of government and submit it to the state legislatures or to "conventions" in the present prescribed manner. But the advantages of approaching this goal by two or more steps, rather than by one, seem to me of determining importance.[19]

Of course, under the parliamentary form of government, once in power the party can reign supreme. Though it has worked well in Great Britain, it certainly didn't work so well in 1930s Germany where it allowed Hitler to create one of the most evil dictatorships the world has ever known.

Who is behind all this? The CCS has a prestigious membership roster, with about one-third of their directors also being CFR members. The group is chaired by C. Douglas Dillon, former Secretary of the Treasury and a powerful Wall Street figure; Lloyd N. Cutler, former counsel to President Jimmy Carter; and Senator Nancy Kassebaum. Other members include former Defense Secretary Robert McNamara, Senator Daniel Patrick Moynihan, Senator Charles Mathias, Senator J. William Fullbright, representatives from the Brookings Institute, the Rockefeller Foundation, and the Woodrow Wilson Center.[20]

Why these powerful men and women want to radically alter our way of government is for them alone to answer. It is clear, however, that the forces of radical Constitutional change certainly appear to be waiting in the wings as soon as the doors of the constitutional convention swing open.

Melvin Laird wrote in a *Washington Post* article in 1984:

> The concept that a constitutional convention would be harmless is not conservative, moderate or liberal philosophy. That concept is profoundly radical, born either of naivete or the opportunistic thought that the ends justifies the means.

States still to ratify a call for a Constitutional Convention as of early 1990 are California, Connecticut, Hawaii, Illinois, Kentucky, Maine, Massachusetts, Michigan, Minnesota, New Jersey, New York, Ohio, Rhode Island, Vermont, Washington, Wisconsin, and West Virginia. All others have already done so. Every year that these state legislatures meet, the well-paid, pro-Con-Con lobbyists are there. And every year, ordinary citizens are there to oppose them, and they have been remarkably successful.

In 1989, the State of Nevada also rescinded its call for a Con-Con, but went much further than Florida or Alabama. Nevada actually had its 1979 call "expunged" from the record of proceedings as if it never existed, saying the legislature was initially led to vote for the Con-Con on the basis of a fraudulent representation that the convention would be limited to a single issue.[21] The vote by the Nevada Assembly to rescind its call for a constitutional convention was unanimous.

Even though no state has passed a Con-Con resolution since 1983, the issue doesn't seem to go away. According to Con-Con observer Marshall Peters:

> You would think something as damning as the Nevada expunge-
> ment would stop the Con-Con movement right in its tracks, but they
> just keep marching straight ahead. Some of these people are making
> a living trying to get Con-Con passed, and as long as they are being
> paid by whoever is paying them, the fight will continue.[22]

If your state has already passed a resolution calling for a Con-Con, start a petition to have your state legislator introduce a resolution to have it withdrawn. You will be surprised that most state legislators have little or no knowledge of the resolution, and will, in most cases, be quite anxious to jump on the issue once the simple facts are explained to them.

If your state has not passed a Con-Con resolution, find out who is heading up the organization to stop it in your state. If the organization has not been started, start it yourself. If your state has passed a Con-Con resolution, work to have your state legislature rescind its call, as Florida did in the spring of 1988. Basic information packets are available by writing to: Joan Collins, Coordinator, 5737 Corporate Way, West Palm Beach, FL 33407.

IN CONCLUSION

So what has been accomplished? We started out with the Nixon Coup of 1973. It is not yet known exactly what the scope of coup-planning was at that time. Surely those brazen enough to consider such a plot were surprised and embarrassed by the swift and negative reaction by the military officers and government officials who helped expose it at the time. Memoirs of several of the principals, such as Alexander Haig, are due out in the near future. Eventually the whole truth will be known, and hopefully, this book will have helped to stimulate it.

Regardless, this book has offered a highly probable hypothesis — that the coup-planning was merely one option being explored in the century-old plans of secret societies to wrench the Constitution from the citizens of the United States. As long as this Constitution is in place as is, their plans for their New World Order are much more difficult to achieve.

Until the dawn of the twentieth century, this plan for a New World Order was centered in Masonry, then Illuminated Masonry, but with the advent of the Round Table Groups (which still exist today), and their American brethren, the Council on Foreign Relations, the torch has been passed from century to century.[23]

This book has shown the following:

1. There has been an elite group hidden within secret societies for thousands of years whose primary goal is to create a world government which they call the New World Order. This group tries to convince mankind that world government is necessary for world peace, but in reality, a single world government can only lead to world dictatorship. This group was probably responsible for coup-planning during the Nixon administration.

2. The elite of the secret societies financed Communism and has used it ever since to help further their goals. Their influence in world events has been very significant, yet previously little-known.

3. By keeping the Soviet Union strong, this group has cost America trillions of dollars and tens of millions of lives. Just as President Roosevelt did in the 1940s with Lend-Lease, this group will again try to persuade the American taxpayer to pump billions of dollars into the ailing Soviet economy. The United States would be wise to consider its course of action very carefully.

4. This group operates on a number of fronts. They not only try to control international events but the domestic policies of nations, including their economic, educational, and religious policies. Their power is multiplied because they have at least substantial influence on the news media.

5. In order to function, this group has developed methods to deceive normally good men. Don't be too quick to condemn these good men. Just because your neighbor is a Mason, or even a member of the prestigious CFR, that doesn't mean he is evil. Yes, most, if not all the time, a CFR member has bought the concept of the New World Order, but most of them just don't understand that world government by definition must culminate in world dictatorship. To lump them all together, however, and call them all conspirators only alienates potential friends, and magnifies the strength of the enemy.

6. This group thrives under an illusion of invincibility. Although they are rich and powerful, they constantly make mistakes. They are not invulnerable. They do not control everything. After all, we are still able to debate these questions openly. The average person can have an effect.

7. Finally, be prepared to deal with this issue permanently. The New World Order is not going away. Until Jesus returns, we will have to face it, and we will have to teach our children how to do so. The future will be a minefield of political trickery and spiritual deception. We have to resign ourselves as individuals, and as a nation, to oppose the New World Order as long as we can.

Merely knowing about this "Great Plan" of the secret societies—what it is, who is behind it, and what they are after in today's world—empowers us and weakens the enemy. Like all creatures of darkness, they do not function well in the light of public scrutiny:

> For we wrestle not against flesh and blood, but against principalities, against powers, against the rulers of the darkness of this world, against spiritual wickedness in high places.
>
> Therefore, take up the full armor of God, that you may be able to resist in the evil day, and having done everything, to stand firm.
>
> Stand firm therefore, having girded your loins with truth, and having put on the breastplate of righteousness,
>
> and having shod your feet with the preparation of the gospel of peace;
>
> in addition to all, taking up the shield of faith with which you will be able to extinguish all the flaming missiles of the evil one.
>
> And take the helmet of salvation, and the sword of the Spirit, which is the word of God.
>
> Eph. 6:12-17

NOTES

ONE
THE NIXON COUP

1. Barry M. Goldwater, *Goldwater*, (New York: Doubleday, 1988), p. 265, 263.
2. National Public Radio broadcast of the Haig Hearings, Jan. 14, 1981.
3. Seymour Hersh, "The Pardon," *Atlantic Monthly*, Aug. 1983, p. 69.
4. Ibid., p. 67.
5. Ibid., p. 69.
6. Ibid
7. Ibid., p. 67.
8. Ibid.
9. Ibid.
10. Goldwater, p. 281.
11. Mustafa El-Amin, *Al-Islam Christianity & Freemasonry*, (Jersey City, NJ, New Mind Productions, 1985), p. 154.
12. Senate Supreme Court confirmations for Robert Bork, Sept. 29, 1987, public television broadcast.
13. John Kenneth Galbraith, "Richard Nixon and the Great Socialist Revival," *New York*, Sept. 21, 1970, p. 25.
14. Gary Allen, *None Dare Call It Conspiracy*, (Concord Press, Rossmoor, CA,) 1971, p. 109.
15. Ibid.
16. Ibid.
17. Ibid.
18. Ibid., p. 109-110.
19. Ibid., p. 109-116.
20. Ibid., p. 114.
21. Ibid., p. 118.
22. James Kunen, *The Strawberry Statement — Notes of a College Revolutionary*, (New York: Random House, 1969), p. 112.
23. James MacGregor Burns, *The Power to Lead*, (New York: Simon & Schuster, 1984), p. 160.
24. *The Phyllis Schlafly Report*, Dec. 1984, p. 3; quoted from original document, Rexford Guy Tugwell, "Constitution for the Newstates of America," Article 1, Section A-8, published in 1974 as part of his book, *The Emerging Constitution*, details of publication unknown.
25. Letter to Bishop Mandell Creighton, April 3, 1887, Life and Letters of Mandell Creighton, 1904 as cited in The Oxford Dictionary of Quotations, Third Edition, 1980, Oxford University Press, Book Club Associates edition, p. 1. Lord Acton was the noted British moralist and historian of the 1860s and although one of the most silent members of Parliment of that day, one of its most influential members. Although a devout Catholic, he opposed the doctrine of Papal infallibility.

TWO
ANCIENT SECRET SOCIETIES

1. Stephen Knight, *The Brotherhood*, (Briarcliff Manor, NY: Stein and Day Publishers, 1984), p. 34.
2. *Holy Bible, Masonic Edition, Cyclopedic Indexed*, (John A. Hertel Co., 1951), p. 49.
3. Manly P. Hall, *The Secret Destiny of America*, (Los Angeles: The Philosophical Research Society, Inc., 1944, fourth printing 1978), p. 74.
4. Manly P. Hall, *The Lost Keys of Freemasonry*, (Richmond, VA: Macoy Publishing & Masonic Supply Co., Inc., 1923, ninth printing 1976), p. 18.
5. *Holy Bible, Masonic Edition*, p. 49.
6. Paul A. Fisher, *Behind The Lodge Door: Church State and Freemasonry in America*, (Bowie, MD: Shield Publishing, Inc., as revised Dec. 1989), p. 248; quoting from New Age, Sept. 1948, p. 535.
7. Ibid., p. 272.
8. El-Amin, p. 115.
9. Ibid.
10. *Holy Bible, Masonic Edition*, p. 49.
11. Albert Pike, *Morals and Dogma of the Ancient and Accepted Scottish Rite of Freemasonry*, (Richmond, VA: L.H. Jenkins, Inc. 1871, Feb. 1921 edition), p. 22-23.
12. Robert K.G. Temple, *The Sirius Mystery*, (London: Futura Publications Ltd., 1976), p. 106.
13. Pike, p. 15-16.
14. Ibid., p. 14-15.
15. *Sky & Telescope* magazine, Feb. 1986, p. 146.

16. Temple, p. 87.

17. Hall, *The Lost Keys*, p. 55.

18. Ibid., p. 61.

19. Ibid., p. 90.

20. Colin F.W. Dyer, Master of the Quatuor Coronati Lodge #2076, *Speculative Craft Masonry*, (published by Lewis Masonic Publishers Ltd. 1976), p. 53.

21. Ibid.

22. Ibid., p. 57.

23. Edith Starr Miller, *Occult Theocracy*, (originally published in 1933, but citation is contained on p. 220 of the 1980 reprint edition, Hawthorne, CA: The Christian Book Club of America); secondary reference from a letter written by General Albert Pike entitled "Instructions" issued by him on July 14, 1889 to the 23 Supreme Councils of the world as recorded by A.C. De La Rive in *La Femme et l'Enfant dans la Franc-Maconnerie Universelle*, p. 588.

24. Ibid., p. 221.

25. Pike, p. 24.

26. Hall, *The Lost Keys*, p. 11-13.

27. El-Amin, p. 116.

28. Dyer, p. 23.

29. Ibid., p. 126.

30. Fisher, *Behind The Lodge Door*, p. 32.

31. Nesta H. Webster, *World Revolution*, (Devon, UK: Britons Publishing Co., 1971 edition, originally pub. 1921), p. 26.

32. Pike, p. 23.

33. Ibid., p. 819.

34. Ibid.

35. El-Amin, p. 362.

36. *Holy Bible, Revised Standard Version*, John 18:20.

37. John Robison, *Proofs of a Conspiracy*, (Boston: Western Islands edition, 1967; originally published New York: George Forman, 1798), p. 65-66.

38. Marie Bauer Hall, *Collections of Emblemes, Ancient and Moderne, by George Wither to which is Added Foundations Unearthed*, (Los Angeles: Veritat Foundation, 1987), p. 14.

39. Hall, *The Lost Keys*, p. 48.

40. Ibid., p. xxiv.

41. Ibid., p. 11-12.

42. *Holy Bible, RSV*, Ezekiel 28:15.

43. Ibid., Revelation 12:4.

44. Knight, p. 15.

45. Ibid., p. 28.

46. Abbé Augusten de Barruel, *Memoirs Illustrating The History of Jacobinism*, (London: T. Burton, 1798), v. 2, p. 311-312.

47. Nesta H. Webster, Secret Societies and Subversive Movements, (Hawthorne, CA: Christian Book Club of America, reprint edition published without date, originally published in 1924), p. 324.

48. Ibid.

49. Ibid.

50. *Holy Bible, Living Bible*, 1 Peter 1:13-14.

51. *Holy Bible, New American Standard version*, 2 Cor. 11:14-15.

52. *Holy Bible, RSV*, Gen. 2:4-5.

53. Hall, *Secret Destiny*, p. 24-25.

54. Ibid., p. 25.

55. Manly P. Hall, *America's Assignment With Destiny*, (Los Angeles: The Philosophical Research Society, 1951), p. 49-50.

56. Hall, *Secret Destiny*, p. 25.

57. Ibid.

58. Ibid., p. 45-46.

59. Ibid., p. 30.

60. Webster, *Secret Societies*, p. 31-32.

61. Ibid., p. 30.

62. Miller, p. 119.

63. Ibid., p. 34.

64. Ibid.

65. *Holy Bible, NAS*, Cor. 11:14.

THREE
The Great Atlantean Plan

1. Hall, *America's Assignment With Destiny*, p. 114.

2. Hall, *The Lost Keys*, p. xxi.

3. *Holy Bible, NAS*, Gen. 6:12, 17.

4. Ignatius Donnally, *Atlantis: The Antediluvian World*, (New York: Dover, 1976, originally pub. New York: Harper & Bros., 1882), p. 192.

5. Hall, *Secret Destiny*, p. 53.

6. Ibid., p. 57-59.

7. Hall, *Secret Destiny*, p. 53-55.

8. Ibid., p. 63.

9. Ibid., p. 55.

10. Ibid., p. 59.

11. Charles Ryrie, *Revelation*, (Chicago: Moody Press, 1968), p. 103.

12. *Holy Bible, Living Bible*, Dan. 7:25.

13. Hall, *Secret Destiny*, p. 72.

14. Ibid.

15. Sherry Baker, "Native-American Masons," *OMNI*, February 1987, p. 37.

16. Hall, *America's Assignment*, p. 27.

17. Ibid., p. 12.
18. Ibid., p. 60.
19. Marie Bauer Hall, *Collections of Emblemes*, p. 9-10.
20. Ibid., p. 7.
21. Elizabeth Wells Gallup, *The Bi-literal Cypher of Sir Francis Bacon*, (Detroit: Howard Publishing Co., 1901), p. 7.
22. *Encyclopedia Britannica*, 15th ed. (1980), s.v. "Elizabeth 1 of England."
23. *Encyclopedia Britannica*, 15th ed. (1980), s.v. "Bacon, Francis."
24. Hall, *Collections of Emblemes*, p. 10.
25. Hall, *America's Assignment*, p. 59-60.
26. Gallup, *The Bi-literal Cypher*, p. 2.
27. Hall, *America's Assignment*, p. 62.
28. Ibid., p. 58-59.
29. Hall, *Secret Destiny*, p. 110.
30. Hall, *Collections of Emblemes*, p. 14.
31. Hall, *Secret Destiny*, p. 107.
32. *Encyclopedia Britannica*, 15th ed. (1980), s.v. "Bacon, Francis."
33. Hall, *Secret Destiny*, p. 111-112.
34. Hall, *Collections of Emblemes*, p. 17.
35. Ibid.
36. John Eidsmoe, *Christianity and the Constitution*, (Grand Rapids, MI: Baker Book House, 1987), p. 48.
37. Colin F.W Dyer, Master of the Quatuor Coronati Lodge # 2076, *Symbolism In Craft Freemasonry*, (Middlesex, UK: Lewis Masonic Publishers Ltd., 1976), p. 64.
38. Peter Marshall and David Manual, *Light and the Glory*, (Old Tappan, NJ: Revell, 1977), p. 81.
39. Ibid., p. 83.
40. Hall, *America's Assignment*, p. 63.
41. *The Complete Works of William Shakespeare*, (London: Murrays Sales & Service Co., Cresta House, 1973), p. 16; The Tempest, Act 11, scene 1.
42. Hall, *Collections of Emblemes*, p. 2-3.
43. Ibid., p. 4.
44. Ibid., p. 5.
45. Ibid., p. 7, 12.
46. Ibid.
47. Ibid., p. 2-3.
48. Ibid., p. 8.
49. Ibid., p. 2-4.
50. Gallup, *The Bi-literal Cypher*, p. 3.

FOUR
EARLY AMERICA & REVOLUTION

1. Marshall Foster and Mary-Ellen Swanson, *The American Covenant, the Untold Story*, (Thousand Oaks, CA: The Mayflower Institute, 1981), p. 55.
2. Ibid., p. 56.
3. Marshall and Manual, *Light and the Glory*, p. 110.
4. Ibid., p. 110.
5. Ibid., p. 120.
6. Ibid., p. 121.
7. Foster and Swanson, p. 83.
8. Ibid.
9. Ibid.
10. Webster, *World Revolution*, p. 85.
11. Hall, *Secret Destiny*, p. 132.
12. Dr. James Kennedy, from a November 30, 1986 sermon.
13. Hall, *Secret Destiny*, p. 133.
14. Hall, *America's Assignment*, p. 95.
15. Hall, *Secret Destiny*, p. 133-134.
16. Fisher, *Behind The Lodge Door*, p. 33.
17. Ibid.
18. Bernard Fay, *Revolution and Freemasonry — 1680-1800*, (Boston: Little Brown and Co., 1935), p. 254-255.
19. Webster, *World Revolution*, p. 305.
20. Fay, p. 256.
21. From an inscription in the entrance of the George Washington Masonic National Memorial in Alexandria, VA
22. Robert W. Lee, "The 250th Anniversary of the Birth of George Washington," *American Opinion*, February 1982, p. 110.
23. John C. Fitzpatrick, ed., *Writings of Washington*, (Washington, D.C.: U.S. Government Printing Office, 1940), v. 36, p. 452-453.
24. Webster, *World Revolution*, p.8.
25. Fitzpatrick, p. 453.
26. Hall, *America's Assignment*, p. 96-97.
27. *Holy Bible, Masonic Edition*, p. 6.
28. "Masonry In America," editorial, *New Age*, April 1940, p. 202.
29. Hall, *America's Assignment*, p. 95.
30. Fay, p. 238-239.
31. Robison, *Proofs of a Conspiracy*, p. 64.
32. Ibid., p. 92.
33. Ibid., p. 125.
34. Verna Hall, *Christian History of the Constitution of the United States of America: Christian Self-Government with Union*, (San Francisco: The Foundation for American Christian Education, 1979), p. 248A.
35. Ibid., p. 22.
36. Ibid., p. 9.
37. Ibid., p. vi.

38. Verna Hall, p. 248A.
39. Ibid., p. 300.
40. Foster and Swanson, p. 107.
41. Verna Hall, p. 64.
42. Hall, *Secret Destiny*, p. 178.
43. Ibid.
44. Hall, *The Lost Keys*, p. 53, 56.
45. Ibid., p. 54-55.
46. Ibid., p. 114.
47. Hall, *Secret Destiny*, p. 177-181.
48. Hall, *America's Assignment*, p. 100-101.
49. Ibid., p. 103.

FIVE
WEISHAUPT'S ILLUMINATI

1. *Encyclopedia Britannica*, 15th ed., s.v. "Illuminati."
2. Webster, *World Revolution*, p. 23.
3. Ibid.
4. Ibid., p. 18.
5. Ibid.
6. Ibid., p. 14.
7. Ibid., p. 23.
8. Ibid., p. 24.
9. Ibid., p. 22.
10. Ibid., p. 34.
11. Ibid., p. 35.
12. Ibid., p. 24.
13. Ibid.
14. Robison, *Proofs of a Conspiracy*, p. 6-7.
15. Ibid., p. vi.
16. Ibid., p. 112.
17. Webster, p. 87.
18. Ibid.
19. *Encyclopedia Britannica*, 15th ed., s.v. "Spartacus."
20. Webster, p. 26.
21. Robison, p. 99.
22. Ibid., p. 92.
23. Ibid.
24. Ibid., p. 93.
25. Pike, *Morals and Dogma*, p. 23.
26. Robison, p. 87.
27. Ibid., p. 85.
28. Ibid., p. 86.
29. Ibid., p. 124.
30. Ibid.
31. Webster, p. 28.
32. Ibid., p. iv.
33. Ibid., p. 89.
34. Ibid., p. 91.
35. Robison, p. vi.
36. Ibid., p. 123.
37. Webster, p. 40.
38. Robison, p. 97, 98.
39. Ibid., p. 98.
40. Ibid., p. 98-99.
41. Webster, p. 33.
42. Ibid., p. 33-34.
43. Ibid., p. 36.
44. Ibid.
45. Robison, p. 84.
46. Webster, p. 31.
47. Ibid.
48. Ibid., p. 38.
49. Ibid., p. 33.
50. Robison, p. 121.
51. Webster, p. 23.

SIX
THE FRENCH REVOLUTION

1. Webster, *World Revolution*, p. 41.
2. As quoted in "How America Saw the French Revolution," William P. Hoar, *American Opinion*, Feb. 1978, p. 12-13.
3. Webster, p. 44.
4. Ibid., p. 57.
5. Hoar, p. 11.
6. Ibid.
7. Webster, p. 40.
8. Ibid., p. 41.
9. Ibid.
10. Hoar, p. 13.
11. *American Opinion*, June 1976, p. 53-54.
12. Ibid., p. 53-54.
13. Webster, p. 46.
14. Ibid.
15. Ibid., p. 43-44.
16. *Encyclopedia Britannica*, 1980, V. 1, p. 866.
17. *Headline News*, Cable News Network, July 14, 1989.
18. Webster, p. 44.
19. Hoar, p. 13-14.
20. *World Book Encyclopedia*, 1980, s.v. "French Revolution."
21. Webster, p. 46-47.
22. *Headline News*, Cable News Network, July 13, 1989.
23. Hoar, p. 17-18.
24. Webster, p. 47.
25. Ibid., p. 15.
26. Hoar, p. 17.

27. Ibid.
28. Alexander DeConde, *Entangling Alliance: Politics & Diplomacy under George Washington*, (Durham, N.C.: 1958), p. 55n.
29. Hoar, p. 17.
30. DeConde, p. 55n.
31. *Encyclopedia Britannica*, 1980, V. 11, p. 1006.
32. Webster, p. 48-49.
33. Ibid., p. 48.
34. Ibid., p. 54-55.
35. Ibid., p. 56.
36. Ibid., p. 56-57.
37. Hoar, p. 17.
38. Ibid., p. 18.
39. *Headline News*, Cable News Network, Dec. 9, 1987.
40. Webster, p. 57.
41. Ibid., p. 59.
42. Ibid.
43. Ibid.
44. Ibid., p. 60.
45. Ibid., p. 61; quoting a letter from a Quintin Craufurd to Lord Auckland, May 23, 1793.

SEVEN

AMERICAN JACOBINS

1. William P. Hoar, "How America Saw the French Revolution," *American Opinion*, p. 20.
2. Ibid., p. 17.
3. Salem Kirban, *Satan's Angels Exposed*, (Huntingdon Valley, PA: Salem Kirban, Inc., 1980), p. 151.
4. Ibid.
5. Des Griffin, *Descent Into Slavery*, (S. Pasadena, CA: Emissary Publications, 1980), p. 135.
6. Knight, *The Brotherhood*, p. 32-33.
7. Hoar, p. 21.
8. Ibid.
9. Ibid.
10. William J. Whalen, *Christianity and American Freemasonry*, (Milwaukee, WI: Bruce Publishing Co., 1958), p. 5.
11. Hoar, p. 21.
12. Ibid.
13. Ibid., p. 21-22.
14. Robert W. Lee, "The 250th Anniversary of the Birth of George Washington," *American Opinion*, Feb. 1982, p. 110.
15. DeConde, *Entangling Alliance*, p. 306.
16. Fitzpatrick, ed., *Writings of Washington*, p. 452-453.

EIGHT

AMERICAN MASONRY

1. Inquire Within (pen name for Miss Stoddard), *Trail of the Serpent*, (Hawthorne, CA: re-published by Omni Christian Book Club, a collection of essays which appeared in the Patriot between 1925 and 1930), p. 10.
2. Ibid., p. 92-94.
3. Ibid., p. 92.
4. Ibid., p. 94-95.
5. Vicomte Leon de Poncins, *The Secret Powers Behind Revolution*, (Hawthorne, CA: re-published without original publication date by the Christian Book Club of America, but probably originally written and published in the late 1920s), p. 92.
6. Captain William Morgan, *Illustrations of Masonry by one of the Fraternity Who has devoted Thirty Years to the Subject*, (Batavia, NY: self-published, 1827), p. 15.
7. Ibid., p. 15-16.
8. Ibid., p. 21-22.
9. Ibid., p. 21.
10. Ibid.
11. *Holy Bible, New American Standard Version*, Matthew 5:34.
12. Morgan, p. 21-22.
13. Ibid., p. 22.
14. Ibid., p. 26.
15. Ibid.
16. Ibid., p. 52-53.
17. Ibid., p. 54-55.
18. Ibid., p. 56.
19. Ibid., p. 75-76.
20. Ibid., p. 76.
21. Dave Hunt and Ed Decker, *The God Makers*, (Eugene, OR: Harvest House, 1984), p. 119.
22. Morgan, p. 77.
23. Ibid.
24. Ibid., p. 74.
25. Rev. Charles G. Finney, *The Character, Claims and Practical Workings of Freemasonry*, 1869, p. 12.
26. Ibid., p. 17.
27. Rev. Martin L. Wagner, *Freemasonry: An Interpretation*, 1912, p. 10.
28. Finney, p. 91.
29. Whalen, *Christianity and American Freemasonry*, p. 9.
30. *Encyclopedia Britannica*, 1980, v. iv, p. 138.

31. Whalen, p. 5.
32. Fisher, *Behind The Lodge Door*, p. 34.
33. Ibid., p. 35.
34. Knight, *The Brotherhood*, p. 36.
35. Ibid., p. 2.
36. El-Amin, *Al-Islam Christianity & Freemasonry*, p. 140.
37. *Holy Bible, Masonic Edition*, p. 10.
38. Ibid., p. 10.
39. Finney, p. 91.
40. Ibid.
41. Knight, p. 36-37.
42. Finney, p. 94.
43. Ibid.
44. Fisher, p. 35.
45. El-Amin, p. 113.
46. Finney, p. 108.
47. Stephen Knight, *Jack the Ripper—The Final Solution*, (Chicago: Academy Chicago Publishers, 1986), p. 178.
48. Knight, *The Brotherhood*, p. 54.
49. Ibid., p. 53-54.
50. Knight, *Jack the Ripper — The Final Solution*, p. 178.
51. El-Amin, p. 122.
52. Pike, *Morals and Dogma*, p. 820-821.
53. Webster, p. 20.
54. Pike, p. 820.
55. Ibid.
56. Ibid., p. 821, 823-824.
57. Webster, p. 20-21.
58. *Holy Bible, Masonic Edition*, p. 10.
59. Ibid.
60. John Wark and Gary Mark, "Shrine grew from 114-year-old seeds of secrecy, fellowship," *Orlando Sentinel*, July 1, 1986, p. A-4.
61. Ibid., p. A-10.
62. *Ancient Arabic Order Nobles of the Mystic Shrine: A Short History*, Shrine General Offices, Tampa, FL, 4/85, p. 3.
63. Wark and Mark, "Shrine grew from 114-year-old seeds of secrecy, fellowship." p. A-14.
64. *Ancient Arabic Order Nobles of the Mystic Shrine: A Short History*, p. 3.
65. Ibid., p. 4.
66. El-Amin, p. 119.
67. Knight, <u>The Brotherhood</u>, p. 211
68. Ibid, p. 211
69. bid, p. 211-2
70. Ibid, p. 213

NINE
ALBERT PIKE & MAZZINi

1. Miller, Occult Theocracy, p. 198.
2. Ibid.
3. Mgr. George E. Dillon, D.D., *Grand Orient Freemasonry Unmasked as the Secret Power Behind Communism*, (Metairie, LA: Sons of Liberty revised edition 1950; original edition New York: Burns and Oats, 1885), p. 50-51.
4. Ibid., p. 50.
5. Ibid.
6. Ibid., p. 54.
7. Ibid., p. 56.
8. Miller, *Occult Theocracy*, p. 197.
9. Dillon, p. 57.
10. Ibid., p. 58.
11. Ibid., p. 58-59.
12. Ibid., p. 59-60.
13. Ibid., p. 64.
14. Ibid., p. 67.
15. Miller, p. 213.
16. Ibid., p. 31.
17. Ibid., p. 32.
18. Ibid., p. 210.
19. Ibid.
20. Fisher, *Behind The Lodge Door*, p. 210.
21. Ibid.
22. Ibid., p. 211.
23. Ibid.
24. Miller, p. 215-216.
25. Ibid., p. 217.
26. Ibid., p. 221.
27. Miller, p. 220-221; secondary quote from A.C. De La Rive, "Instructions" issued by Gen. Albert Pike on July 14, 1889, to the 23 Supreme Councils of the world as recorded in *La Femme et l'Enfant dans la Franc-Maconnerie Universelle*, p. 588.
28. Henry Tanner, "Behind the Italian Lodge: A Secret Ideological Aim?" *New York Times*, May 31, 1981.
29. Miller, p. 247-248.
30. Ibid., p. 248-249.
31. Dillon, p. 88-89.
32. Kirban, *Satan's Angels Exposed*, p. 161.
33. Marie Bauer Hall, *Collections of Emblemes*, p. 11.
34. Kirban, p. 162-163.
35. Griffin, *Descent Into Slavery*, p. 39.
36. Richard Wurmbrand, *Marx & Satan*, (Westchester, IL: Crossway Books; a division of Good News Publishers, 1986, fourth

printing, 1987), p. 42.
37. Ibid., p. 43.

TEN
KARL MARX

1. Dillon, *Grand Orient Freemasonry Unmasked*, p. 87.
2. Wurmbrand, *Marx & Satan*, p. 18.
3. Ibid., p. 19.
4. Webster, *World Revolution*, p. 167.
5. Ibid., p. 11.
6. Ibid.
7. Ibid., p. 13.
8. Ibid.
9. Ibid., p. 15.
10. Ibid.
11. Ibid., p. 20.
12. Ibid., p. 15.
13. Ibid., p. 21.
14. Ibid., p. 23.
15. W. Cleon Skousen, *The Naked Communist*, (Salt Lake City, Ensing Pub. Co., 1958), p. 12.
16. Ibid.
17. Ibid., p. 37.
18. Webster, p. 167.
19. Wurmbrand, p. 20.
20. Ibid., p. 25.
21. Ibid., p. 56.
22. Ibid., p. 25.
23. Skousen, p. 72-73.
24. Ibid.
25. Ibid., p. 73.
26. Wurmbrand, p. 27.
27. Ibid.
28. Ibid.
29. Pierre-Joseph Proudhon, *Philosophie de la Misere (The Philosophy of Misery)*, (Paris: Union Generale d' Editions, 1964), p. 199-200.
30. Ibid., p. 200-201.
31. Webster, p. 169.
32. Wurmbrand, p. 32.
33. Webster, p. 169.
34. Wurmbrand, p. 48.
35. Ibid., p. 31.
36. Ibid., p. 32.
37. Webster, p. 172.
38. Griffin, *Descent Into Slavery*, p. 33; secondary reference from Frederic Morton, *The Rothschilds*, (New York: Fawcett Crest, 1961), p. 18-19.
39. Ibid., p. 37.
40. Ibid., p. 52.
41. Webster, p. 172-173.
42. Ibid., p. 182.
43. Ibid., p. 183.
44. Ibid.
45. Ibid., p. 195.
46. Skousen, p. 3-4.
47. Ibid., p. 187.
48. Webster, p. 187-188.
49. Wurmbrand, p. 109.
50. Ibid., p. 57.

ELEVEN
SOVIET REVOLUTION

1. Allen, *None Dare Call It Conspiracy*, p. 68.
2. Ibid.
3. Ibid.
4. Ibid.
5. Skousen, *The Naked Communist*, p. 108.
6. Allen, p. 68.
7. Webster, *World Revolution*, p. 275.
8. Ibid.
9. Ibid., p. 278.
10. Skousen, p. 115.
11. Ibid., p. 116.
12. Ibid., p. 120.
13. Wurmbrand, *Marx & Satan*, p. 49.
14. Ibid.
15. Skousen, p. 121.
16. Wurmbrand, p. 50.
17. Skousen, p. 125-126.
18. Ibid., p. 103.
19. Ibid., p. 104.
20. Allen., p. 71.
21. Ibid., p. 72.
22. Ibid., p. 71.
23. Ibid., p. 73.
24. Ibid., p. 75.
25. Griffin, *Descent Into Slavery*, p. 72.
26. Carroll Quigley, *Tragedy and Hope*, (New York: Macmillan, 1966), p. 398.
27. Ibid., p. 401.
28. Wurmbrand, p. 69.
29. Ibid.
30. Webster, p. 20.

TWELVE

CFR, AND FDR

1. Skousen, *The Naked Communist*, p. 3; from Disraeli's novel *Coningsby, or the New Generation*, 1844.
2. Quigley, *Tragedy and Hope*, p. 62.
3. Karl Marx & Frederick Engels, *Communist Manifesto*, (New York: International Publishers, 1948), p. 30.
4. Ibid.
5. Quigley, p. 325.
6. James Perloff, *The Shadows of Power: The Council on Foreign Relations And The American Decline*, (Appleton, WI: Western Islands, 1988), p. 20.
7. Lewis Paul Todd and Merle Certi, *Rise of the American Nation*, second edition (New York: Harcourt, Brace & World, 1966), p. 266-267.
8. Ibid., p. 266.
9. Perloff, p. 21.
10. Todd and Certi, p. 266-267.
11. Dallas Plemmons, *The Illuminati*, (self-published tract, 1979), p. 4.
12. Ibid.
13. Fisher, *Behind The Lodge Door*, p. 101.
14. Ibid., from *Forum*, November, 1925, p. 799, 811.
15. Griffin, *Descent Into Slavery*, p. 37.
16. Perloff, p. 22.
17. Ibid.
18. Ibid.
19. *National Economy and the Banking System*, Senate documents, Col. 3, No. 23, 75th Congress, 1st Session, 1939.
20. Theodore White, *The Making of the President*, 1964, (New York: Atheneum, 1965), p. 67.
21. Perloff, p. 23.
22. Allen, *None Dare Call It Conspiracy*, p. 51.
23. Plemmons, p. 28-29.
24. Ibid., p. 28.
25. Ibid.
26. Griffin, *Descent Into Slavery*.
27. Congressman Cliff Stearns, "Citizens' Summary: Revenues & Expenses of the United States Government: 1989," (Washington, D.C.: Government Printing Office, 1989), p. 2-3.
28. Skousen, *The Naked Capitalist*, p. 27.
29. Ibid., p. 31.
30. Quigley, p. 954-955.
31. Ibid., p. 955.
32. Norman Dodd radio interview, May 30, 1977, distributed by American Opinion, 395 Concord, Belmont, MA., 02178.
33. Ibid.
34. Ibid.
35. Fisher, p. 217; quoted from an editorial, "Abuse Of The Public Press," *New Age*, September 1952, p. 519.
36. Ibid., p. 217-218.
37. Norman Dodd radio interview, May 30, 1977.
38. Perloff, p. 29.
39. Ibid., p. 29-30.
40. Norman Dodd radio interview, May 30, 1977.
41. Ibid.
42. Allen, p. 33.
43. Skousen, *The Naked Capitalist*, p. 38.
44. Ibid., p. 38; secondary quote from *Mao Tse-tung, Problems of War and Strategy*, ii, 6 Nov. 1938.
45. Ibid., p. 39.
46. Quigley, p. 287.
47. Colonel Edward Mandell House, *Philip Dru: Administrator: A Story of Tomorrow*, (New York, no publisher mentioned, 1912), p. 222.
48. Ibid., p. 8.
49. Ibid., p. 45.
50. Skousen, *The Naked Capitalist*, p. 21.
51. Ibid., p. 11.
52. Ibid., p. 31.
53. Perloff, p. 11.
54. Ibid., p. 13.
55. Ibid., p. 11.
56. Ibid., p. 14.
57. Ibid., p. 10.
58. Ibid., p. 9.
59. Ibid., p. 8.
60. Ibid., p. 7.
61. Fisher, p. 246.
62. Ibid.
63. Perloff, p. 53.
64. Ibid.
65. Ibid., p. 55.
66. Ibid., p. 56.
67. Curtis B. Dall, *FDR: My Exploited Father-In-Law*, (Washington, D.C.: Action Associates, 1970), p. 49.
68. Perloff, p. 56-57.
69. Ibid., p. 55.
70. Ibid., p. 57.
71. Herbert Hoover, *The Memoirs of Herbert Hoover: The Great Depression 1929-1941*,

(New York: Macmillan, 1952), p. 420.

72. *Congressional Record*, June 19, 1940, Vol. 86, p. 8641.

73. Perloff, p. 66.

74. John Toland, *Infamy: Pearl Harbor and Its Aftermath*, (New York: Doubleday, 1982), p. 115-118.

75. Perloff, p. 68.

THIRTEEN
WORLD WAR II

1. Joseph Carr, *The Twisted Cross*, (Lafayette, LA: Huntington House, 1985), p. 87.

2. Ibid., p. 85.

3. Ibid.

4. Ibid., p. 89.

5. George Moshinsky, *Behind the Masonic Curtain*, (Denver: ZZYZX Publishing Co., 1986), p. 4.

6. Carr, p. 85.

7. Fritz Thyssen, *I Paid Hitler*, (New York: Farrar & Rinehart, 1941), p. xxiv.

8. Antony C. Sutton, *Wall Street and the Rise of Hitler*, (Seal Beach, CA: 76 Press, 1976), p. 35.

9. Perloff, *The Shadows of Power*, p. 48.

10. Skousen, *The Naked Capitalist*, p. 8.

11. George Racey Jordan, *Major Jordan's Diaries*, (New York: Harcourt, Brace and Co., 1952), p. 33-34.

12. Ibid., p. 34.

13. Ibid.

14. Ibid., p. 66.

15. Ibid., p. 79.

16. Ibid., p. 81-84.

17. Ibid., p. 92.

18. Ibid., p. 93.

19. Ibid., p. 94.

20. Ibid., p. 95.

21. Ibid., p. 113.

22. Ibid., p. 96.

23. Ibid., p. 217-218.

24. Antony Sutton, *Western Technology and Soviet Economic Development, 1917-1930*, (Stanford, CA: Hoover Institution on War, Revolution and Peace, Stanford University, 1968), p. 292, as quoted by Gary Allen, *None Dare Call It Conspiracy*, (Rossmoor, CA: Concord Press, 1971), p. 101.

25. Jordan, p. 218-219.

26. Ibid., p. 31.

27. Griffin, *Descent Into Slavery*, p. 155; quoting from Mark Clark, *Calculated Risk*, (1950), p. 368-370.

28. Ibid., p. 154-156.

29. Ibid., p. 154.

30. Plemmons, *The Illuminati*, p. 12.

31. Griffin, p. 178.

32. Quigley, p. 790.

33. Griffin, p. 187; secondary quote from John F. Montgomery, *Hungary, The Unwilling Satellite*, p. 210.

34. Personal interview with author.

35. Fisher, p. 194; quoting from *The New York Times*, Feb. 18, 1933.

36. Ibid., p. 12.

37. Ibid., p. 12-13.

38. Ibid., p. 247.

39. Perloff, p. 69.

40. Perloff, p. 87.

41. Ibid.

42. Ibid., p. 87-88.

43. Ibid., p. 88.

44. Ibid.

45. Charles A. Willoughby and John Chamberlain, *MacArthur, 1941-1951*, (New York: McGraw-Hill, 1954), p. 402.

46. Douglas MacArthur, *Reminiscences*, (New York: McGraw-Hill, 1964), p. 375.

47. Allen, p. 86.

48. Ibid.

49. Griffin, p. 214.

FOURTEEN
THE PRESENT

1. Quigley, *Tragedy and Hope*, p. 950.

2. Ibid., p. 954.

3. *Moles in High Places; Part 1* (transcript of video tape), Alexandria, VA: Western Goals, 1984), p. 6.

4. R. Harris Smith, *OSS: The Secret History of America's First Central Intelligence Agency*, (Berkeley, CA: University of California Press, 1972), p. 150.

5. *Moles in High Places*; Part 1, p. 6.

6. Ibid.

7. Peter Wright, *Spy Catcher*, (New York: Dell, 1987), p. 238.

8. *Moles in High Places*; Part 1, p. 8.

9. Ibid., p. 9.

10. Ibid.

11. Perloff, *The Shadows of Power*, p. 109.

12. Letter-to-the-Editor, New York Times, September 26, 1979, p. A24.

13. Perloff, p. 109.

14. Wurmbrand, *Marx & Satan*, p. 59.
15. Ibid.
16. Paul C. Vitz, *Censorship: Evidence of Bias in Our Children's Textbooks*, (Servant, 1986), p. 87.
17. *Moles in High Places; Part 1*, p. 15.
18. Ibid.
19. *Humanum Genus Encyclical Letter of His Holiness Pope Leo XIII on Freemasonry*, (originally published on April 20, 1884; republished, Hawthorne, CA: Christian Book Club of America, 1982), p. 27.
20. "Norman Dodd radio interview," May 30, 1977, distributed by *American Opinion*, 395 Concord, Belmont, MA, 02178.
21. Ibid.
22. Ibid.
23. Ibid.
24. Ibid.
25. Perloff, p. 141.
26. Ibid., p. 142.
27. Ibid., p. 144.
28. Ibid., p. 146.
29. Ibid.
30. William R. Corson, Susan B. Trento and Jospeh J. Trento, *Widows*, (New York: Crown Publishers, 1989), p. 55.
31. Ibid., p. 56.
32. Ibid., p. 94-95.
33. Ibid., p. 95.
34. Ibid., p. 97.
35. Ibid., p. 98.
36. Ibid., and author's personal interview with another senior intelligence analyst still in the employ of one of the intelligence agencies who must remain anonymous.

FIFTEEN

THE CONSTITUTIONAL ASSAULT

1. It has been erroneously reported that only three states passed resolutions in 1975. The confusion stems from the fact that at least three states passed more than one Con-Con resolution. The six states which passed Con-Con resolutions in 1975 were Alabama, Deleware, Louisiana, Maryland, Mississippi, and North Dakota.
2. Warren Burger, speech, as quoted by Irene Mitchell and Elaine Donnelly, "Update on Campaign for a Constitutional Convention," *Republican Women's Federation of Michigan*, September 16, 1987, p. 1.
3. Melvin R. Laird, "James Madison Wouldn't Approve," *Washington Post*, February 13, 1984, p. A-13.
4. Ibid.
5. Senator William B. Spong, Jr., "An Enduring Document," *Loudoun Times Mirror*, July 2, 1987.
6. Laird, "Madison Wouldn't Approve."
7. Perloff, *Shadows of Power*, p. 28.
8. Bertram F. Collins, *Anatomy of a Conspiracy: The Constitutional Convention Con Game*, (West Palm Beach, FL: Bertram F. Collins Awareness/Action Seminars, 1988), p. 6.
9. Perloff, p. 4.
10. Robert L. Preston, *The Plot to Replace the Constitution*, (Salt Lake City: Hawkes Publishing, 1972). The original document, written by Rexford Guy Tugwell, entitled "Constitution for the Newstates of America," Article 1, Section A-8, was published in 1974 as part of his book, *The Emerging Constitution*. Details of publication unknown because the original book has become extremely scarce.
11. Colonel Curtis B. Dall and E. Stanley Rittenhouse, "A Review and Commentary on Rexford G. Tugwell's Book *The Emerging Constitution*." (Washington, D.C.: Liberty Lobby), p. 4, 3, 8, and 9.
12. Henry Steele Commager, *A Declaration of INTERdependence*, (Philadelphia: World Affairs Council, 1975), photocopy of original document.
13. Marshall Peters, *How To Stop The Crisis: Plot to Rewrite the U.S. Constitution*, (Feeland, MD: self-published, no date), p. 5.
14. Nita Scoggan, *Prayer Alert*, (Manassas, VA: Royalty Publishing Co., 1989), p. 51.
15. *The Phyllis Schlafly Report*, Dec. 1984, p. 4.
16. Burns, *The Power to Lead*, p. 160.
17. DeConde, *Entangling Alliance*, p. 175.
18. Ibid.
19. Henry Hazlitt, *A New Constitution Now*, (Irvington-On-Hudson, NY: Arlington House, 1974); originally published in New York by McGraw-Hill and London by Whittlesey House. The Arlington House edition notes that some 80 pages of material was deleted from the original edition.), p. 132.
20. Ruth Marcus, "Constitution in Need of a 200-Year Tune-Up?," *Washington Post*, Jan. 15, 1987.
21. Nevada Assemby Resolution 20, June 24, 1989.
22. Personal telephone interview, February 2, 1990.
23. Although the author does not have the date, during the initial talks concerning German reunification in early 1990, it was announced on NBC's evening news that the planning for reunification was being handled by the German Round Table

Select Bibliography

Allen, Gary. None Dare Call It Conspiracy. Rossmoor, CA: Concord Press, 1971.

Buechner, Col. Howard A., and Bernhart, Capt. Wilhelm. Adolf Hitler and the Secrets of the Holy Lance. Metairie, LA: Thunderbird Press, Inc., 1988.

Burns, James MacGregor. The Power to Lead. New York: Simon & Schuster, 1984.

Carr, Joseph. The Twisted Cross. Lafayette, LA: Huntington House, 1985.

Collins, Bertram F. Anatomy of a Conspiracy: The Constitutional Convention Con Game. West Palm Beach, FL: Bertram F. Collins Awareness/Action Seminars, self-published tract, 1988.

Corson, William R., Trento, Susan B. and Joseph J. Widows. New York: Crown Publishers, 1989. Current, Richard N. Daniel Webster and the Rise of National Conservatism. Boston: Little, Brown and Co., 1955.

Dall, Colonel Curtis B. and Rittenhouse, E. Stanley. "A Review and Commentary on Rexford G. Tugwell's Book The Emerging Constitution." Washington, D.C.: Liberty Lobby, 1972.

Dall, Curtis B. FDR: My Exploited Father-In-Law. Washington, D.C.: Action Associates, 1970.

de Barruel, Abbé Augusten. Memoirs Illustrating The History Of Jacobinism. London: T. Burton, 1798.

DeConde, Alexander. Entangling Alliance: Politics & Diplomacy under George Washington. Durham, N.C: 1958.

Dillon, Mgr. George E., DD. Grand Orient Freemasonry Unmasked as the Secret Power Behind Communism. Metairie, LA: Sons of Liberty revised edition 1950; original edition New York: Burns and Oats, 1885.

Donnally, Ignatius. Atlantis: The Antediluvian World. New York: Dover, 1976, originally published New York: Harper & Bros., 1882.

Dyer, Colin F.W., Master of the Quatuor Coronati Lodge # 2076. Speculative Craft Masonry. Middlesex, UK: Lewis Masonic Publishers Ltd., 1976.

Dyer, Colin F.W., Master of the Quatuor Coronati Lodge # 2076. Symbolism In Craft Freemasonry. Middlesex, UK: Lewis Masonic Publishers Ltd., 1976.

Eidsmoe, John. Christianity and the Constitution. Grand Rapids, MI: Baker Book House, 1987.

El-Amin, Mustafa. Al-Islam Christianity & Freemasonry. Jersey City, N.J.: New Mind Productions, 1985.

Fay, Bernard. Revolution and Freemasonry — 1680-1800. Boston: Little Brown and Co., 1935.

Finney, Rev. Charles G.. The Character, Claims and Practical Workings of Freemasonry. Republished, Hawthorne, CA: Christian Book Club of America, no date, originally published 1869.

Fisher, Paul A. Behind The Lodge Door: Church State and Freemasonry in America. Bowie, MD: Shield Publishing, Inc., as revised Dec. 1989.

Fitzpatrick, John C., ed. Writings of Washington. Washington, D.C.: U.S. Government Printing Office, 1940.

Foster, Marshall and Swanson, Mary-Ellen. The American Covenant, the Untold Story. Thousand Oaks, CA: The Mayflower Institute, 1981.

Gallup, Elizabeth Wells. The Bi-literal Cypher of Sir Francis Bacon. Detroit: Howard Publishing Co., 1901.

Goff, Kenneth. Brain Washing: A Synthesis of the Russian Textbook on Psychopolitics. Originally self-published in 1939 in Englewood, CO; now published by Mrs. Beth P. Skousen, 8233 Racine, Warren, Mich. 48093.

Goldwater, Barry M. Goldwater. New York: Doubleday, 1988.

Griffin, Des, Descent Into Slavery. S. Pasadena, CA: Emissary Publications, 1980.

Hall, Manly P. America's Assignment With Destiny. Los Angeles: The Philosophical Research Society, 1951.

Hall, Manly P. Freemasonry of the Ancient Egyptians. Los Angeles: Philosophical Research Society, 1973.

Hall, Manly P. The Lost Keys of Freemasonry or The Secret of Hiram Abiff. Richmond, VA: Macoy Publishing and Masonic Supply Company, Inc., 1923, ninth printing, 1976.

Hall, Manly P. The Secret Destiny of America. Los Angeles, The Philosophical Research Society, Inc., 1944, fourth printing 1978.

Hall, Marie Bauer. Collections of Emblemes, Ancient and Moderne, by George Wither to which is Added Foundations Unearthed. Los Angeles, Veritat Foundation, 1987.

Hall, Verna M. Christian History of the Constitution of the United States of America: Christian Self-Government with Union. San Francisco, The Foundation for American Christian Education, 1979.

Hazlitt, Henry. A New Constitution Now. Arlington House, 1974; originally published in New York by McGraw-Hill and London by Whittlesey House. The Arlington House edition notes that some 80 pages of material was deleted from the original edition.

Holy Bible. Masonic Edition, Cyclopedic Indexed. Chicago: John A. Hertel Co., 1951.

Hoover, Herbert. The Memoirs of Herbert Hoover: The Great Depression 1929-1941. New York: Macmillan, 1952.

Humanum Genus Encyclical Letter of His Holiness Pope Leo XIII on Freemasonry.

Originally published on April 20, 1884; republished, Hawthorne, CA: Christian Book Club of America, 1982.

Hunt, Dave and Decker, Ed. The God Makers. Eugene, Oregon: Harvest House, 1984.

Inquire Within (pen name for Miss Stoddard). Trail of the Serpent. Hawthorne, CA: republished by Omni Christian Book Club, a collection of essays which appeared in the Patriot between 1925 and 1930.

Jordan, George Racey. Major Jordan's Diaries. New York: Harcourt, Brace and Co., 1952.

Kirban, Salem. Satan's Angels Exposed. Huntingdon Valley, PA: Salem Kirban, Inc., 1980.

Knight, Stephen. Jack the Ripper - The Final Solution. Chicago. Academy Chicago Publishers, 1986.

Knight, Stephen. The Brotherhood. Briarcliff Manor, NY: Stein and Day, 1984.

Marshall, Peter, and Manual, David. Light and the Glory. Old Tappan, NJ: Revell 1977.

Martin, Walter. Kingdom of the Cults. Minneapolis, Minnesota: Bethany House Publishers, April 1985.

Marx, Karl & Engels, Frederick. Communist Manifesto. New York: International Publishers, 1948.

Miller, Edith Starr. Occult Theocracy, originally published in 1933, but citation is contained on p. 220 of the 1980 reprint edition, Hawthorne, CA: The Christian Book Club of America; secondary reference from a letter written by General Albert Pike entitled "Instructions" issued by him on July 14, 1889 to the 23 Supreme Councils of the world as recorded by A. C. De La Rive in La Femme et l'Enfant dans la Franc-Maconnerie Universelle .

Moles in High Places; Part I (transcript of video tape). Alexandria, VA: Western Goals, 1984.

Morgan, Captain William. Illustrations of Masonry by one of the Fraternity Who has devoted Thirty Years to the Subject. Batavia, NY: self-published, 1827.

Morris, Robert. Self Destruct: Dismantling America's Internal Security. Arlington House, 1979.

Moshinsky, George, Behind the Masonic Curtain. Denver: ZZYZX Publishing Co., 1986.

Perloff, James. The Shadows of Power: The Council on Foreign Relations And The American Decline. Appleton, WI: Western Islands, 1988.

Pike, Albert. Morals and Dogma of the Ancient and Accepted Scottish Rite of Freemasonry. Richmond, VA: L. H. Jenkins, Inc. 1871; Feb. 1921 edition.

Plemmons, Dallas. The Illuminati. self-published tract, 1979.

Proudhon, Pierre-Joseph. Philosophie de la Misère (The Philosophy of Misery), Paris:

Union Générale d'Editions, 1964.

Quigley, Carroll. Tragedy and Hope. New York: Macmillan, 1966.

Robison, John. Proofs of a Conspiracy. Boston: Western Islands edition, 1967; originally published New York: George Forman, 1798.

Ryrie, Charles. Revelation. Chicago: Moody Press, 1968.

Schnoebelen, William J., and Spencer, James R. Mormonism's Temple of Doom. Idaho Falls, ID: Triple J Publishers, P.O. Box 3367, 83403, 1987.

Scoggan, Nita. Prayer Alert. Manassas, VA: Royalty Publishing Co., 1989.

Shea, Robert J. and Wilson, Robert Anton. Illuminatus. New York: Dell, 1975.

Skousen, W. Cleon. The Naked Capitalist. Salt Lake City: self-published, 1970.

Skousen, W. Cleon. The Naked Communist. Salt Lake City: Ensing Pub. Co., 1958.

Smith, R. Harris. OSS: The Secret History of America's First Central Intelligence Agency. Berkeley, CA: University of California Press, 1972.

Sutton, Antony C. Wall Street and the Rise of Hitler. Seal Beach, CA: 76 Press, 1976

Temple, Robert K.G. The Sirius Mystery. London: Futura Publications Ltd., 1976.

Todd, Lewis Paul and Certi, Merle. Rise of the American Nation. (second edition) New York: Harcourt, Brace & World, 1966.

Toland, John. Infamy: Pearl Harbor and Its Aftermath. New York:

Doubleday, 1982.

Vitz, Paul C. Censorship: Evidence of Bias in Our Children's Textbooks. Servant, 1986.

Wagner, Rev. Martin L. Freemasonry: an Interpretation. 1912.

Webster, Nesta H. Secret Societies and Subversive Movements. Hawthorne, CA: Christian Book Club of America, reprint edition published without date, originally published in 1924.

Webster, Nesta H. World Revolution. Devon, UK: Britons Publishing Co., 1971 edition, originally pub. 1921.

Whalen, William J. Christianity and American Freemasonry. Milwaukee, WI: Bruce Pub. Co., 1958, p. 9.

White, Theodore. The Making of the President. 1964. New York: Atheneum, 1965.

Willoughby, Charles A. and Chamberlain, John. MacArthur, 1941-1951. New York: McGraw-Hill, 1954.

Wright, Peter. Spy Catcher. New York: Dell, 1987.

Wurmbrand, Richard. Marx & Satan. Westchester, IL: Crossway Books; a division of Good News Publishers, 1986, fourth printing, 1987.

INDEX

NEW WORLD ORDER:
THE ANCIENT PLAN OF SECRET SOCIETIES

For thousands of years, secret societies have cultivated an ancient plan, which has powerfully influenced world events. Until now, this secret plan has remained mysteriously hidden from view. Its primary objective is to bring all nations under one-world government–the biblical rule of the Anti-christ. Today, its proponents simply call it the New World Order.

Millions of lives and trillions of tax dollars have been spent fighting the tyrannical regimes of the Soviet Union, China, Cuba, and even that of Nazi Germany–all spawned in the womb of secret societies. Evidence shows that all major wars of the twentieth century have been linked in some way to the administrators of this ancient plan. If the secret societies have their way, even the United States Constitution will be at risk by being opened up to massive changes at a constitutional convention.

This book presents new evidence that a military takeover of the U.S. was considered by some in the administration of one of our recent presidents. Although averted, the forces behind it remain in secretive positions of power, maneuvering for another opportunity.

Written by a descendant of both Patrick Henry and Woodrow Wilson, *New World Order: The Ancient Plan of Secret Societies* reveals just who is behind this New World Order, what they want, how they are affecting your life today, and what you can do about it.

William T. Still is a former newspaper editor and publisher. He has written for *USA Today*, *The Saturday Evening Post*, the *Los Angeles Times* syndicate, *OMNI* magazine, and produced the syndicated radio program "Health News." He and his wife, Cynthia, have two children.

"Regardless of your views about the coming of a world government, Bill Still's new book will make you reassess the odds. He traces the historic role of secret societies and their influence on the 'Great Plan' to erase nationalism in preparation for a global dictatorship. He allows the facts to speak for themselves as he sounds an ominous warning for the 21st Century."
    D. James Kennedy, Ph.D.
    Senior Minister
    Coral Ridge Presbyterian Church

ISBN 0-910311-64-1

51099

9 780910 311649

HUNTINGTON 〖HH〗 HOUSE, INC.

ISBN 0-9 10311-64-1